INSTANT NATIONALISM

McArabism, al-Jazeera and Transnational Media in the Arab World

---

Khalil Rinnawi

University Press of America,® Inc.
Lanham · Boulder · New York · Toronto · Oxford

Copyright © 2006 by
University Press of America,® Inc.
4501 Forbes Boulevard
Suite 200
Lanham, Maryland 20706
UPA Acquisitions Department (301) 459-3366

PO Box 317
Oxford
OX2 9RU, UK

Library of Congress Control Number: 2006920423
ISBN-13: 978-0-7618-3439-7 (clothbound : alk. paper)
ISBN-10: 0-7618-3439-7 (clothbound : alk. paper)
ISBN-13: 978-0-7618-3440-3 (paperback : alk. paper)
ISBN-10: 0-7618-3440-0 (paperback : alk. paper)

To all the peace seekers

Table of Contents

Foreword   vii

Preface   ix

Acknowledgments   xi

Introduction Instant Nationalism: McArabism al-Jazeera and Transnational Media in the Arab World   xiii

Chapter One Literature Review   1

Chapter Two McArabism: Engagement, Globalization and Localization in Arab Media   7

Chapter Three Emergence and Erosion: a Brief History of the Electronic Media in the Arab World and Structures   25

Chapter Four Arab Satellite TV Stations: Main Players and Classifications   49

Chapter Five Regulation and Control of the Transnational Media   73

Chapter Six Mc-Arabism through Transnational Arab News: the Case of al-Jazeera   97

Chapter Seven Pan-Arab Media: Implications and Effects   127

Chapter Eight Conclusion   151

Appendix 1 Nilesat TV Channels   155

Appendix 2 Channels Available on Arabsat   161

Appendix 3 Channels Available on Nilesat Banquet   165

Appendix 4 List of Governmental TV Stations   167

Appendix 5 Channels Available on ART   169

Bibliography   171

About the Author   179

Index   181

List of Tables

Table 3.1: Selected satellite channel start-ups, 1990-98   41

Table 3.2: Satellite penetration in the Arab world: 43

Table 4.1: Classifications according to ownership and location   66

Foreword

Half a century ago the currents of Arab identities flowed through the state-controlled radio stations or on the pages of the state-dominated press. In contrast, the Arab world today reveals rushing streams of information, commentary and news, not to mention burgeoning images of mass culture. The region is inter-connected in the 21st century by a confluence of media that, in the aggregate, have sparked a new vitality for Arab nationalism. The explosion of mass media often stokes skepticism not only toward regional governments but toward the projects of global powers and related economic forces, not least the United States and the phenomenon of globalization.

As western observers now realize these developments are complex, confusing and often hard to comprehend given limited fluency in Arabic in the West. Moreover, while the new media may lend force to demands for peaceful political reform and democratization, they may also spread messages of angry dissent and alienation. Khalil Rinnawi has performed a great service by writing a book that will lend clarity to these phenomena by offering descriptive insight, conceptual lucidity and what amounts to a primer on the new media, which he glosses as "McArabism".

This is not simply a book about al-Jazeera, the now famous Arab world cable news station, which resembles a cross between CNN, Fox News and BBC International, but it examines the broad panoply of satellite broadcast media, and state attempts to regulate these media. Many readers will find his discussion of popular music both novel and informative. His reflections on how the Arab world has moved closer to standard dialect of Arabic due to the spread of satellite broadcasting are also thoughtful. Moreover, McArabism has lent a new salience to Islam as a facet of Arab identity, as Rinnawi capably explains.

McArabism is not just a catchy term, but it is an innovation that is profoundly affecting Arab political identities and therefore Arab and global politics. The book shows how the Arab-Israeli conflict resonates in the media, since this conflict is central to the political imaginings of most Arabs. Rinnawi has performed an important service for western readers who are anxious to learn how ideas about politics and culture are transmitted in the Arab world. This is all the more urgent because of the horrific developments in Iraq, which have deeply engaged Arab sensibilities and influenced Arab perspectives on the west and the United States in particular.

At a time when the topics of political reform and extremism are much on the lips of westerners, Instant Nationalism is a timely and judicious book. No doubt, it will enjoy a well-deserved enthusiastic reception.

Augustus Richard Norton
Boston University

Preface

Instant Nationalism: McArabism, al-Jazeera and Transnational Media in the Arab world

The roots of this book can be traced to a summer gathering in Amman, where a regional conference was taking place. Participants from Morocco, Egypt, Jordan, Kuwait and Palestine were discussing the performance of Sami Haddad on the al-Jazeera talk show, *al-Ittijah al-Mu'akas* (The Opposite Direction). It soon became apparent that Arabs residing in different countries, with traditionally sealed media borders, could share a common discourse regarding Arab mass media.

In November 2001, the American President George Bush asked the pro-American Qatari government to exert pressure upon al-Jazeera to alter its broadcasts—a pointed reference to return to traditional Arab broadcasting, influenced by local, regional and global state-regime needs, rather than Arab screens.

One of the inadvertent effects of September 11, 2001 in intellectual and political Anglo-European imaginings was al-Jazeera. As if from nowhere (for those who had been oblivious to Arab screens), al-Jazeera impudently emerged on 'white' screens, beating the big Western satellite television stations at their own game—breaking big stories, making controversial news.

It soon became apparent to the participants, including myself, that al-Jazeera has created a new space in the Arab world. The Arab media environment, long dominated by state-sponsored or state-run terrestrial and local television stations, aimed at contemporary nation-state building, has essentially been a state-sponsored monologue addressed to citizens affirming and reaffirming the legitimacy of the state-regime. New Arab transnational satellite TV in the Arab world, particularly al-Jazeera, has offered a new participatory space to engage Arab screens, and importantly, convey new imaginings of a regional Arab identity.

Even as this book was being written, the Arab media map I have outlined and discussed underwent significant shifts. Sections on the Middle East Broadcasting Center were reviewed, taking into account the unexpected rise of its new news and current affairs channel, al-Arabiya. In the year this book was reviewed and edited, other newcomers came to the scene, *al-Hurra* (The Free), *al-Ikhbariya* (The News) and others, surprising many with the seriousness governments and private investors have given alike to the idea of news and current affairs in the Arab world.

It would be difficult to think of another region that has seen the dramatic rise of so many news and current channels. Time will tell whether Arab skies are overcrowded, whether Arab screens will absorb all these new comers, who will rise and who will fall and more importantly, whether transnational journalism in the Arab world will firmly and irrevocably establish itself as the fourth pillar for the region, or whether contradictions between the Arab regional and local-national will skew media development, creating two media tiers that will neither help nor strengthen local societies towards positive change.

Nevertheless the major shift, which prompted me to write this book remains the major seismic movement on the Arab world's media map. As a historical text then, this book shall hold currency for those seeking to understand the then-heady days of a new Arab media speaking what had been previously, the unspeakable.

There are a few important notes for the reader of this book, *Instant Nationalism: McArabism, al-Jazeera and Transnational Media in the Arab world*. I have made minimal use of detailed references and footnotes for simplicity's sake. Transliteration of the many terms used in this book has followed a relatively simple method, based closely on the style used in *The Journal of Palestine Studies*.

Khalil Rinnawi
Haifa
June 2005

Acknowledgments

This book could not have been completed without the help of many people. First, I am particularly grateful to professor Dov Shinar, Dean of the School of Media, and Dr. Amichi Zelberman, Head of the Behavioral Science Department in the Academic Track of the College of Management in Tel-Aviv. They encouraged me to undertake this project. I want to thank Dr. Hillel Nossek and Dr. Yoram Metal for reviewing the book as it was being prepared and Professor August Richard Norton for his valuable advice for publishing of the book. Special thanks are in order for Clark Hoover, Roze Manasrah, Abeer Nahas, Susan Makhoul, Samah Diab and Nabeel Al-Saleh for their assistance. Finally, I would like to thank Diaa Hadeed for editing and preparing this book for publication.

Introduction
Instant Nationalism: McArabism al-Jazeera and Transnational Media in the Arab World

On April 9, 2003 U.S.-led coalition forces took control of Baghdad, thus ending the reign of Saddam Hussein. While Western and Arab news outlets broadcast images of Iraqi citizens happily welcoming the "liberators" into their capital, the reaction throughout the Arab world outside Iraq was marked by a sense of sadness, for this city rich in Arab history and symbolic of shared Arab values and interests had fallen to the West. With this event, the divide between the pan-Arabic and specific localized Arab agendas became apparent.

One of the main purposes of *Instant Nationalism: McArabism, al-Jazeera and Transnational Media in the Arab World* is to understand this paradox, which resulted from the transnational media broadcasting content prior to and during the war that created a shared sense of Arab nationalism which we call *McArabism*. Named for the McDonald's food chain, McArabism refers to a situation in which citizens throughout the Arab world receive identical nationalist pan-Arab content via transnational media, just as one can get the same Big Mac at any McDonald's outlet. But when the television is turned off, Arab citizens return to their respective local lives and specific realities, where their interests likely differ from those portrayed in the transnational media.

Based on field-work and research, this book uses al-Jazeera as a case study to examine the emergence of critical transnational television within the Arab world, new imaginings of identity it has offered, and its implications for political, social and cultural spheres in the region.

I examine those factors, which have transpired to create an environment allowing for the emergence of an Arab transnational television station like al-Jazeera, describing in detail the subsequent new and continuously evolving media map and provide a classification of the various types of transnational television broadcasts in the Arab world today.

Importantly, the book shall also examine how satellite broadcasting has eroded previous existing means of mass media in the Arab world, and the effects of these new media technologies upon Arab political, social, cultural and religious arenas.

I observe various responses of Arab states to these changes, including regulation and deregulation, and explore whether these state-regimes can maintain their direct and indirect mechanisms of exerting control over the media.

The emergence of an Arab transnational television station such as al-Jazeera points to new conditions in the mass communication environment, such as globalization and the advent of new media technologies, just as CNN during the Gulf War. It also points to changing relationship systems between the Arab and Anglo-European world. Hence al-Jazeera, which has set the Arab media agenda since the mid-1990s, is now influencing major networks such as CNN and BBC in a manner unprecedented by a non-Anglo-European media outlet. Three major trends have contributed to these recent developments: the emergence of new media technologies in reinvigorating regional imagined communities, in a communicative environment where borders and the state's ability to exert control over media content have become obsolete; dramatic changes in the Arab media environment, and the appearance of a unique kind of regionalization process in the Arab world, which I call *McArabism*.

Changes in the Arab media environment

Al-Jazeera's emergence in the Anglo-European world points to larger changes in the media environment in the Arab world. Over the last decade, Arab skies have become crowded with satellites beaming an array of content from governmental, semi-governmental and commercial television stations. While early global and regional channels such as CNN, Star TV and the BBC might have been perceived by some as instruments of Western media imperialism, they have been followed by channels partially created within and targeted at Arab markets in the region. Other channels have emerged, such as the Lebanese Broadcasting Company (LBC) based in Beirut and the London-based Middle Eastern Broadcasting Company (MBC), targeting Arab communities in the diaspora.

Importantly, the traditional role of small, often marginalized Arab states to take on the vanguard (or image) of a proactive, free media has influenced the emergence of transnational satellite broadcasters. Without constraints of vying for leadership roles in the Arab world while simultaneously seeking influence in Arab affairs, we find throughout this book that it has been the small states, such as Lebanon, the UAE and Qatar which have produced the most critical, relatively open political and social programming. Thus our focus in this book is particularly upon al-Jazeera, Abu Dhabi TV, LBCI, al-Manar and ANN.

McArabism

Benjamin Barber (1992) argues that *Jihad* (localization and tribalism) and *McWorld* (globalization) are two major opposing trends at work in the Arab

World[1]. By drawing on these concepts and my own fieldwork, I suggest the resulting tension between them is the unique regionalization process I call *McArabism*. This process finds statement in the Arab media and has serious implications on the relationship between the Arab and Anglo-European world.

For Barber, *Jihad* and *McWorld* distinguish between two possible political futures for the world. Jihad is a kind of re-tribalization characterized by "threatened 'Lebanonization,' where culture is pitted against culture, people against people and tribe against tribe" (Barber 1992). Meanwhile McWorld, originating in the Anglo-European world, refers to the integration and uniformity caused by the "onrush of economic and ecological forces" that "mesmerize" the world toward one common form of cultural consumption, thus "pressing nations into one commercially homogenous global network . . . tied together by technology, ecology, communications and commerce." Although acting in opposition to one another, neither trend offers much hope to citizens looking for practical ways to govern themselves democratically.

The penetration of new media technologies into the Arab world and their expansion via the transnational media has created a confrontation between the localism and tribalism of Jihad and the globalization forces of McWorld. The outcome of this confrontation in the Arab world is *McArabism*: a kind of regionalism quite different from the pan-Arabism(s) formulated during the 1950's and 1960's in the Arab world. In terms of formation, it is a product of interaction between new media technologies and local trends and powers. Without a clear ideology, spokesperson or political representation, it is open to external influences. Moreover, new media technologies allow it to bypass central or statist political, social or cultural agencies. McArabism is evident in political, socio-cultural and religious spheres.

In order to understand McArabism, it is necessary to consider that over the last seventy years, media institutions in the Arab world have traditionally been oriented towards local needs and nation building. The state regime typically manipulates the media to ensure its own survival in the name of the state. The survival of the regime *is* the survival of the State, according to tribal media. In other words, the process of establishing the nation-state, and the subsequent need to strengthen and ensure its survival (and the regime's), are characterized by the developmental media model (Siebert 1992) in the spirit of tribal media as depicted by Barber's Jihad. Based on a local orientation, this tribal media creates needs-consumption systems and local discourses that are confined by the geopolitical borders of each Arab state. Thus, the geographic borders of each Arab state delineate the borders for the respective tribal media systems in each state.

McArabism finds statement on three main levels in the media: *structure, content* and *audience*. *Structure* refers to the complex game over control and ownership that takes place between transnational media stations, owners, and political, social and religious elites. *Content* points to tension found in political and socio-cultural arenas. It is reflected in which content the media broadcasts.

---

[1] In this context Jihad does not refer to its more widespread meaning in the West as a holy war, nor to its literal meaning in Arabic as struggle or effort (primarily dictated against the self).

While transnational media pushes for freedom to select content attracting the largest audience possible, political and social elites try to prevent the broadcast of content challenging political and socio-cultural status-quos. This opposition of interest also finds statement in the media's struggle to select content that is attractive to the audience and also takes into consideration political and socio-cultural redlines. *Audience* refers to the audience-media relationship reflected in competition between traditional local tribal media - controlled and manipulated by the political regime and socio-cultural elites - and Arab transnational media, especially satellite television stations, oriented according to commercial needs and interests.

Methodology and research questions

Research for the book is based on document and literature analysis including publications and electronic materials. Most of the data and materials used in this paper were obtained from research trips to Arab countries and their respective television stations. A great deal of information was gathered from media professionals working in these television stations, and from other media analysts and observers in the Arab world.

For our purposes, 'Arab world' refers to all Arab countries in the Middle East and North/Arab Africa. In this definition we exclude Turkey, Iran and Israel, although part of the Middle East, are not Arab states. The one exception I use throughout this book is the inclusion of Palestinian citizens of Israel as engaged in socio-cultural, and occasionally, political, imaginings in the Arab world. When using the term 'Arab screen,' this also applies to the definition I have given of the Arab world. The term 'Arab state regime' is used interchangeably with 'Arab state' and 'Arab regime' to describe the general norm of power sharing (or power exclusivity) within borders throughout the Arab world.

It *is* problematic to speak of the Arab world as one bloc. In each individual state there is a huge discrepancy in socio-economic standards between tiny groups of elites and the rest of the population living a day-to-day existence under extremely difficult socio-economic conditions. There are also tremendous differences between various Arab states, as evident when comparing the incredibly wealthy Gulf states to the rest of the Arab world. There are also distinct cultural differences between villages, cities, and regions in individual states, as indicated by different levels of westernization or globalization, dialects, religious practice and so forth. However, there is academic worth in making a broad study of the Arab world. Primarily, the nature of regional, pan-Arab television encompasses these boundaries rather than accentuating them. There is a shared daily discourse significantly influenced by what Arab audiences are watching on television (al-Hitti 2000).

Television was decided as the locus for this book. In comparison with other media, television is the most accessible to Arab audiences (Karam 1999; al-Hitti 2000, among others). Arab governments have historically reduced taxes on televisions in an effort to encourage people to buy them. It has always been the state-regime's interest to ensure widespread ownership of television sets (but not satellite dishes), providing a tool of mobilization over citizens.

Moreover, television broadcasting has always been a means of bypassing the print media and its primarily literate, elite audience, able to afford publications and overcome different obstacles facing the traditional print media to cross hermitic geopolitical borders between the different Arab states.

Meanwhile, television is far more accessible to Arab audiences than print media due to high illiteracy rates in the Arab world (Sreberny 2001). Therefore, audiovisual media can reach a larger audience, potentially serving as a means to construct a national audience and bring people into a shared cultural-political space for the first time.

Television, like radio in the Arab world, is a participatory, communal activity. This both adds in quantitive mass to the amount of people with access to television—family, extended family, neighbors, etc, and qualitatively to interaction *between* audience members and *engagement* with the screen.

Book Outline

This book, *Instant Nationalism: McArabism, al-Jazeera and Transnational Media in the Arab world,* is divided into seven chapters, combined of two different, related sections—classification & background, theory & analysis. Chapter one offers a literature review of various media theories, particularly of developing nations. Chapter two then offers a theoretical vision of McArabism, exploring engagement, globalization and localization in the Arab media. Arab Satellite TV is examined in structural detail in chapter three, *Main Players and Classifications.* Chapter four examines *regulations and control of the transnational media* and chapter five examines *Mc-Arabism through transnational Arab news: the case of al-Jazeera.* Finally, I conclude with the pan-Arab media, discussing possible implications and effects.

Chapter two, McArabism: Engagement, Globalization and Localization in Arab media argues that McArabism can be viewed in a context of both increasing globalization (McWorld) and localization (Jihad), according to Benjamin Barber's (1992) discussions of a new, bi-polar model. Ideas of identity are first contextualized. I argue that the rise of regional information entities has reinvigorated a sense of common destiny among many in the Arab world. The formation of McArabism from Nasserite pan-Arabism is discussed, alongside other new forms of imaginings of regional Arab identity, which have contributed to the messages McArabism conveys today. Importantly, I discuss McArabism in reference to Subaltern Studies, finding that McArabism, although relatively divorced from real power structures in the Arab world, is rather an upper-middle class imagining.

In chapter three, Emergence and Erosion: a brief history of the electronic media in the Arab world, I examine the history of the electronic media's development in the Arab world and the media structure that subsequently developed, followed up by discussing the emergence of transnational television in the region and its effect on the Arab 'media map.' The direct role transnational television plays in transmitting media content via satellite both within Arab states and across national borders is explored. Two main processes are focused upon: the emergence of the Arab transnational media, and how satellite broadcasting has eroded existing means of mass media in the Arab world.

I find that the emergence of Arab transnational television in the Arab world has significantly eroded the media structure that existed relatively unchanged for more than forty years, maintained by the Arab governments and ruling elite. More importantly, as I argue, television is constructing a national public space that addresses men and women, old and young, educated and poorly educated, urban and rural (Sreberny 2001).

Chapter four, *Arab Satellite TV Stations: Main Players and Classifications,* examines Arab transnational TV channels, which are Arab speaking or Arab owned or run, transmitted inside or outside the Arab world and/or to the Arab Diaspora. I introduce main Arab satellite TV stations and players in detail, including structural information about each station, the establishment process and history, ownership, management, location and network correspondents and offices. Satellite television is then classified according to different categories, providing a map of Arab transnational TV.

Ultimately, I find that despite the rapid development and popularity of satellite TV in the Arab world, development has not emerged through any progressive pan-Arab policy supporting the media as a fourth estate, or a move towards encouraging civil society or democracy. Rather, a mixture of Arab domestic politics in individual states and technology has allowed the formation of satellite TV—particularly news-based channels. While many transnational Arab broadcasters have returned to the Arab world, it appears clear that this has not impacted upon the quality or tone of the serious news stations. These stations have positioned themselves into structures whereby their positions are essentially 'safe': either in Qatar or the UAE, or broadcast from abroad (ANN), with no possibility of return to the Arab world.

Chapter five, *Regulations and control of the transnational media,* discusses different reactions and policies taken in order to deal with transnational broadcasting in the Arab World, taking into consideration difficulties of regulating media based upon new media technologies, transversing geo-political borders, penetrating to varying degrees all levels and classes of Arab society. This analysis functions on two levels: audiences and their access to transnational Arab TV; and Arab transnational broadcasters and their possibilities for 'free' operation in the Arab world.

Through the chapter, the book finds agreement with the quote "new media technology has made the battle impossible to wage" (al-Umran 1996). Already existing strategies, media regulations and control policies are not sufficient to deal with the new broadcasting technologies.

Chapter six, *Mc-Arabism through transnational Arab news: the case of al-Jazeera,* introduces al-Jazeera as the primary context for the emergence of McArabism. This channel is introduced in detail; its programs (current to time of publication) are listed, introducing the station's uniqueness as a news and current affairs channel, not simply in the Arab world but globally. I provide a comparison and analysis of CNN, terrestrial Jordanian TV and al-Jazeera in eight newscasts, offering a broad context for understanding al-Jazeera's importance as a critical Arab transnational channel. I discuss in some detail arguments of al-Jazeera's bias, finding that in many cases it is such critiques which have demonstrated the impact of al-Jazeera, and the willingness of Arab viewers to grant the station legitimacy, to engage with their screens and to subvert through viewing, the sovereignty of reigning state-regimes.

Chapter seven, *The pan-Arab media: implications and effects* explore some implications of Arab satellite TV, discussing different ways the emergence of transnational TV in the Arab world, particularly al-Jazeera, has impacted upon the media itself. This has been particularly important in altering broadcasting agendas to reflect commercial success rather than nation-state building, changing popular broadcasting styles. It has also introduced previously taboo social and political topics and issues, changing the nature of audience participation and providing access to politically or socially marginalized minority groups and audiences.

I conclude by noting that the relationship of transnational TV to Arab audiences is principally of *engagement*, whereby new technologies, combined with individual policies specifically conveying a sense of Arabism of several (critical) transnational channels, such as ANN, Abu Dhabi TV, al-Jazeera, and an already existing background of Arab identity, have coalesced on varying levels towards a new regional identity: McArabism.

Chapter One
Literature Review

Since the end of the 1950s, academic research related to international media systems and mass communication has been dominated by three approaches: communications, modernization and development; media and cultural imperialism; and a revisionist cultural pluralism and globalization approach still searching for a coherent theoretical form.

Communications, modernization and development approach

The *world media system* perspective was first introduced in the book *Four Theories of the Press* (Siebert et al., 1956) and subsequently in Daniel Lerner's *"Modernization Theory"* (1963), Wilbur Schramm (1964) and others. Media systems reflect the prevailing philosophy and political system of the society in which they operate (Siebert et al., 1956). To understand the *international* media system one must identify "the philosophical and political rationales or theories which lie behind the different kinds of press we have in the world today" (ibid). Society's media development and operation reflects the degree of modernization or traditionalism in that society, where modern modes of mass communication are not only identified with modern society but are also important in the transition process from traditionalism to modernity.

Lerner's (1963) *modernization theory* offered the most coherent view of how a modern communication system (supposedly) contributes to this transition. By extending their horizons on both the social, cultural and political levels, Lerner argued modern communication systems socialize people into wanting more out of life.

But this is not how modernization in fact took place in many developing countries. The *national development model* was actually used to justify repressive political systems and the arbitrary exercise of political power, as was the case in the developing countries of Asia and Africa. The media system was thus directed toward maintaining control over the population. In practice modernization theory was used to restrict freedom of expression and to justify political indoctrination.

Furthermore, the creation of independent states from former European colonial enterprises in the period following World War II spurred academic debates about the very nature of development and the unique obstacles faced by newly independent nations. Among other critiques, Lerner (1958) and Schramm (1964) cited the traditional values prominent in the developing world as constituting the central obstacle to political participation and economic activity—the two key elements of the development process. They suggested promoting mass media in order to alter attitudes and values. The degree of media development could be quantified by media indicators, including the number of radios, televisions, newspapers and cinemas in relation to the minimum number deemed necessary for development. This approach, which was adopted by UNESCO and widely touted in the developing world, was subsequently criticized for its ethnocentrism and reinforcement of dependency.

Modernization theory ultimately came under fire for insufficiently accounting for the role local factors play in regard to media access and for paying too little attention to developing a pluralistic media system. Indeed, tradition was often featured in modernization theory as something to be overcome rather than as a legitimate element of civil society. Mass communication was thus viewed as a trust-building exercise between leaders and the led, rather than as an open-ended system of collective dialogue.[2]

Media and cultural imperialism

Critical theorists have coined a number of phrases that fall under the *media and cultural imperialism* approach, such as "media imperialism" (Boyd-Barrett 1977); "structural imperialism" (Galtung 1979); "cultural dependency and domination" (Link 1984, Mohammadi 1995); "cultural synchronization" (Hamelink, 1983); "electronic colonialism" (McPhail, 1987); "communication imperialism" (Sui-Nam Lee 1988); "ideological imperialism" and "economic imperialism" (Mattleart 1994).

The media/cultural imperialism approach has come to embody the view that globalization, which has enabled the spread of (largely) American media content, has resulted in the obliteration of local cultures. This perspective, developed in the late 1960s, contends that American aid programs to developing countries and U.S.-sponsored "free flow of information" policies actually help the American media industry achieve international domination (Schiller 1969 and 1998). The so-called modernization of developing countries fosters dependency within an exploitative system of global homogenization rather than promoting self-sufficiency.

The dependency approach, which was initially developed in Latin America and developing countries throughout the world, was built upon older critiques of imperialism (Gunder-Frank 1964) that recognized the global structures and interrelationships conditioning development, especially in regard to the multiple and diverse legacies of colonialism. It was critical of the post-independence economic dynamics that kept developing countries in a condition of economic

---

[2] For instance, see Schramm (1963,55): "It is probably wrong for us to expect a country which is trying to gather together its resources and mobilize its population for a greater transitional effort to permit the same kind of free, competitive, and sometimes confusing communication to which we have become accustomed in this country."

dependency on ex-imperial powers and argued that development could not be achieved by merely mimicking Western structures, but rather had to be conceived as an autonomous, self-chosen path that built upon the rich and ancient cultures of developing countries.

The great merit of the *cultural imperialism* (Schiller 1976, Matterlart, 1979) and *media imperialism* (Boyd-Barrett 1977) models was their recognition of *global* dynamics and relationships and the suggested linkages between foreign policy interests, capitalist expansion and media infrastructures and content. But in the 1980s and 1990s, due in part to a rightward shifting political climate, the media imperialism thesis came under fire for several reasons, the major points of which follow:

Some questioned the theory's assumption that there is a one-way flow of communication and influence from the West and claimed that global communication flows are actually "multidirectional." Giddens (1999) points to "reverse colonization," as exemplified by the export of Brazilian television programs to Portugal and the "Mexicanization" of southern California. There are arguments that global media enterprises are compelled to adapt to local cultures and link up with local partners in order to sustain their expansion (Croteau and Hoynes 1997).

Similarly, developing countries have shown cultural resistance and a preference for indigenous programs (Silj 1998). This is expressed politically, with some states adopting policies that support local media production (Humphreys 1996, Raboy 1997) and culturally as rooted in local traditions and social networks.

Some claim that because this approach sees indigenous non-Western cultures as vulnerable, it does not acknowledge that for centuries—before the advent of globalization in its current form—cultures have been encountering each other. Some critics point out that the current panic over American cultural imperialism tends to overlook the fact that media globalization is only the most recent example in a centuries-old series of cultural encounters through which the values, beliefs and symbolic forms of different groups have been exchanged.

The cultural imperialism model was also based on a situation of relative media scarcity in many developing countries that no longer exists. By 1990 the international media environment was far more complex than that suggested by the cultural imperialism model frozen in the realities of the 1970s (Curran and Park 2000).

Cultural pluralism and globalization

Partly in response to the criticisms of the aforementioned perspectives, a new approach began to appear in the 1980s that reflected the new neoliberal temper of the time. The *cultural pluralism and globalization approach* shifts the focus of researchers from the modernization or exploitation of developing societies to a perception of globalization as a universal phenomenon transforming the entire world. According to Giddens (1999), this perspective proposes that the globalization process taking place "is only partly westernization" and "is becoming increasingly decentered" such that it is "not under the control of any group of nations" nor of large corporations (ibid). Thus, he says that the effects of globalization "are felt as much in Western countries as elsewhere" (ibid.).

A central claim of this approach is that globalization is actually extending the very basis of communication and cultural exchange. This argument is often presented in the simple form first suggested by McLuhan (1964), according to which the rise of new communications technologies, which compress time and space and transcend national frontiers, creates a "global village." As Ang (1990) notes, "The transnational communication system . . . offers opportunities of new forms of bonding and solidarity, new ways of forging cultural communities." Thus, new international channels of communication break down divisions between nations and increase understanding and empathy between peoples around the world.

Thus, a new global-local connection is being created that is eroding the national. Globalization is promoting ethnic, cultural, religious and linguistic diversity within nation states (Robins et al., 1997). For example, German Turks can be exposed to the Turkish media in Berlin and Frankfurt. The identity of diaspora communities can now be sustained through daily engagement via global media (Dayan 1998).

Some cultural theories that fall under this approach contend that globalization "pluralizes the world by recognizing the value of cultural niches and local abilities" (Waters 1995). Globalization also selects elements of neatly partitioned national cultures and remixes them in new ways for an international public (Robins 1995).

The cultural pluralism and globalization approach also poses a conceptual challenge to the media and cultural imperialism theory. Arguments about "the active audience" and "polysemy" (Fiske 1987) suggest that there is a diversity of audience members, with each bringing his/her own interpretive frameworks and sets of meanings in order to understand media texts, thus resisting, reinterpreting and reinventing any foreign "hegemonic" cultural products (Mohammadi 1992).

New directions—the bipolar model

New theoretical approaches have developed in addition to the three mentioned above. Sreberny-Mohammadi's (1992) "globalization and localization bipolar" model. Sreberny-Mohammadi contend that a third conceptual term is needed, somewhere between "global" and "local," that takes account of the "state" structures and national policy making apparatus which still embody the essential level on which political, economic and cultural decision making take place (ibid 1992). A triangular model, with the "national" element re-inserted, reflects the multiple and deeper tensions and contradictions that constitute the present world order (ibid).

The new media environment and international mechanisms which were created by the global flow of information and the expanding use of new media technologies have led to a very complicated situation in the international communications arena in which it would be superficial to argue that the influence of the media is one directional. Media effects are multi-directional and a variety of different players—such as global economic powers, local governments and the nation state apparatus—compete with one another in the communication arena. The rapidity and complexity of change in the media environment demands new terms and vantage points than those offered by older perspectives, which often seem frozen in a bygone communications era as Sreberny-Mohammadi argues.

Proposal for a new perspective - McArabism

Based on the limitations of the approaches discussed above, I contend that while globalization in the field of international communication has significantly affected developing countries, this has been especially true in the Arab world where new flows of information and the transnational media revolution have simultaneously weakened the nation state and strengthened a trend toward a new type of regionalism, a new form of pan-Arabism that I call *McArabism*. New media technologies prompted the creation of transnational media, particularly satellite television, in the Arab world, which developed McArabism, a new kind of instant nationalism. I shall first introduce the implications of transnational broadcasting in the Arab world, discussing McArabism in this context.

Media globalization and localization in the Arab world

In general, the implications of transnational broadcasting in the Arab world can be discussed according to two level of analysis: the Arab world *vis à vis* the rest of the world (especially industrialized Anglo-European states) and the Arab word as a whole in relation to its components, which include nation states, ethnic and religious groups and geographic areas.

The use of new communication technologies in the Arab world is reflected by the appearance and subsequent growth of transnational media, chiefly satellite television. This trend has challenged the previously existing media system. Importantly, it has transformed the entire media paradigm which includes self-perceptions, terms of reference, modes of functioning and the very basis of the relationships between the media and the state-political leadership on one side and society, its cultural elites and social and religious values on the other (Sreberny 2001, Karam 1999 & Alterman 1998 among others).

As I discuss later in more depth, television media institutions in the Arab world were established with an orientation toward local needs, consumptions and nation building, where the state regime apparatus manipulates the media on all levels, justified in the name of the state's survival. During the last 70 years since the creation of the new Arab nation state—until the appearance of the Arab transnational media in the beginning of 1990s, localism or statism became not only the orientation of the media but also the reality in society.

In other words, the process of the establishment of the nation state and the subsequent need to ensure its survival and strengthen it, characterized the developmental media model created according to the spirit of the Barber's (1992) term "Jihad," meaning a kind of "tribal media." This tribal media is based on local orientation and creates a local/tribal media needs-consumption system and a local discourse that end at the geopolitical borders of each Arab state. In this situation, the borders of each Arab state are also the borders for the tribal media system.

The introduction of transnational media into the Arab world has had the effect of strengthening globalization and localization processes acting in opposition to one another. In this state of affairs, the media plays a central role and reveal the tensions between macro and micro levels of socio-economic structures, cultures and development dynamics. But first we must define these central concepts: *Globalization* refers to "the intensification of worldwide social relations which link distant localities in such a way that local happenings are shaped by events occurring many miles away and vice versa" (Giddens 1990). In contrast, *localization* is the tendency to preserve the local, tribal collective identity, indigenous culture and the local systems of values and norms of each state, nation or any other ethnic collective (Barber 1992).

Chapter Two
McArabism: Engagement, Globalization and Localization in Arab Media

McArabism can be viewed in a context of both increasing globalization (McWorld) and localization (Jihad), according to Benjamin Barber's (1992) discussions of a new, bi-polar model. I first place ideas of identity in context, exploring the notion of the Arab world as an Andersonian (Anderson 1998) imagined community, tensions between localism/tribalism and global pulls and forces, leading to a fuller discussion about McArabism in these contexts.

McArabism as an imagined community

A regionalization effect produced by the emergence of transnational media in the Arab world can be traced to the concept of "imagined community" as suggested by Benedict Anderson (1983, 1998). This suggests that a new nationalism, such as McArabism is a form of imagined community, principally composed of Arabs inside the Arab world, but also Arabs in diaspora and indigenous Arab minorities in other Middle Eastern countries.

According to Anderson, the emergence of new nationalisms results from a process of "re-imagination" conditioned by drastic transformations in the conscience and media within a modern framework (ibid). The relationship between ancient (imagined) nations, itself a process of re-imagining positioned in the rise of contemporary nationalism based upon philosophies of ethnic solidarity, is a process of imagination framed by radical social changes, which have taken place after the industrial revolution. In the case of the Arab world (which in most parts has undergone an extremely skewed model of development, not resembling the industrial revolution model contexted upon Anglo-European states), the entrance of the Arab transnational media is a strong factor impacting upon the process of re-imagination, built upon histories put forward in the most part by the new Arab historians and intellectuals from the *al-Nahda* period in the Arab world and among Arabs in diaspora.

The creation of an Arab nationalism such as McArabism requires the development of new space thinking and time understanding among Arabs. Anderson argues that for this to occur, in the first stage huge groups and collectives of human beings must be able to perceive themselves as societies living in parallel to other large groups with whom they share the same language, religion, customs and heritage, even if there is no interaction or contact between them. The Arab transnational media has had the same process in Arab societies in Arab state regimes and also among some Arabs in diaspora.

According to Anderson (1998):

> The nation is *imagined* because the members . . . will never know most of their fellow-members, meet them, or even hear of them, yet in the minds of each lives the image of their communion. Communities are to be distinguished, not by their falsity/genuineness, but by the style in which they are imagined. Moreover, it is imagined as *limited* because even the largest of them, encompassing perhaps a billion living human beings, has finite, if elastic, boundaries, beyond which lay other nations. It is imagined as *sovereign* because the concept was born in an age in which Enlightenment and Revolution were destroying the legitimacy of the divinely ordained, hierarchical dynastic realm. Finally, it is imagined as a *community*, because, regardless of the actual inequality and exploitation that may prevail in each, the nation is always conceived as a deep, horizontal comradeship

The conditions Anderson describes above are relevant to the Arab world (and Arabs in diaspora) and as I argue, with transnational media facilitating an Arab imagined community.

Elsewhere in his book, Anderson uses the term "re-imagination" which is relevant to the Arab world, clarifying a situation where Arab past/history is being rehabilitated to be positively perceived by Arabs today; recontextualized for relevancy and reintegrated into a system of perceiving the past, present and future. Arab heritage and Islam are two basic elements in these processes. Other nationalisms also draw upon religion to some extent, such as the Jews and the creation of Israel.

Re-imagination is facilitated, or spontaneously drawn upon through an Arab history of cultural hegemony (as opposed to cultural monopoly) from Andalusian Spain to Iraq. Notions of the Arab-Islamic world as participating in a shared culture, language, religions and even economy draw upon *ayyam al-'Arab*, the pinnacle of Arab intellectual and cultural achievement (Hourani 1979).

Islamism is today strongest in those Arab state regimes where the contemporary ethnic does not enjoy a credible historical re-imagining. Similarly, Islamism in the Arab world is more easily accommodated and integrated into those Arab state regimes where there is a historical notion of an ethnic community— such as Egypt and Morocco, as opposed to for instance, Syria and Algeria.

Just as importantly, Islamism (itself contemporary re-imaginings of Islam) is an important factor in strengthening McArabism as an imagined community in the Arab world. Although Islam emphasizes the relevancy of an Islamic community over the ethnic, state regimes tend to allow two contradictory factors to merge, whereby Islam as a unifying bond within the state (or more appropriately, state regime), but is however limited to contemporary state boundaries. Nevertheless, state regimes also pay service to Islam as forming a sense of solidarity with non-Arab, Muslim countries and hence, the fluctuating importance of the Organization of Islamic Conferences.

According to Anderson, the novel and the newspaper were the two basic "imagined forms of activities" which contributed to creation of the imagined community of European nations in the 18th century (ibid). In this regard, the mass media plays a central role in the process of creating imagined communities, mediating between members of the same community who in reality enjoy no real interaction. Continuing this approach in our case, it can be argued that the Qur'an initially formed the first unifying text for an imagined community—the new converts to Islam and the non-Muslim (often large) minorities under Islamic rule and later the large body of Arab and Islamic literature shared between the Islamic world, with one (and later two and three) unifying languages, Arabic, Persian and Turkish.

With the contemporary formation of the Arab world with relatively stable borders (with the clear exception of Palestine, which remains an imagined community with imagined, as opposed to geo-political boundaries), I suggest that transnational media in the Arab world is the means by which Arab screens are exposed to the same socio-cultural media content. The daily consumption of the media in modern communities in fact resembles the Islamic five prayers a day. In both cases, the ritual—prayers or exposure to media content—is performed daily by members who participate in similar socio-cultural rituals and are aware that others are also participating in the same ritual, providing a sense of belonging to the same community even without personally knowing its members (ibid).

Unlike print media that developed in Arab countries, with some exceptions, which worked towards individual state regime building, Arab transnational media weakens nation state orientation and strengthens McArabism—a regional form of localization, however paradoxical this appears at first.

In this context, new media technologies have presented important elements of a televisual environment and a new collective space in the Arab world. This mass media language—the television medium—constructs the basis of a new consciousness in the Arab world, building a unified or common field of communication through images and voices broadcast on television. The use of Modern Standard Arabic, a language understandable to most Arabs, regardless of geographic location, conveying transnational (shared) media content, creates a participatory importance to Arabs. The growth of new media technologies and the capitalist drive to expand its reach into more markets maintain the expansion of a televisual environment. Consequently, the combination of capitalism and media technology have lead to new forms of imagined communities, laying the groundwork for the appearance of new/old collective identities, such as that depicted by McArabism.

Localization, Globalization

The appearance of new media technologies in the Arab world—and transnational media in particular—creates tension between forces of localism and tribalism, which Barber calls "Jihad"—and between globalization, which Barber calls "McWorld." I suggest this clash has produced *McArabism*. The tensions between these trends operate on three main levels: structural-organizational; media content and audience.

Structural-organizational level

The *structural-organizational level* refers to the very complex game that takes place in the struggle for control and ownership between transnational media organizations, private owners and political, social and religious elites. The balance in this struggle has changed over the last two decades as globalization and the entrance of transnational media in particular, has cost national governments a portion of their sovereignty. This trend poses a problem for virtually every type of government and society as well as socio-cultural institutions (Park & Kim & Sohn 2000, Dahlgren 2000). These vast transformations and innovations in media technology reenergize globalization processes.

Cable, satellite and digital technologies have facilitated the launch of new commercial television channels that are eroding the audiences, revenues and legitimacy of public service channels provided by the state, in addition to the rise of giant media corporations as a political lobby and the spread of neoliberal ideas. These have all worked to prompt the adoption of deregulatory broadcasting policies. Increasingly, the forces of commercial globalization are encroaching upon and undermining, publicly owned and regulated broadcasting media (Tracey 1998).

These trends result in a weakening of the powers of political and socioreligious elites, especially over their control and influence over mass media. In today's global era, these elites, who in the past almost completely controlled the flow of content via the state's ownership of mass media, must now struggle against economic interests that own transnational media and search for alternative means to regulate content. In a globally deregulated world, all economies, especially those related to the media, are subject to market pressures (Kit-Wai Ma 2000, Hallin 2000 and Lee 2000). The ability of the state and socio-cultural elites to resist these pressures and to support values and social standards that reflect the will of the people as expressed in the democratic system, has diminished everywhere. But this is also true of non-democratic systems, which characterize most of Arab countries, where societies are even more vulnerable to these external effects (Alterman 1998).

Until the entrance of satellite broadcasting, electronic media in the Arab world was almost completely owned and controlled by the state (Boyd 1993). This enabled state regimes to act as gatekeepers and thus was able to effectively manage external effects transmitted via electronic media. In this situation, tensions between global and local forces were relatively low. The emergence of transnational broadcasting—accompanied by commercialization and privatization of the electronic media—has lead to increasing tensions between owners, regimes and other social-religious elites. This tension in the context of the Arab world was (and is) based upon the assumption that transnational media, television in particular, would shatter all of the existing ideologies, axioms and conventions in the political, social and cultural-religious spheres as represented by traditional elites, transferred by the manipulative efforts of the tribal mass media found in each state (Karam 1999). Conversely, one finds that the efforts of Arab transnational television broadcasters to succeed in competition between themselves and with other non-Arab transnational broadcasters for audience and rating have prompted them to make organizational changes.

Consequently, Arab transnational television stations must use new media technologies and content in order to survive. Censorship—a parameter for the degree of control over the media—is one criterion for analysis on this level. The specific question is to what degree do censorship apparatuses deal with new media technologies and the global media environment? And what happens organizationally in regards to self-censorship in the Arab world?

The questions regarding censorship on an organizational level focus upon three dimensions: *Target* refers to against whom censorship is imposed or pressure applied, to prevent the flow of information. For example, is the target the owner of the information, the communications channel, the media professional (editor, journalist, producer, etc.), advertiser, advertising agency or distributor? The dimension of *social spheres* (political, economic, legal or others) refers to the pressures exerted with the intent to prevent publication of information. The third dimension is the *motive* for censorship and refers to such questions as: Is censorship motivated by moral-ideological factors (political, religious, etc.), or other interests (political party, economic, etc.)? Does it concern the entire Arab population or specific groups, such as content deemed inappropriate for women or children?

The tension on the structural-organizational level is reflected by the interests of political elites and ruling regimes, which also represent social-religious values, to control the flow of information through ownership of transnational media or in other indirect ways. They strive to secure hegemony over the media, while the interest of transnational media stations is to try to function in a free manner without any limitations that prevent them from success in market place competition.

Media content level

The level of media content refers to tensions in political and socio-cultural arenas, as reflected in the content of media broadcasts. While transnational media tends to push for freedom of content selection in their bid to attract larger audiences, political and social elites try to restrict this freedom in order to prevent the dissemination of content that poses a challenge to the political and socio-cultural status quo. This clash of interests also finds expression in the media's struggle to select content that is both attractive to the audience, yet also takes into consideration socio-cultural redlines of what is permissible. Thus media globalization and the emergence of transnational broadcasting in particular, also escalate tension with the local sphere on the level of media content.

Privatization of the broadcast media in most developing countries has led to further commercialization of content and to American-style programming, in contrary to Gidden's (1990) argument. The "global village" has been transformed into a global market where transnational broadcasters are the primary sellers of cultural products and information (Kumar 1999). Conversely, commercial media outlets, mainly transnational broadcasters, must practice a great degree of flexibility and adjust their selection of media content according to the tastes of relevant political powers and social norms found in each country, in order to be granted access to the audiences of these countries.

Furthermore, transnational broadcasters adopt media content that is relevant to local audiences of specific states (much like terrestrial media) and also content relevant to audiences in other states. The main area for analysis here is the tension between media gatekeepers and media professionals. Unlike the first level, the censorship question in this context is in regard to content and not organization. To what kinds of content: news, entertainment, advertising, culture, is censorship applied?

Generally speaking, transnational broadcasting in the Arab world can be said to either stifle or stimulate local production of media content. Thus, Western content genres such as news bulletins, soap operas, sitcoms and game shows have significantly influenced local products, which are often no more than imitations. But local channels have also developed indigenous versions of these genres. This suggests that local appropriations of global formats can actually be very productive. Furthermore, as Shoesmith (1999) argues in the case of Southeast Asia, transnational broadcasting services in the Arab world has introduced competition into national television systems, for in many respects television production in authoritarian regimes generated pretty dull stuff, making Western produced materials look quite attractive when they became available.

Whatever their misgivings about so-called traditional or Islamic values, transnational broadcasters in the Arab world have demonstrated that in order to gain the favor of national governments needed to obtain access to valuable domestic markets, they can either adapt their program content themselves or have it be adapted for them. As in most developing countries, the bulk of transnational broadcasters seem to have realized that to attract sizable audiences in the Arab world, they must provide programming—be it news or entertainment—that does not offend the sensibilities of mainstream audiences, let alone government officials and politicians. Thus pragmatic business considerations have compelled even liberal minded transnational broadcasters to acknowledge local values and at the very least, make cosmetic changes to content (Thomas 1999).

Audience level

The tension on the audience level can be found in the relationship between the audience and the media as expressed by competition between traditional, local, tribal media, controlled and manipulated by political regimes and sociocultural elites on one side and the Arab transnational media, which is oriented by economic commercial forces, on the other. This tension is reflected by a variety of indicators for different television stations, such as ratings and viewer penetration. Moreover, prior to the appearance of transnational media, Arab viewers were considered a target audience, meaning that state controlled media offered a brand of content specifically tailored for local audiences living within the borders of each Arab state. After the appearance of transnational media, especially satellite television, this new media began to steal these audiences from local-tribal media, usually without violating socio-cultural redlines.

To summarize, the tension between localism, tribalism and Jihad on the one hand and globalization and McWorld on the other, is reflected in the three levels mentioned above. It also operates in two other spheres: the socio-cultural/religious sphere and the political/public sphere. While the first sphere is a reflection of Arab-Islamic traditions and traditional social values, the second expresses the considerations of the political or state level, which can differ between states, but tend to be nearly identical among the different Arab political regimes.

Regionalization, new pan-Arabism, McArabism: Old traditions, new frameworks

The tension discussed above reveals the process of McArabism, which has become evident among Arab communities within and beyond the Arab world. McArabism in the Arab media is a specific case of regionalization, emerging through the simultaneous flow of Arab-produced programs within the Arab world and among Arab communities, chiefly news, political discussion shows and historical Arab-Islamic programs, specifically those broadcast from al-Jazeera, Abu Dhabi TV and ANN, although with emphasis upon the former. While traditional state run media in a post-colonial context has worked towards creating and solidifying national identities,[3] transnational media undermines this in favor of a regional identity, based both upon individual beliefs in the pan-Arab nature of the Arab world and the need to appeal to a regional, Arab market.

Terrestrial identities

As a part of the nation state building process during the pre-satellite period, the operation of state run electronic and other media was oriented in positive and negative senses, towards shaping collective ethno-national identity according to the post-colonial boundaries of each Arab state. This in turn nurtured the development of a national collective identity, by creating and propagating national products, such as literature and sports. Repressive measures, like censorship, were used in combination with state sponsored media as a means to prevent the infiltration of media from beyond the state's borders and to create a closed ethno-national media environment to strengthen a sense of national identity among the population of each state. One of the primary goals of creating a tribal media was to shape a narrow national identity, oriented towards and controlled by, respective political regimes.

---

[3] Few modern Arab states can be considered to have nation state identities in the Western or Marxian concept of the term. These states would arguably be: Egypt, Mount Lebanon, Tunis and Kuwait.

New technologies and Arab actors in satellite media

Since the early 1990s there has been a new wave of regionalization and new pan-Arabism, created by and based on the significant increase of regional (transnational) Arab media actors. There is a process of regionalization of media structures and its content, spurred by the use of new technologies. Quite obviously, new technologies facilitate the transmission of information regardless of geographical distance. Whereas national differences could once be maintained with relative ease because geography and governmental efforts combined to create distinct markets for information, it has become much more difficult, with new technologies making it cheaper, faster and easier for information to transcend those obstacles, creating something much more closely resembling a single target group.

Creation of a regional market

Another factor, which has enhanced the stature of a regional Arab identity are advertisers seeking to enter this part of the world to sell mainly Anglo-European products/labels. This is more easily achieved by unifying separate (state border segregated) Arab media markets. The expansion of Arab transnational media has been heavily enhanced and pushed by economic and capitalist forces from within and beyond the Arab world seeking new markets. Here, the lack of separate discernable structures between economic and political forces has merged within new media markets (Sakr 2000). For example, Kazan (1993) argues that Arab capitalists, especially from Gulf States, entered the media industry and transnational media in particular, to provide a new realm for investing capital generated by oil sales. To a large extent, regional print media and television broadcasts have combined to create a regional media market, known to marketers as the pan-Arab market, which is becoming increasingly influential (Alterman 1998).

Interestingly, while the pan-Arab market is becoming increasingly influential, *pan-Arab consumers,* as a bloc, are not. This can be seen in repeatedly failed or weak attempts to boycott Israeli or American products. In the context of our study, it can be seen in the consuming of American media products, such *Radio Sawa* (Radio Together), clearly and openly made with the intention of influencing or garnering a pro-American Arab culture in the Arab world (broadcast from Washington) among Arab youth. *Radio Sawa* has become one of the most popular, if not the most popular, radio station in the Arab world today. However, the continuing consolidation of McArabism may strengthen notions of Arabs as a consumer bloc—the strongest calls for boycott to date have emerged in the al-Jazeera age. Similarly, it may have no impact at all, tied to a process of pure economic survival, not undermined by any emotional, cultural or social ties, or notions of an imagined community, acting out a sense of mutual concern or responsibility.

The effect of transnational (Arab) broadcasting has had in creating a regional pan-Arab identity is strengthened by the formation of a pan-Arab media market, where the imperative is to create media products that enlarge and unite the market rather than fracture it. This is notable for several reasons: First, the pan-Arab media market has the characteristics of a market. Based on forces of supply and demand, programming is not tailored to simply meet the needs of government broadcasters. Rather it actively seeks viewers by offering a variety of news and entertainment options. The result is enormous empowerment of the audience and dramatic increase in viewer satisfaction with content.

Second, viewers of commercial regional broadcasting are perceived as free consumers. This means each viewer has the freedom to choose from a large variety of television stations according to their preferences. This is in contrast to the pre-satellite period during which viewers were considered a passive audience, with no alternative but to view the state run television stations.

Third, regional markets are indeed regional. To a great degree, identical programming can be seen throughout the Arab world. Although market driven programmers direct their broadcasts primarily to groups highly valued by advertisers—which in the Arab world, generally means those in wealthy Gulf states—programming reaches and influences many throughout the region who may not fit the targeted socioeconomic profile of each station.

Fourth, some regional broadcasting players are not subject to censorship apparatuses of Arab states. As a result, they have been able to bring onto Arab screens content that was absent in the past. Arab viewers have thus been introduced to debate and argument over current events by politicians, intellectuals and other personalities, many of whom previously lacked access to television because they were identified with opposition groups and dissenting opinions that state regimes wished to silence.

Backgrounds and contexts to McArabism: pan-Arabism

McArabism is an outcome of new media technologies (external influences) interacting with local trends and powers, most importantly, a pan-Arab regional notion of *self,* particularly in—but not exclusive to—Egypt and the Levant, of one Arab people, rooted in a common history, religions (Christianity and Islam), with a common present (against colonialism, imperialism) and a common future. Clearly, notions of one Arab people and a common present against colonialism and imperialism may not appeal to the (very imperial) state regimes or people of the Arab Gulf, or even North Africa. However, the media professionals influencing notions of pan-Arabism or McArabism on transnational Arab broadcasters tend to come from these two regions, Egypt and the Levant. It has been their ideas (or ideals), which have had the most currency in the Arab world. Other media professionals not from these regions also tend towards a pan-Arab slant, whether because of individual beliefs or the influence of the media stations where they work.

Pan-Arabism was left to drift for decades without meaningful state sponsorship, supporting economic structures and few civil society institutions to develop its ideas, despite its strong evocative nature in the Arab world. This drift was compounded by the death of Nasserite pan-Arabism—unsuccessful in terms of economic empowerment (on some levels), human rights building and democracy, but entirely successful in giving, for the first time, Arabs a significant historical era, where their collective (whether created through that era or not) aspirations that could be crafted into reality.

Pan-Arabism has suffered keeling physical, intellectual and political blows since then: Camp David (1978), isolating Egypt from the Arab world. The end of the seventeen year Lebanese War through an American-Syrian understanding (1991), the first major invasion (1990) of one Arab country (Kuwait) by another (Iraq), leading to the Gulf War (1991), allowing Iraq to decay under sanctions. The first Intifada (1987), in the West Bank and Gaza Strip, which, ironically enough for its appeal to pan-Arabism, formed a catalyst for the Madrid Peace Conference (another catalyst being the Gulf War and PLO leader Yasser Arafat supporting Iraq) and the Oslo Peace Process (1993) that allowed individual Arab regimes to negotiate with Israel, rather than as a bloc. The list is almost inexhaustible. Each has made their own impact on the ideal and practicality of pan-Arabism.

Backgrounds and contexts to McArabism: new, tentative visions of Arab identity

McArabism is posited in another important context: articulations of a shared identity emerging in recent years. These have been the outcome of long and short term processes in the Arab world, including the failure of Nasserite pan-Arabism; a period of state-state disengagement and isolation, marked with increasing foreign intervention, inflicted both by state regimes and international actors; the rise of pan-Islam as an alternative to Arabism and the marginalization, discrediting and diminishment of the secular Left in the Arab world.

The strengthening that Arab-Islamic groups, including al-Qaeda, Hizbollah and Hamas have offered disempowered and disillusioned publics in the Arab world; small but occasionally powerful cultural productions reviving the role of cultural producers in the Arab world as the bastion of secular pan-Arabism and individual policies of Arab transnational channels have emerged from this background to offer new visions of Arab identity, which have formed an important background to McArabism. These new articulations have initiated the direction of McArabism, shaped and reshaped through new technologies and transnational Arab television channels.

New shared feelings of identity have been expressed as an articulation or confirmation of identity (through culture, politics, arts, economics), unity upon important issues affecting Arab people: a just solution to the Palestinian issue, the Iraqi crisis, economic and legal justice in the Arab world, independence from former and present imperial powers, a more prominent role for Islam in society. Nevertheless, these expressions have been problematic: ambiguous on how Islam should assume a role in Arab society, gender relations and human rights (as a secular construct positioned in citizenship). While there has not been one voice or group in the Arab world powerful enough to individually articulate these different aspirations and engage directly with Arab publics, it is the sum total of the parts which becomes important.

Arab-Islamic movements

Arab-Islamic movements have been, and continue to be, the strongest articulators of this new vision, particularly Hizbollah, which has worked towards cognizing to Arab publics a vision of Arabism and Islam together. Al-Manar, the Lebanese Shiite terrestrial/transnational television station has had the strongest influence in this regard, consistently emphasizing the indivisibility of Islam and Arabism (whether in secular or religious articulations). Every address and debate has emphasized Islam and Arabism together, addressing Arab Christians and Muslims. Meanwhile, Hamas draws upon secular notions of nationhood (Palestine as a state, Palestinians with their own ethnic identity) to justify its activities.

Through providing much advertised social services to forgotten groups in Arab society (the rural poor, homeless, unemployed, widowers and orphans, the disabled, etc.); many Arab-Islamic groups call for social and economic justice, with their bases firmly in grassroots work.

Many Arab-Islamist political analyses of the Arab world are critical and articulate. Drawing upon traditional Arab-leftist critiques of imperialism, indigenous power, the need for economic and moral unity (i.e., shared stances on issues of importance to the Arab world, such as Palestine and Iraq), religious leadership from this group (including Sheikh Yusuf Qaradawi, Laith Shbeilat and Hassan Nasrallah, although from different schools of thought) cognize new visions of the Arab world based in indigenous roots. Their influence only increases with political persecution.

Cultural groups and productions

Cultural productions have offered a different vision of regional Arab identity, in part based upon new notions of Arab empowerment, although revived for its relevance to contemporary Arab realities.

In terms of new visions, quite possibly the strongest articulation of this was al-Hilm al-'Arabi (The Arab Dream), released in 1998, bought together entertainers from all over the Arab world to sing and evoke common aspirations: unity, peace and justice. The song itself was a clumsy mixture of folksy and clichéd evocations which tended to remind one of Arab failure more than Arab success.

The chorus mourns:

Generations after generations will live on our dream
And what we say today we are accountable for through our lives
It is possible that the darkness of night will keep us apart for a day but
The rays of light reach the furthest skies
This is our dream all our lives, gathering all of us

More powerful than the song was the video clip it offered (indicative of the producer's understanding of new technologies), an amalgamation of Intifada footage, including children throwing stones, to 'Abd al-Nasser charismatically speaking.

The video clip was controversial enough not to be screened in Egypt, although easily obtainable through black music markets. Indicative of its ability to inspire, evoke and engage, the song culminated in a concert in 2000, *Sawt Malyun 'Arab* (The Voice of a Million Arabs), which bought together hundreds and thousands of Arabs to attend the concert (Hadid 2000). An interesting side note—the concert was later discredited in much of the Arab world later, with reports of infighting among different singers and poor organization, leading to internet postings and editorials drawing upon the concert as a reason why Arabs could never achieve the pan-Arabist ideals called for in the song (ibid 2000).

Just as popular, with the withdrawal of the Israeli forces from south Lebanon and the on set of the second Intifada, have been re-appropriated older songs. These songs have been blared over radio stations, repacked and resold all over the Arab world and importantly, used frequently on television—whether as a part of clichéd montages about the Intifada, used at the beginning of programs to direct the audience's mood, or on commercials advertising programs about Palestine/Iraq.

These have included Ahmad Qa'bour's *Unadikum* (I call on You), first released in the late seventies, which calls upon Arabs to support and join Palestinians:

I call on you
And I pull on your hands
And I kiss the ground
Under your feet
And I tell you I will be your sacrifice . . .
For the tragedy you live is also my fate

The Lebanese diva, Fairouz, had her 1967 song *Zahrat al-Mada'in* (Flower of the Cities) return to the airwaves. The song mourns the loss of Jerusalem and promises its return:

> Our eyes turn to you every day
> They wander in the corners of prayer places
> Embrace old churches
> Wipe the sadness from the Mosques
> ... the door of our city will not be closed and I am going to pray
> I will knock on the doors and they will open
> I will wash my faces in the holy waters of Jordan
> And you will wipe away the footprints of the occupiers

Marcel Khalife's *Samiduna Huna* (Steadfast here) defiantly opposes the destruction bought upon Lebanese and Palestinians in Beirut, now re-appropriated to express defiance to occupation and re-occupation (ibid 2000):

> Steadfast here
> Above this great destruction
> And in our hands
> We gather thunder
> In my heart is the ancient branch of loyalty

Another part of this cultural context is the re-broadcasting, dubbing, private viewings and much discussion about 'Adel Imam's (a famous Egyptian comedy actor) movies and Durayd Lahham's plays—Lahham is one of the Arab world's most popular playwrights, specializing in black comedies satirizing Arab state regimes. Lahham was actually jailed for six months, some years ago, for including a scene in one his plays, where he refuses to buy new shoes. Lahham refuses, claiming that his old shoes are a great brand—the Lion brand *(markat al-Assad)*, a play upon the then-ruler of Syria, Hafiz al-Assad.

The re-appropriation of such cultural products has been crucial in understanding subaltern aspiration, which leans towards pan-Arab identity, desires empowerment and agency. Most importantly, these are not *imposed* products, indicative of their importance to ordinary Arabs. In this context, transnational Arab media has emerged, not simply broadcasting or re-broadcasting, but re-creating and directing new forms of Arab regional identity, particularly al-Jazeera, through open discussions and debates, investigative journalism programs and most immediately, through its news broadcasts.

This has operated as a formative part of the process towards McArabism: the potential for it to be embraced, while also directing it in part. In this regard, McArabism is not a state sponsored ideal, nor is it a movement, in the sense of enjoying a generated history, process or supposed future. There are no clear tenants expressed. It does not have a leader, nor does it have members. The formation of McArabism is premised upon the erosion of state control expressed through state limits as information borders. Thus McArabism often works in antagonism to the state, enjoins upon Arab audiences to critically think and respond to events around them—a radical drift from Arab leader-follower models—and also the model inspiring many historical Arab movements. McArabism reflects a neoliberal trend for choice: the audience is exposed to multi-layers of information, different viewpoints and news directly from the source and is encouraged to make up their own minds. Inevitably, the audience is also encouraged to be a good consumer.

McArabism is primarily a pan-Arab, regional expression of Arab identity conveyed through Arab transnational television, particularly al-Jazeera and other main Arab regional channel players. As a regional expression of identity, relatively beyond the control of one evocative voice, it appears to be more democratic (reflecting the identities and aspirations of viewers). Thus it evokes Islam—or Islamic symbols and religious elements. It appears that the influence of Islam over McArabism also has a direct relationship to the Palestinian issue as the yardstick of Arab development—its influence, its success, the place of Arabs (as a people) in the world, their influence and their ability to reach their aspirations. Like the old Arabism, it has linguistic and historical roots, but creates a stronger sense of immediacy and unmediated community, with the birth of new technologies. The greater exchange of ideas through the region and a concomitant increased strength of transnational movements in the region are not only possible but also likely.

Nevertheless, McArabism is not Subaltern, as offered in analysis by Gayatri Spivak or Ranjit Guha and other intellectuals. Its proponents are clearly upper middle class media professionals—men and women. News and political discussion programs are mainly drawn from individuals and structures (governments, civil society institutions, think tanks, etc.), which are clearly focused around other upper middle class professionals, despite a plethora of views expressed.

However, for those wishing to pursue a line of Subaltern analysis in Arab transnational media, it is important to note that news and political discussion programs draw their legitimacy from *ordinary* people confirming views or creating contexts in which (then) upper-middle class professionals respond to. For example, in a news bulletin, middle-aged women from a refugee camp will speak about a bomb she witnessed falling onto a crowded apartment. The footage then switches to a Hamas representative confirming events taking place, offering commentary. Moreover, the upper middle class, the overwhelming majority of people working for transnational media, or asked to appear on such media, are beyond the only real power structure in the Arab world: political structures, represented in the ruling state regime.

It is helpful to return to the terms coined by Benjamin Barber (1992) to understand the tendencies I am speaking of in McArabism. As I noted earlier, in Barber's paper *Jihad vs. McWorld,* he distinguishes between two "political futures." One is "Jihad," a kind of retribalization of large swaths of humankind characterized by "threatened Lebanonization of national states in which culture is pitted against culture, people against people and tribe against tribe" (ibid). The alternative is "McWorld"—a reference to the spread of American cultural and capitalist interests throughout the world as embodied by McDonalds, which refers to a kind of integration and uniformity caused by the "onrush of economic and ecological forces" that "mesmerize" the world toward one common cultural consumption (music, food, communication, computer usage, etc.) and "pressing nations into one commercially homogenous global network . . . tied together by technology, ecology, communications and commerce" (ibid). According to Barber, the two tendencies of Jihad and McWorld

> . . . operate with equal strength in opposite directions, the one driven by parochial hatreds, the other by universalizing markets, the one re-creating ancient sub-national and ethnic borders from within, the other making national borders porous from without.

The emergence of McArabism is accomplished via six main processes, which complete each other. The first process is *intensification* using and broadcasting regional (pan-Arab) media content expressed on several levels.

News: Intensification refers to the dramatic increase in frequency of newscasts, which are broadcast several times daily on entertainment satellite channels like MBC or LBCI and every hour on the all-news television stations such as al-Jazeera and Abu Dhabi TV. This is in contrast to terrestrial television stations, which have only one or two news broadcasts each day, providing only limited opportunity for people to tune in.

Shared concern: Intensification also refers to addressing issues on transnational television of interest to a pan-Arab audience. These issues include crises between Arab states and non-Arabs, problems facing the Arab world as whole and political, social and cultural phenomena in Arab societies. This is significant on two levels: Many of these issues were previously hidden from the eyes of the Arab audiences, while a shared (new) pan-Arab engagement in these issues have intensified the nature of their concern on a pan-Arab level.

Pan-Arab and Islamic programs: The process of intensification, which has led to McArabism, has been facilitated through the regional broadcasting of historical, educational and political programs aiming to educate (Arab) audiences about the history, development or issues regarding the Arab and Islamic world. Through virtually simultaneous broadcasting, it encourages audiences to engage in symbolic events, developments and milestones of Arab-Islamic culture, to draw their relevance to the viewer and to re-create or emphasize the viewer's worldview based upon their ethnic/religious identity.

Entertainment programs: Intensification is also expressed through entertainment programs, such as movies and dramas that have traditionally been popular on Arab television screens. Alongside the traditional fare of Egyptian movies and Syrian soap operas, it has encouraged a new pan-Arab music market, with regular music shows and a new emphasis upon video clips. In contrast to the period of terrestrial television where music programming offered locally produced songs in local dialects, difficult to understand beyond a geographic area, or the traditional fare of Egyptian classics; transnational broadcasting offers a pan-Arab selection of music, encouraging at once a new understanding and appreciation of different Arabic dialects (although the majority of songs are in Gulf, Lebanese or Egyptian dialects). More importantly, the creation of a new entertainment market, specifically targeted for regional Arab audiences has created a common framework of entertainment trends.

The second process is a *shared stance* on pan-Arab and Islamic issues or crises like the Palestinian Intifada, the Arab-Israeli conflict, the Iraqi crisis with the U.S. or Usama Bin Laden and al-Qaeda in Afghanistan. Thus a regional pan-Arabist dialogue among intellectuals has begun to emerge, not only in such regional Arab newspapers as *al-Hayat* and *al-Sharq al-Awsat,* but more importantly and effectively through satellite television stations like ANN, Abu Dhabi TV and al-Jazeera. This dialogue has expanded the bounds of debate in the Arab world, representing the injection of both new views and back-and-forth discussion into areas where such things had been relatively rare. But this dialogue has also tended to merge into an 'Arab consensus,' which can become its own form of restraint.

The third process is emotive footage, also described as *sensationalism* of the news through the use of various kinds of rhetoric in reporting language as well as pictures, style of presentations and other effects. I address this issue in more detail specifically regarding al-Jazeera in a later chapter. Importantly, the process of allowing viewers to see, often live, footage clearly intended to provoke an emotional effect allows audiences to experience deeper forms of engagement. Beyond a rational level of acknowledgement or sharing issues of concern, the use of emotional footage posits the audience in an imagined community, or a participant/viewer of a part of his/her community on screen.

The fourth process is *direct engagement:* This refers to the use of modern styles of news and broadcasting which allow the audience to understand the news with minimal state intervention, including using different broadcasting effects and techniques such as live broadcasts, figures and maps; having reporters stationed in both Arab and non-Arab countries; providing in-depth reports on various issues and conducting interviews with people, leaders and groups representing different points of views. This was rarely, if ever, done on state owned terrestrial television stations. The use of these tools (maps, reporters, interviews) has lead to a low degree of intervention in the process of bringing reality to audiences; less intervention from internal gatekeepers of news programming, less intervention from political regimes and other television station owners—as occurs with state owned terrestrial stations where news is subject to heavy manipulation and ultimately represents the formal attitude and interests of the regime, its partners and friends.

The fifth process is *language.* Transnational television broadcasts news and serious programs in Modern Standard Arabic. This is based upon classical Arabic, with a simplified grammar system and the inclusion of contemporary terms in their Arabized form, rather than in English or French, the two main colonial languages of the region. For instance, broadcasters use terms such as *hatif* (telephone—commonly referred to as *telefon), 'ala al-hawa* (live—commonly said as *layv).* Although there is no one dialect of Arabic, which can be understood among all levels of Arabic society (plagued as it is by low levels of school attendance among women, and illiteracy), Modern Standard is perhaps the most widely understood, based in Qur'anic Arabic and taught through school systems all over the Arab world.

This is in contrast to the period before transnational television, when many terrestrial stations used local dialects. On the other hand, the status of Egyptian and Lebanese dialects has strengthened through transnational broadcasting. This has occurred both through their prominence prior to transnational broadcasting, transferred to the new medium; the over-representation of Lebanese professionals on transnational television (broadcasters and entertainers) and the volumes of entertainment programs (video clips, movies, soap operas, etc.) the two countries churn out. Meanwhile, Gulf dialects are enjoying a new prominence on transnational television, apparently due to the power of Gulf consumers to marketers.

Sixth, *the formation of an independent press corps.* Transnational television tends to be identical in terms of news coverage and delivery. Many of these news organizations are based outside the region, or in states that the majority of staff is not from—such as Qatar-based al-Jazeera, Abu Dhabi-based Abu Dhabi TV and Dubai-based al-Arabiya, giving a degree of independence unprecedented in many countries. One consequence of this is the emergence of a press corps that both remains independent of the agendas of the most prominent Arab states and seeks an audience that transcends national borders.

As suggested through this discussion, McArabism requires that Arab audiences be exposed simultaneously to identical content, to enjoy opportunities for interaction. Just as importantly, McArabism is achieved not only through media content but also *through the medium itself.* The medium itself is a vital element in this process, providing Arabs in different locations a greater opportunity to engage with content. This helps create a collective discourse that raises issues that have meaning to all Arabs. Transnational television channels play a central role in the rising quality of television news, scientific and entertainment programs, while also creating more harmonious Arab public opinion on crucial regional and pan-Arab issues.

For example, some argue that the rise in Arab public opposition to the U.S. attack on Iraq in 1998 and the boycott of the al-Doha economic conference with Israel in 1997 were partly due to the existence of the transnational Arab television, especially the more independent of them (Ghareeb and Mansour 2000). Following the televising of the latest Intifada and the U.S.'s attack on Iraq, far stronger opinions can be nuanced towards Israel and the U.S.

This is important in terms of discussing the implications of McArabism: At this stage, it is uncertain how widespread the regional impact of McArabism is. Is it defined through the amount of discussions revolving around events, which could have only been known through transnational television? Is it through the amount of people (increasingly so) participating in debate over the Palestinian issue through watching repeated assaults upon the West Bank and Gaza Strip? Is it defined through the increasing legitimacy given to news broadcasts on transnational stations, above all al-Jazeera? Or is it through the increasing hostility (occasionally expressed through preventing transmission and removing press cards from journalists) via governments and their institutions towards transnational television? Is it through satellite dish ownership?

It is clear that class barriers have emerged to the spread of McArabism, chiefly in rural areas, with relatively poorer populations and less access to satellite television. However, the notion of watching television as a *communal act* in much of the rural Arab world may even diminish this barrier. For instance, the emergence of the influence of radio broadcasts in the Arab world only emerged through the act of *communal listening*—whether in houses, cafes, or the re-broadcast of transmissions in mosques and discussions. It appears at this stage, that Arab transnational television is also enjoying influence among poorer groups with little access to such technology, through communal behavior.

Chapter Three
Emergence and Erosion: a Brief History of the Electronic Media in the Arab World and Structures

This chapter concentrates upon a description and analysis of historical and social processes in the development of the electronic media, above all, transnational media in the Arab world over the last seventy years, including the media structure that subsequently developed.

I then look at the emergence of transnational television in the region and its effect on the Arab media map. The direct role transnational television plays in transmitting media content via satellite both within Arab states and across national borders is examined. Two main processes are concentrated upon: the emergence of the Arab transnational media and how satellite broadcasting has eroded existing means of mass media in the Arab world.

Since the last decade of the last century, Arab skies became full with satellites beaming an array of governmental, semi-governmental and commercial television stations throughout the region. While early global and regional channels such as CNN and BBC might have been perceived by critics as instruments of Western media imperialism, they were followed by channels partially created within and directed at national markets, chiefly Saudi Arabia and the other smaller Gulf states, as well as sub-national/ethnic language channels aimed at specific Arab communities transplanted from their original location to sites across the Arab world or in diaspora. Most Arab governments have even taken to beaming their domestic governmental channels via satellite, which are specifically directed towards other countries in the region. Some pan-Arab satellite channels have specialized in business, entertainment, film, news, educational programming, children's programming and women's channels.

Brief history of media technology in the Arab world

The following overview of broadcasting in the Arab world is intended to be a starting point and a general context for discussing electronic media systems.

Radio broadcasting

Broadcasting and the electronic media in the Arab world began in the 1920's with the operation of colonial radio stations in some Arab countries. The first local radio broadcasting initiative occurred in Egypt with several private commercial stations, most of which were located in Cairo (Dabbous 1994). Over the next two decades, due to limitations and obstacles in receiving radio broadcasts and a shortage of radios, the medium's popularity was limited to Arab elites. However, colonial powers and later, the creation of the Arab nation state accelerated the media development process. Radio became one of the basic instruments for the nation building of the new Arab states (Boyd 1993).

State initiatives, in the form of sponsorship, funding and regulatory measures, were adopted as a means to develop the new medium. This approach was taken so that radio could be used for domestic sociopolitical aims and importantly, for regional purposes as the former Egyptian president Jamal 'Abd al-Nasser did with the famous Egyptian radio station *Sawt al-'Arab* (Voice of the Arabs), broadcast from Cairo during the 50s and 60s when Nasser's pan-Arabism reached almost every corner of the Arab world (Karam 1999). Arab leaders were interested in rapid social and economic change and also desired a new form of regional influence that only radio broadcasting systems could provide.

A substantial decrease in radio prices during the latter part of the 1950's and early 1960's expanded the availability of radios for lower income segments of the population. It is hardly a coincidence that the transistor revolution coincided with political movements in North Africa, Egypt and Iraq that overthrew ruling royal families or were successful in gaining independence from colonial powers (Boyd 1993). The rapid spread of radio also coincided with rising independence from colonial powers. Consequently, by the end of the 1970s every Arab country boasted at least one state owned radio station.

With the exception of Lebanon, where most radio stations were privately owned in the same manner as other electronic media (especially television) (Kraidy 1998), radio stations were state run (Boyd 1993). In most Arab countries the Ministry of Information is responsible for running radio stations, determining its media policy, content and operating framework. The Minster of Information *is* the radio director (Karam 1999).

From the early 1980s, Arabic-language radio stations physically located outside the Arab world became the main source of competition for local state run radio stations. *BBC Arabic* broadcasting from the U.K., the Paris-based *Voice of America* and *Radio al-Sharq* (Radio East) (Kraidy 1998) and the Washington-based *Radio Sawa* (Radio Together) have become popular with Arab listeners within a relatively short time, particularly the latter. This new phenomenon, evident throughout Arab world, is largely due to the allure of Anglo-European stations' entertainment programming and the high level of credibility regarding news coverage. This also testified to the unreliability Arab listeners attributed to state run stations (Boulos 1996). This trend in radio broadcasting from beyond the Arab world has continued with privately owned Arab communication companies.

The turn to foreign radio stations (or stations broadcast from outside the Arab world) has left state run radio stations far behind their privately owned counterparts, which after almost one century of radio broadcasting in the Arab world is a major factor causing these traditional radio stations to rethink how they function in the new media environment.

Nevertheless, judging from the quick rise in popularity of radio stations broadcast from outside the Arab world over a twenty year period certainly suggests that local Arab (principally government owned) stations have not yet formulated a model attractive to local listeners. Indeed, as we shall see throughout this book, the same can be said of terrestrial television.

Television Broadcasting

Television broadcasting in the Arab world can be traced to the creation of the Arab nation state. Television broadcasting began with international television viewing, mostly in the Gulf. Up to the 1960's there were no local television stations in most Arab countries. The government owned Iraqi television, established in Baghdad in 1956, was the first television station in the Arab world (Hurrat and Leidig 1994).[4] Egypt followed with its own television station in 1959, resulting from a joint venture between the Egyptian government and Radio Corporation of America (Nassr 1963). The Saudi government introduced television in the 1960s, countering deep-seated religious opposition to the medium with various political imperatives, including the need to divert Saudi listeners away from Nasserist propaganda broadcast by Egyptian radio stations from Cairo.[5]

Entertainment however, did not take precedence over religious programming, especially given Saudi responsibility for guardianship of Mecca and Medina, the holy places visited by Muslims on pilgrimage from all over the world. Saudi television began live coverage of Ramadan prayers and pilgrimage rituals in 1975. In 1980, after the siege of the Grand Mosque of Mecca by religious extremists and the revolution that created the Islamic Republic of Iran, the proportion of religious programming in Saudi television was dramatically increased.

During the 1960s and early 1970s television stations were established in every Arab state, with the last three being Qatar (1970), Bahrain (1972) and finally Oman (1974) (Karam 1999).

By the end of second millennium, for every 1000 persons in the region there are 96 television sets as compared to 120 television sets for every 1000 persons in the world (Karam 1999). Figures of television set ownership indicate differences between different Arab countries. In Saudi Arabia, there is one television set for every three persons, while in Bahrain and Jordan there is one television set for two persons. Lebanon has only one television set for four persons and in

---

[4] This small station was imported as a part of a British trade fair with Iraq.
[5] Douglas Boyd recounts the history in *Broadcasting in the Arab World,* 3rd edition (Ames: Iowa, 1999, 152-3).

Egypt there is one television set for five persons. In comparison, in the United States, there is one television set for each person (ibid).

The main challenge terrestrial television faces is its limit range, compared with radio, which can cross borders in the same region with relative ease. With more sophisticated equipment, radio can cross the borders of continents, with Anglo-European-sponsored radio stations broadcasting to the Arab world from Europe since 1920.

Arab terrestrial television broadcasting is limited to the borders of each Arab state and to parts of neighboring countries. Unlike radio, terrestrial Arab television failed to broadcast content throughout the Arab world, indeed, failed to open media borders in the Arab world. In fact, it has consistently done the opposite, creating small media consumption units limited to the geopolitical borders of Arab nation states, from its establishment in the 1960s, until new technology was introduced in the late 1980s.

Indicative of this failure, television stations were created in the Arab world as a result of state regime initiatives (with the exception of Lebanon), not from individuals, private interests or other commercial entities (Kraidy 1998). Furthermore, even today all television stations not directly controlled by the state are still oriented to serve the general goals of the state, with a primary focus on unifying the nation and promoting social integration.

There are two main types ownership in the Arab world. In most Arab countries, including Syria, Egypt, Saudi Arabia and Libya, the broadcasting system is owned by the state. Ownership is direct in nature. Television stations are formally owned and funded by the state. All station employees are state workers. State officials and political leadership dictate media policy and the selection of content for these stations (Boyd 1993). The second and less common type of television ownership in Lebanon, Bahrain, Jordan and Morocco, refers to a situation where stations are jointly owned by the government and the private sector (ibid 1993). In this situation, the initiative to create electronic media entities originally comes from private companies and entrepreneurs who operate with the approval of the state.

Until the early 1990s, state control over the electronic media meant that privatization and commercialism was very limited in almost every Arab state. This was a result of various factors, most importantly being strict regulations limiting private ownership of electronic media.

Broadcasting content

Generally speaking, terrestrial Arab television and radio programming is based on two main components: political propaganda for the regime and entertainment. A significant percentage of programming time is devoted to political information and propaganda, though in general such non-entertainment content, including news and commentary, merely extols the (so-called) accomplishments of the political leaders, regardless of their political appearances (Karam 1999).

In addition, every terrestrial Arab television and radio station has a large amount of religious-oriented programming, with hours given over on Friday, the Muslim holy day, to broadcasting the sermon given in a (usually prominent) mosque and filming the Friday prayer. Arab television content corresponds with current political and cultural-religious circumstances in the Arab world, generally religious and traditional. Arab television programmers informally adopt a kind of unwritten but clearly understood codes of ethics that befits local norms and values.

Simultaneously, the trend toward permissiveness in Anglo-European television programs has served to narrow the choices available to Arab countries. In many cases, programs must undergo editing for excessive sex, violence and in the case of Saudi Arabia, any references to Christianity (Boyd 1993).

As tends to be the case in non-Latin developing countries, most programs broadcast on the majority of terrestrial Arab television stations are imported from Anglo-European countries, especially from the United States (Karam 1999) and Latin America. In comparison, Arab media industries have failed to export even one media product to any country outside the Arab world. The second most prevalent type of programming on Arab television is local-based, orientated solely towards the audience of each Arab state. This includes newscasts (most of them on local issues) and educational and social programs. Until the end of the 1990s, most Arabic-language programming broadcast by terrestrial television stations was produced in three countries: Egypt, Lebanon and Syria, while most Arab countries did not have the ability or resources to produce television programming. In most Arab countries (save for Egypt), with the exception of newscasts, religious programs and programs on local issues, virtually all programming was imported from Anglo-European countries, Latin America or from other Arab countries.

Broadcasting Control

Media in the Arab world—and electronic media in particular—is controlled by the respective ministries of information *(Wizarat al-I'lam)* in each state—i.e., state officials rather than professionals run the media. The main interest guiding these officials is to ensure the media adheres to the editorial lines of the regime, rather than to media guidelines, in terms of quality, content, programming or audience needs. Ministers of information may intervene when action is required to ensure that television stations operate according to state regime interests.

This is achieved not only through an official office of censorship, which can be found in virtually every Arab state, but also in every way deemed suitable to achieve particular objectives, including self-censorship, the use of emergency laws, or other legal and illegal applications of power or pressure.

During the 1970s and 1980s, television systems in the Arab world were constrained by three major problems: insufficient production of local programming, which lead to external television imports; close government scrutiny and control, leading to prohibitive working environments; and shortages of human and financial resources, leading to dull and low-quality programming output (Ayish 2001).

This situation creates a serious obstacle for the Arab media and the broadcast media in particular, preventing the press from serving as a fourth estate to criticize state institutions, functioning little more than an extension of the regime. Over the last 60 years—from the 1920s to the late 1980s—a kind of tribal broadcasting media developed in the Arab world.

From their very inception, Arab television and radio were closely controlled by state broadcasting authorities. News programs were heavily scripted and almost invariably opened with extensive coverage of the activities of the head of state.[6] Entertainment programs trod delicately on social (let alone political) issues, the consequence of which was a diverting yet not especially exciting extension of the state information apparatus into the homes of the populace. As Alterman (1998) writes, television programming was the product of government bureaucrats and it often showed.

Tribal broadcasting media

Tribal media, as briefly mentioned above, refers to the mass media system that developed in every Arab state over a 60 year period: from the 1920s to the late 1980s. It consisted of written, electronic and other medias, operating within a defined geopolitical unit (state or other sociopolitical entities), with closed borders. This arrangement put limitations on the infiltration of external mass media content, including logistical obstacles, such as a limited broadcast range of terrestrial television stations, as well as limitations created by political regimes, such as various regulations and censorship, in order to prevent local communities being exposed to external media. This included preventing the importation of newspapers, magazines, books and videocassettes or jamming external electronic broadcasts.

In the post-colonial era, the governments of the newly established Arab states, based on a single ruling group (whether ethnic/religious, party-based, monarchical) turned to print media to exhort the public to support the new rulers. Many governments closed party presses and replaced them with government entities that reflected official viewpoints. Much like radio, the written word was to be employed in the service of the state (Alterman 1998). Throughout the region—in Syria, Iraq, Libya and South Yemen, among others—governments took over the ownership of the press. Hence the characterization of these newspapers by the Arab media analyst William Rugh as the "mobilization press" is apt, since their purpose was to rally support for authoritarian governments.

Programming content within state-delineated media units was directed according to a rigid media policy set by political elites and regimes, intended to control information flows and to do so in a way that would also ensure its control over the masses. Not only did this not leave any space for external media, as was already mentioned above, but neither was there any possibility for any alternative, independent, domestic, non-state produced programming.

This was achieved through a variety of mechanisms. The first was the use of rigid internal media regulations, which actively discouraged the establishment of private or non-state mass media organizations. In some cases, privately

---

[6] It is not uncommon for example, for the national evening news broadcast in an Arab country to begin with a silent ten-minute shot for the head of the state greeting a large delegation of visiting dignitaries by kissing each one another on both cheeks.

owned media outlets are forbidden by law. Second, state censorship was heavily used, both directly and indirectly, to control media content of both state and private media. This included economic, political and administrative pressure, as well as various sanctions, including shutting down media outlets and even violence against journalists and others working in the media. But the most effective means was the development of a culture of self-censorship, which became one of the rules of media survival. In addition to these constraints, modern Arab nations also made use of moral structural norms to enforce their media regulatory policies during this 60 year period.

During the 1970s and 1980s, in a framework "resembling democratization acts," state regimes sought to absorb public frustration by permitting the appearance of allowing the expression of liberal media and free press. This was done through a combination of coercion and co-option, with careful monitoring of public opinion to understand what might lie beyond the bounds of popular acceptance. In addition, many governments allowed for the emergence of a kind of loyal opposition, permitting a diversity of views within understood boundaries. Doing so allowed new ideas to gestate and kept the intelligentsia in line without actually threatening the government's ultimate grip on power. The media— initially print and followed by radio and television—played an important role in this equation by both disseminating government viewpoints and providing a forum for carefully modulated criticism and commentary on government policies (Alterman 1998).

Consequently, the use of these means of media control shows that state media (in what ever form) not only survives but is also hermetically sealed from external messages. State regimes and professionals produce a media that is continuously manipulated, preserving balances of power and dominant perceptions of reality. With television, this was achieved mainly by producing programs— carefully selected by station managers and other media professionals—with a political orientation suiting state leadership (Kraidy 1998).

Importantly, developments in the Arab world over the past 50 years seem to have put political news on top of media agendas. One implication of this trend has been the production of elitist news programs that show little concern with developments related to grassroots organizations or groups that fall outside existing political arrangements at local and regional levels in the Arab world. The emphasis on political news has also come at the expense of human interest coverage describing ordinary individuals (Ayish 2001).

Furthermore, nightly newscasts were not only the major component of television journalism but were themselves dull and monolithic in their format, content and delivery. Television news gatekeepers selected their topics with a view guided mainly by existing political, social and cultural arrangements. Political news dealing with speeches by political leaders, official visits and protocol activities always topped the news agenda in the Arab world. Under these conditions, opposition groups had less access to government monopolized television, as did large segments of the population living outside urban centers. During the 1970s and 1980s, a single channel environment provided viewers with limited exposure to regional and international television content from neighboring countries or around the world (ibid 2001).

This tribal media arrangement was set up by political elites not only to preserve political regimes, but also to maintain the socio-cultural order and cultural religious values that provide the foundation for the existing political order's legitimacy. The reinforcement of the traditional patriarchal society, which is part of this media policy, also aims to sustain the existing media model. This is reflected in the large and consistently positive media coverage of political elites, ruling families and leadership by all media outlets without allowing any kind of criticism or even indirectly negative representations.

Daoud Kuttab (1999) argues that this media is given to covering the rulers of the Arab countries rather than providing quality entertainment, documentaries and current affairs programming. In practice, video footage or photographs of leaders and their families and reporting on their activities appear on the front page of leading Arab newspapers.

Moreover, the structure of domestic or independently produced radio and television programs is organized in a manner that preserves and supports existing sociopolitical orders. Simultaneously, imported programs are selected to provide a means of escapism and to ventilate the audience's collective frustration with the situation they find themselves in, but without allowing for side effects of such programs, which could lead to changing domestic sociopolitical and religious cultural orders and values. Arab television programming typically consists of a diverse, mostly pirated, menu of American police series, French and American news, British comedies, Egyptian soap operas, German documentaries and Mexican telenovelas (Kraidy 1998).

In this tribal media, there is a palpable lack of participation by audiences and rarely any deviation from mainstream ideas and opinions held by ruling elites. Consequently, under these circumstances, the public sphere is virtually non-existent. Media is one-directional, from the regime to the population, without any feedback. Audiences are passive rather than active consumers. Public discourse regarding social or political issues is alien to this kind of media. Consequently, we can understand why a mass media almost totally incorporated into the ruling regime gives such attention to the political leadership. This reality defines how journalists perceive themselves, the government and audiences, as well as how overlapping responsibilities between these parties are understood. In this paradigm, the ruler becomes the chairman of the "journalism" institution, the intelligence chief is the editor and the journalist is reduced to a shadow (Fouda 2001).

Therefore, tribal media in the Arab world and especially state run television, can be described as "a mélange of various inconsistent programs, policies and structures, predominantly foreign in orientation and barely relevant to the needs of state population or the Arab world" (Dajani 1999). For tribal media, the concept of television journalism was virtually non-existent as a part of television services, which for four decades had functioned more as government propaganda machines than independent sources of information (Ayish 2001). Furthermore, talk show programs are not a true representation of real life, but are rather a montage adapted for broadcasting. As such, participants on live talk shows are carefully screened and selected to ensure that their comments do not cross red lines, but are instead good representatives for the regime's ideas and the hegemonic ruling ideology. Similarly, no individuals belonging to political opposition groups or holding non-mainstream ideas are given the opportunity to participate. Finally, as Lent (1989) argues concerning the media in Asia; Arab media professionals have repeatedly been instructed in regards to their correct roles and are urged to support and cooperate with authorities by stressing positive news, ignoring much negative and adverse information and supporting government plans and ideologies.

In the tribal media framework, television has played the main role, mainly over the last 30 years, when it displaced radio from the prominent position it held from 1920-1960. Until the emergence of television, radio and print were the main players in the creation of tribal media in the Arab world. Traditional state run media has accompanied the establishment of the Arab state, has assisted in the nation building process and in shaping the (assumed) ethno-national collective identity in each state while prepping Arab communities to different new states and solidifying (local) national identities (Alterman 1998).

This can be seen in the Lebanonization of the Lebanese population, the Jordanization of communities on the eastern side of the Jordan River, etc. Until the end of the 1980s, the tribal media and television in particular, in the Arab world, functioned according to a government monopoly model of broadcasting. This model draws upon the notion of broadcasting as a tool for national development placed under government control. Although this model drew partly out of the broadcasting systems that were dominant in former colonial nations such as Britain and France, it deprived broadcasters of editorial discretion and autonomy as a result of ubiquitous government control.

For several reasons, television replaced print and radio as the main medium of the tribal media. First, the range of terrestrial television is very limited and its reach cannot extend far beyond the geopolitical borders of each state. This means that access to terrestrial television channels for each state is generally limited to the population that lives there. Second, it is difficult to extend its broadcasting to areas outside this state, except for populations of neighboring countries located near the borders of that state. Third, it is relatively very easy for ruling elites to control television through its ownership of particular channels, which require a large amount of capital investment and operation costs that are difficult for most private interests to obtain. This is one reason why Lebanon remained exceptional in its plethora of privately owned television stations. In three other states: Jordan, Morocco and Kuwait, partnerships between private interests and the state own television stations. In the remainder of Arab states, television stations are fully owned by the state (Boyd 1993). In addition, a very firm package of laws and regulations were imposed by regimes to prevent private ownership of television stations; a media considered to be very effective among traditional populations with high illiteracy rates, as is the case in the Arab world.

Over time, especially after television sets became easier for Arab citizens to purchase or access, a televisual environment developed in Arab societies that strengthened by the end of the 1980s. This televisual environment, developed within the framework of the tribal media, constitutes its cornerstone, as a result of the increased importance of television as a medium, compared with print and radio in the 1980s.

Emergence of satellite television in the Arab world

One of the major effects of transnational broadcasting in the Arab world, the creation of the pan-Arab media and its mass communication outlets, has been the erosion of earlier existing forms of television broadcasting. To discuss this process we will first chronologically present the development of the pan-Arab media, especially broadcasting.

The first pan-Arab media outlet in the Arab world can be traced to Nasser's weekly radio addresses in the 1950s and the 1960s. During his weekly radio address on *Sawt al-'Arab* (Voice of the Arabs) from Cairo, one would find streets empty in Egypt and throughout the Arab world as people gathered around radio transistors. Nasser's speeches became the main topic for discussion in every Arab home, club or social gathering (Ghareeb & Mansour 2000).

The mobilization media in each respective Arab state did not always function as a purely domestic operation. During the 1950s and 1960s, Egypt was particularly active in promoting its views throughout the region, not only through the semi-official Egyptian daily *al-Ahram*, but also through vigorous radio broadcasting. The pan-Arab station broadcast from Egypt, *Voice of the Arabs* combined the attraction of Egyptian singing stars like 'Abd al-Halim Hafez and Umm Kalthoum with pro-regime news reports broadcast to a wide audience. Readers in all Arab countries closely followed the columns of Mohammad Hassanein Heikal, editor-in-chief of *al-Ahram* and widely known as a Nasser confidant. In Egypt's bid for leadership of the Arab world, the country instituted a bold media strategy that was also an essential component of the country's political program. At this time, state ownership of the press was not standard in every Arab country. In some, governments worked out understandings with local newspapers allowing them to operate in private hands as long as they were generally supportive of government policies (Alterman 1998). Rugh (1987) refers to these publications, many of which still exist, as the "loyalist press," because they are "consistently loyal to and supportive of the regime in power despite the fact that they are privately owned."

The media at this time operated in the context of a radio war between stations of different Arab countries for listeners throughout the Arab world. Nasser's death in 1970, the turning of Egyptian policy from the Soviet Union to the U.S. and Anwar Sadat's signing of the peace agreement with Israel at Camp David not only reduced Egypt's importance as leader of the Arab world, but also marked the end of pan-Arab radio. The result was that different radio stations attained a high level of importance as local radio and not in its pan-Arab form.

With the diminished importance of Egyptian radio, other radio outlets could flourish locally.

The second generation of pan-Arab media emerged in the 1980s with the advent of new satellite technologies, leading to the creation of daily satellite newspapers, most importantly, *al-Sharq al-Awsat* (The Middle East), *al-Quds al-'Arabi* (Arab Jerusalem) and later *al-Hayat* (Life), which are all physically located outside the Arab world and do not face the limitations and censorship that comes with operating inside Arab states. In 1978, a company called Saudi Research and Marketing began producing *al-Sharq al-Awsat* in London and used satellite technology to beam the newspaper's contents to printing plants in Saudi Arabia.[7] Because the new newspaper was headquartered in London, it had ready access to Anglo (British and American) news sources. Furthermore, because it was written, edited and printed in London, it could not be subject to the same kinds of restrictions the government could apply if produced in Saudi Arabia (Alterman 1998).

Al-Sharq al-Awsat was the harbinger of a new kind of Arabic press and was followed by a reborn *al-Hayat* (a Beirut paper that had stopped publishing during the war, resurrected in 1988 and given new life in 1990 with an infusion of cash from the Saudi prince Khalid bin Sultan) and *al-Quds al-Arabi.*

Importantly, the third major newspaper, *al-Quds al-Arabi,* published out of London is in no way part of a publishing empire. *Al-Quds al-Arabi* is created by a handful of reporters out of somewhat threadbare offices in the London. Nevertheless, the newspaper has emerged as an important voice in expatriate Arab circles and to a lesser extent in the Arab world itself. The newspaper's strength can be found in its reporting—generally based on anonymous sources—of decisions and events in the Arab world. The newspaper also features an important innovation: a full page every day with complete translations of articles from the Israeli press. Editorially, *al-Quds al-Arabi* is consistently the most patriotic and critical of the major Arabic papers. Finally, *al-Quds al-Arabi* is the only one of the big three that does not rely on Saudi funding. As a consequence, the paper enjoys a freedom to talk about Gulf politics and events that its competitors do not.

London became the locus for a vibrant Arab press scene. In addition to the newspapers, London-based Arab publishing houses also began turning out an impressive array of glossy full color magazines, such as *al-Majalla* (The Magazine), *al-Wasat* (The Middle) and others. These publications thrived on the United Kingdom's editorial freedom and all were available to varying degrees throughout the Arab world, although on occasion issues would not make it past local censors in one country or another.

These publications are transmitted via satellite from their European headquarters in London to major population centers throughout the Arab world. Although owned by private Saudi interests, these papers target a pan-Arab audience, as is reflected in the make up of their staff, editors and columnists. Furthermore, these publications share something in addition to their heavily

---

[7] The Gannet Corporation relied on similar technology when it launched *USA Today* as a national U.S. newspaper in the early 1980s. The technology has since become common.

Lebanese cast of writers and editors: To a large degree, they have relied on sub-sidies from the Gulf. In fact, London's dominance over Paris in fostering the development of a vibrant press testifies to the importance of money in operating these enterprises. Generally speaking, the Lebanese, who represent the majority of expatriate Arab editors and writers in diaspora, would be much more com-fortable in Paris than in London. French, rather than English, is Lebanon's sec-ond language. But Gulf Arabs are much more comfortable with English and it was mostly to London rather than Paris that they traveled when the oil boom of the 1970s brought new prosperity to the Arab world. Not surprisingly, journal-ists followed the money.

Over the last twenty-five years, London ironically has emerged as one of the world's great Arab capitals, with banks, restaurants, shops and a vibrant and open press previously unknown in the Arab world itself. Whereas such regional Arabic newspapers and magazines reach only the elites in most countries, they still constitute an important means for regional dialogue and they play a signifi-cant role expanding the sphere of public debate.

The third generation of pan-Arab media, which is the main focus in this book, begins in 1990 with the satellite broadcasting in the Arab region. Alter-man (1998) cites three main developments in the Arab world that led to the rise of satellite television in the 1990s. The first was the multilateral response to Saddam Hussein's invasion of Kuwait. To a great extent, the U.S.-led Operation Desert Storm and the events that preceded it in 1990-1991 made for extremely attractive television programming. As gripping as CNN was to watch, during the war, it was not available in most Arab homes. The requisite antennas were large and expensive and distribution was oriented to commercial establishments rather than to the home market. In addition, CNN's English-language broadcasts proved a barrier to easy comprehension by many Arabs. Nevertheless, CNN's presence helped forge a market for a new kind of Arabic broadcasting.

The second crucial development for the sudden emergence of Arab satellite television was the launch of a new generation of satellites. Arabsat, a consortium comprising the members of the League of Arab States, launched its first com-munications satellite in 1985. As satellites become more powerful and occupy lower orbits in the sky, there will likely be a continued increase in broadcasting capacity as well as a continuing diminution in the size and cost of satellite dishes.

The third important development Alterman identifies is the emergence of a substantial class of Arab professionals who studied and in some cases worked in Anglo-European countries before returning to their countries of origin. The growing numbers of Arabs who lived overseas were more consumer-oriented than their parents and their wealth gave them many more options for consump-tion.

The emergence of satellite broadcasting can be traced to two starting points. The first was on December 12, 1990, when the Egyptian Satellite Channel started transmission. In the final buildup to the war that began on 15 January 1991, the state owned Egyptian Radio and Television Union (ERTU) arranged to lease an Arabsat transponder to broadcast television programs across the Arab world all day, every day, for the next three years (Sakr 2001). Within days the ERTU was using the facility to send news and entertainment programs to the Gulf, for the benefit of Egyptian soldiers and local viewers with the necessary receiving equipment. The series became known as the Egyptian Space Channel (ESC).

The second was MBC. In September of 1991, Saudi Arabia launched the Middle East Broadcasting Center (MBC), a privately owned network (Ghareeb & Mansour 2000). Saudi Arabia is the heart of the Islamic world and therefore religious programming has a special importance in official Saudi television programming and dominates a good part of the schedule on the national television channels. This station, which is owned by Saudi royal family members, has been revolutionary not only in its technology and use of satellite facilities, but also in regard to content. Unlike the content broadcast by state terrestrial television stations, which emphasize local news and entertainment and serve as an organ of the state, MBC broadcasts content aimed at all Arab countries, covering pan-Arab issues in all spheres of life such as news, entertainment and sport.

Nile TV International was the second Egyptian satellite channel and began experimental broadcasting in October 1993 in English and French. The main objective of this network is to promote the image of Egypt in Europe and to attract tourism (Amin 2000). In the years after the Gulf War, satellite dish ownership was stimulated by the growth of available international programming, increase in satellite power and transmission range, decline in cost of satellite dishes and an increase in the number of companies that marketed, serviced and manufactured satellite dishes.

The spread of satellites has also been dramatically accelerated by the creation of other two privately owned Arab satellite television broadcasting systems, which are both owned by Saudi business interests with links to members of the Saudi royal family. The first was in October 1993 with ART and the following year with Orbit television's two stations broadcasting from Italy: ART from Avezzano and Orbit from Rome. Both are privately owned by Saudi businessmen. These stations differ from MBC in two aspects: First, each station has more than one channel and second, unlike MBC, which is FTA, these two stations are pay-TV and require subscription fees from viewers. By the end of 1994, some 21 pan-Arab satellite television channels were launched other than MBC: Orbit (a bouquet with 16 of its own channels and other Anglo-European channels such as CNN) and ART (with four channels). Gulf states were among the first to utilize satellite broadcasting as they faced little problem financing these projects.

Following the 1991 Gulf War, Kuwait found it essential to start its own network and the Kuwaiti Space Network began on December 8, 1991. Star TV from Hong Kong started on Asiasat in October 1991, reaching audiences in Kuwait and other Gulf countries. One of the network's new digital pay-TV platforms comes from Gulf DTH, which was made available by the Showtime Company and has the support of English-language programming provided by Viacom Inc. The new offering is co-financed by Kuwait Investment Projects Co. (KIPCO) and is now operating on Nilesat (Amin 2000).

The Jordanian Radio and Television Corporation began broadcasting the Jordanian Arab Space Channel on February 1, 1993, utilizing channel 24 on Arabsat 1-C, which blankets most of the Arab world and Europe. It has also expanded to include transmission of the service to Canada and the United States.

In the North African countries of Morocco, Algeria and Tunisia, national television stations were broadcast via satellite. The main reason behind the move was to develop bridges to improve communication between expatriate labor in Europe and the home country. North African countries have a unique Arabic dialect that is not well understood in other Arab nations. This may be why their satellite services cater mainly to Arabs in North Africa (ibid 2000).

In 1996, Qatar made initiatives to introduce the first Arab all-news and public affairs satellite channel. The al-Jazeera Satellite Channel from al-Doha in Qatar was obliged to start out on Arabsat Ku-band, which was less widely received. It was not until a C-band transponder became available on Arabsat on 1 November 1997 that al-Jazeera began to be seen by large numbers of people throughout the Arab world.[8]

As a channel devoted to news and current affairs, it soon made up for lost time by astonishing viewers with uncensored political coverage quite different from any Arabic-language television programming previously seen. It was encouraged in this direction by the new Qatari Emir and was supported by the unusual background of its founding staff (Sakr 2001).

Lebanon may have had no state owned satellite service in 1996, but this did not signify that Lebanese broadcasters were absent from the scene. In fact, satellite television in the Arab world entered a new phase in 1996, with the launch of al-Jazeera and two players from Lebanon. All three broke the mould, but in different ways. Despite traditional Lebanese renown in media affairs, the early 1990s found Lebanese broadcasters recovering from their country's 1975-90 War. In October 1994, the Lebanese parliament passed the Audiovisual Media Law, to close most of the myriad stations that had mushroomed during the war and regulate the rest. This law, put into effect in September 1996, officially revoked the state's broadcasting monopoly, making Lebanon the first Arab state to authorize private radio and television stations to operate within its borders. Another law of 1996 specifically catered for satellite channels. Armed with a license under these laws, the private Lebanese Broadcasting Corporation (LBC, founded as a Christian militia station in the 1980s) launched its own satellite station. So did Future television, a private station partly owned (and heavily influenced) by the Lebanese Prime Minister, Rafiq al-Hariri.

In 1996, LBCI (Lebanese Broadcasting Corporation International) became the first satellite television station to operate from within the Arab world (Kraidy 1998). Future Television and LBCI had an instant impact on viewing patterns in the Gulf, with their relaxed and informal approach and LBCI's uninhibited game shows. Unlike other Arab satellite television stations, these two Lebanese stations were originally privately held, terrestrial television stations operating from Lebanon and can be watched by viewers in countries neighboring Lebanon.

---

[8] Interview with Mohammed Jassem al-Ali, then-director of the al-Jazeera Satellite Channel, May 27, 1998.

The motive behind the upgrade of these two stations came to compete with other private Saudi stations for potential audiences in the Arab world and Arab viewers in diaspora. The Lebanese satellite television stations have flourished in the wake of this decision, which itself is unique in the Arab world. Lebanon is also unique because most of its satellite television stations are indirectly owned by political parties and leaders and not the state, which makes Lebanon the most liberal in this regard to media policy in the Arab world. Indeed, the Lebanese entrance instantly challenged the dominance enjoyed until then by Egyptian and Saudi satellite channels.

Despite the fact that from the late 1970s to the end of the 1990s, Egypt lost its leading position in the Arab world in regard to media initiatives, development and content, as a result of the isolation from the Arab world after its peace agreement with Israel, the Egyptian film and television production industry continues to have a large role in the Arab world. In addition, the Egyptian accent continues to be among the most popular in Arab productions. Furthermore many Egyptian producers and artists avoided the boycott by working in other Arab countries, especially Jordan and the Gulf states. Television stations in the Arab world have always broadcast classic Egyptian cinema as a main category of Arabic-language programming, but it was not until after the 1967 Arab-Israeli War and the termination of the conflict in Yemen (in which Egypt played a role) that Gulf states started importing new Egyptian films and videotapes.

By the mid-1970s, such productions were an important source of hard currency for the Egyptian Radio-Television Federation, but their high prices and former President Sadat's moves toward the eventual signing of a peace treaty with Israel caused some states to reduce or stop their Egyptian program purchases altogether. At the same time, the Egyptian political and economic situation led to a new system of production, with artists preferring to work outside the country to earn more money by receiving cash payments, avoiding personal income taxes. Their new productions were mainly Egyptian written, produced, directed and acted, but were taped in London, Athens, Amman, or Dubai. The natural result was a Western-style television program in Arabic (Boyd 1993).

Satellites were heavily underutilized until the 1990s and it is not surprising that during the period of 1985-1990 Egypt was excluded from Arabsat. Thus Egyptians entered the satellite game at a very late stage, unlike the case in previous generations of media in the Arab world. By the time they did so, state television, as well as Saudi and Lebanese private sector interests had already created satellite channels in the wake of the Gulf War. Many Egyptian media professionals were very active with Arab satellite media institutions from different Arab states especially those pan-Arab stations broadcasting from Europe.[9] Some argue that the emergence of so many regional players and non-Egyptian centers of production meant that Egypt's media hegemony in the 1950s and 1960s would not be repeated.[10]

---

[9]Abdallah Schleifer, "Video Cairo Sat: Breaking New Ground as Usual, But This Time on Nilesat" Transnational *Broadcasting Studies. 1999, No. 3, Fall.*
[10] Interview with Dr. Shibley Telhami in *Transnational Broadcasting Studies.* No.4, Spring 2000.

But similar to the private media sector in Lebanon, the public media sector in Egypt—and the Egyptian government in particular—wanted to return to the Arab media field by getting a piece of the satellite cake and exploiting two factors in the country's favor: Egyptian culture, which is the most dominant in the region and the Egyptian Arabic dialect, which is still by far the most well known in the Arab world. Nilesat, the Egyptian government's first satellite, was Cairo's answer to this challenge. Launched on 28 April 1998, Nilesat provides services in various fields, especially in education, media and culture. Its main relevant product to our discussion is Nile TV, which is unique in the history of Arab satellite television. It marked the first time that the satellite of an Arab state—in this case Egypt—was used not only by other Arab states or media companies to transmit broadcasts, but also for Egypt to establish a state owned television company, containing around 20 stations. Most of the stations are thematic in nature, offering a large variety of content and authentic programs. Egypt's specialized channels on Nilesat 101 (Nile News, Nile Culture, Nile Sports, Nile Children and Nile Variety) are increasingly gaining popularity with viewers. The Egyptian private sector is also making its mark in the region.

Egypt's gigantic Media Production City provides space for private and international production houses. A recent change that marked Egypt's open policy is reflected in the contract signed between al-Jazeera and the Media Production City, whereby al-Jazeera is given facilities to produce and transmit without any censorship of content whatsoever.

The launch of Nilesat 101 and 102, in addition to the already existing Arabsat A and B, increased significantly the capacity of satellite television broadcasting in the region. From 1996-2002 there was a flourishing increase of satellite television stations in the Arab world, which can be classified according to two categories other than private and state owned as discussed above.

As explained above, the process of erosion into traditional media that was prompted by the creation of satellite television stations in the Arab world suggests that most of these television stations, except Egypt's, are privately owned or initiated. But the last few years indicate two new categories: The first category refers to government efforts to enter the satellite broadcasting game, reflected by the creation of at least one state owned satellite television station in every Arab country without exception. This state of affairs has resulted from the initial trend of private-commercial satellite television, which posed a threat to Arab state regimes, challenging their ability to influence Arab screens via the traditional media and terrestrial television in particular.

Arab state regimes have sought to find a way to exist in the new transnational media environment while preventing the creation of space for other transnational media players that would allow the latter to compete on an equal basis, which would ultimately undermine state credibility by eroding media content. Hence, each state has made every effort to create a niche on Arabsat, which is owned by most countries, or to broadcast content on Egypt's Nilesat. By the end of 2000 every Arab state in Asia, the Gulf and North Africa had their own satellite television station, while some—such as Egypt and Saudi Arabia—had more than one.

The second category is reflected in the trend of satellite television stations founded by political and religious parties and groups. This category includes the London-based satellite station ANN, owned by Rif'at al-Assad, the brother of the late Syrian president Hafez al-Assad. ANN is considered very controversial, screening political and talk show programs that enjoy good ratings among Arab audiences. This category also refers to *al-Manar*, a television station located in Lebanon and owned by the Lebanese Shiite party Hizbollah. The station's political-ideological broadcasting agenda is partly oriented towards fighting Israel. There are also two Islamic and two Christian stations broadcasting in Arabic.

Table 3.1: Selected satellite channel start-ups, 1990-98

Start-up	Name	Country Link	Ownership
1990	ESC	Egypt	State
1991	MBC	Saudi Arabia	Private
1992	EDTV	Dubai, U.A.E.	State
1993	JSC	Jordan	State
1994	ART	Saudi Arabia	Private
	Orbit	Saudi Arabia	Private
	RTM	Morocco	State
1995	STV	Syria	State
1996	LBCSat	Lebanon	Private
	Future Int.	Lebanon	Private
	Al-Jazeera	Qatar	Independent
1997	ANN	Syria	Private
1998	Nile Thematic Channels	Egypt	State

Source: Sakr 2001

One expected result of the increasing market orientation of Arab media in general and satellite television in particular, is the likely migration of foreign-based channels back to the region for at least some of their production and the establishment of new channels within the Arab world. Producing material in high-cost cities like London, New York and Washington cannot compete economically with the much lower production costs found in Amman, Cairo, Beirut (TBS 2000) and now Dubai.

Yet the time will come when economic considerations will induce these organizations to return to the region. Their move will be eased by the generally more open media environment currently prevailing in the Arab world, especially in the cities mentioned above. Saudi-run organizations will have the most difficult choice to make, however, because the kingdom is among the least open societies in the region and the considerations for doing business there are among the least compelling. Observers may therefore see Saudi-owned companies setting up shop in other Arab countries, as was the case when ART moved to Cairo.[11]

Satellite television penetration and access in the Arab world

Today, satellite dishes are sprouting up all over the Arab world. It is difficult to obtain accurate figures about the penetration of satellite television in the region, mainly because no one group or organization exists to track data. Observers of the satellite broadcasting scene estimate that some two-thirds of the population in the Gulf have access to satellite television, about 20% of Palestinians and perhaps 10% of Egyptians and Syrians.[12] According to Sreberny's (2001) partial picture of the exposure to transnational television in the Arab world, Algeria, Kuwait, Oman and the U.A.E. have satellite penetration of more than 20% and Saudi Arabia has 17%. In 1997 there were some 1.2 million dishes in Morocco. Officials of the most widely viewed channel, MBC, optimistically estimate their audience "at least 100 million to 120 million viewers."[13] While such estimates may be fanciful, the audience for Arab satellite television is nonetheless substantial, even in authoritarian countries like Iraq and Syria. Alterman's (1998) own estimates, which are based on marketing information, as well as discussions with broadcasters and scholars of the Arab media, suggest that somewhere between 10% and 15% of Arabs in the region regularly watch satellite broadcasts.

According to Showtime's current estimates there are approximately 19 million television households (TVHH) throughout the Arab world. Saudi Arabia and Egypt have around 4 million and 8.5 million TVHH respectively, while Lebanon and Syria have an estimated 3.5 million TVHH.[14]

The Star-select Company has the following figures of satellite penetration in the Arab world (1999):

---

[11] "Transnational Media and Social Change in the Arab world: Public Opinion and Arab Identity" *Transnational Broadcasting Studies*. 1999, No. 2, Spring.

[12] Estimates of access to satellite broadcasts come from Prof. Hussein Amin, American University in Cairo, and others. *Access* is an estimate based on the number of dishes multiplied by a factor estimating the number of people who watch television on each dish (generally, about six). Khawla Al-Otaiky of the Kuwaiti International Information Center estimates Egyptian viewer ship at only 2 million, or less than 4 percent of the population. Hala Kaloti, 1997. "Arab Satellite TV Channels Prove Ineffective," *Inter Press Service*, November 10.

[13] Interview with MBC officials in London, March 17, 1998.

[14] www.showtime.com

Table 3.2: Satellite penetration in the Arab world:

Satellite Television Homes	
Levant*	1,599,000 (27.0%)
GCC**	2,684,000 (56.3%)
North Africa***	2,447,000 (20.8%)
Total	6,730,000

Cable & MMDS Subscribers	
Levant	277,000
GCC	53,000
North Africa	27,000
Total	357,000

DTH Households	
Levant	1,322,000
GCC	2,631,000
North Africa	2,420,000
Total	6,373,000

(Source: www.starselect.com)
*Levant includes Jordan, Syria, Lebanon, Iraq and Palestine.
*Gulf countries (GCC) includes Saudi Arabia, Oman, United Arab Emirates, Kuwait and Bahrain.
***North Africa includes Egypt, Morocco, Sudan, Libya, Tunis, Algiers, Somalia and Djibouti.

The Europe-based Eutelsat Company has also its own figures. According to these figures (see diagrams below), in 1994 some 3.6 million Arab homes were connected to Eutelsat cable and satellite cable or satellite television in the Middle East and North Africa, while by 2001 this increased to 16.2 million. Furthermore, countries in the Middle East and North Africa display the highest growth rate of satellite television penetration, with a 23% increase between 2000 and 2001, while the increase of penetration to cable or satellite in the world has shown an upward trend of 8% annually since 1994.[15] In 2001 in Western Europe, some 53% of television households have either cable or satellite reception, as compared to 35% in North Africa and the Middle East and 27% in Eastern Europe.[16]

According Eutelsat, by mid-1998, dish ownership had spread to over 58% of households with television, or (as 99% of homes in Saudi Arabia own one or

---

[15] Interviews conducted mainly in urban areas due to lack of information available in rural regions.
[16] www.Eutelsat.com.

more televisions) nearly 58% of all households in the kingdom.[17] With the U.A.E. emirate of Dubai renowned as a regional enterpot for trade in consumer electronic equipment and with foreign workers eager for television programming in their own languages, satellite penetration soon reached predictably high levels. An academic survey published in 1995, based on questionnaires circulated to students at the Emirates University in al-Ain, found that 81% of respondents or their families in this group had access to satellite channels.[18] Meanwhile, most middle-class Arab couples, especially in oil rich Arab countries, for the most part in the Gulf, consider a satellite dish a necessity, not a luxury (El Sherif 2001).

Clearly, access to transnational television is not available to all segments of the population in the Arab world. In particular, working and lower economic classes cannot afford the monthly fees of pay-TV, the cost of a satellite dish or decoder fees which can take up a high percentage of the regular salary of a state official in most Arab countries (except the Gulf States) (Amin 2001). There remain large segments of the population for which the development and changes outlined above are irrelevant to their lives. But the effects of the media content will undoubtedly exhibit some degree of a trickle down effect.

Moreover, I suggest that official figures do not account for real ownership numbers in the Arab world. High illiteracy rates, a media climate based on political news, the weather and a culture of family entertainment all indicate the potency of satellite TV. Additionally, surveys conducted in Saudi Arabia and the U.A.E. have shown a high proportion of respondents watching television for more than three hours a day, with those on lower incomes spending most time in front of the screen.[19]

For example, one can find some residents of Palestinian refugee camps in Jordan who lack a roof over their homes on which to place a satellite dish, but they still have a dish.[20]

Consider for instance, that by mid-1997, satellite access in Lebanon was estimated at less than 8%. From that point on, however, the situation began changing dramatically (Sakr 2001). By March 1998, the proportion of households receiving satellite television is believed to have increased around fivefold, to over 40%. The sudden increase was achieved through a boom in the informal, unregulated cabling of neighborhoods, bringing groups of up to 300 households together to share a dish or dishes, along with pirated subscriptions to pay-TV channels. Anecdotal evidence suggests that news of al-Jazeera's arrival spread rapidly by word of mouth. This factor, together with entrepreneurship that facilitated cheap and easy access, provided a major incentive for families to join neighborhood networks.

---

[17] Eutelsat survey for mid-1998.

[18] Atef Adli al-Abd and Fawzia Abdullah al-Ali, 1995. *Dirassat fi'l Ilam al-Fada'i* [Studies in Satellite Media], Cairo, p. 112.

[19] See for example the Fortune Promoseven study quoted in *Gulf Marketing Review*, October 1997, and Al-Abd and al-Ali, 1995; pp. 113, 143.

[20] "Transnational Media and Social Change in the Arab world: Public Opinion and Arab Identity" *Transnational Broadcasting Studies*. 1999, No. 2, Spring.

By the mid-1990s, an estimated 9 million Algerians, or nearly one-third of the population, had access to satellite broadcasts, in rural and urban areas. Around 90 % were organized into groups of 100-300, subscribing to an informal cable system based on one or two shared dishes, one used mainly for Arabic-language programming and the other for French channels.[21]

Consequently, as a result of the emergence and the acceleration of the third generation of pan-Arab media, we are witnessing the creation of a transnational version of the Sreberny's (2001) "televisual atmosphere." This is apparent from several factors. In contexts of considerable illiteracy, audiovisual media reaches larger audiences than print, potentially serving to construct a national audience while bringing poor and uneducated segments from different parts of the Arab world into a shared cultural-political space for the first time (Sreberny 2001, Sakr 2001).

Meanwhile, although national and international radio broadcasting is well established and popular, its audience is being challenged by television as it becomes more visually attractive (Boyd 1999). In contexts where patriarchal culture remains dominant, supported by religious values and social tradition and there is an often an intense masculinization of public space, the penetrative reach of television into the family home may have profound consequences. As Amin (2000) argues, in the era of broadcasting privatization, the audience is more important and exerts greater influence on the broadcasting process than it did during the era of government controlled broadcasting, when the audience had no alternative to state run television. The privatization-broadcasting era is working with audiences that are more active, more sophisticated and able to select alternative media sources from which they can compare and select what they like.

Additionally, in a milieu where people are most often addressed as consumers, clients or as an audience, rather than as citizens or political participants, mediated culture may play a more significant role (Sreberny 2001). The press often faces difficult challenges within the Arab world as various forms of censorship are brought to bear on its overt political discourses (Ghareeb & Mansour 2000). But the advent of television may be even more seductive and subversive than the political press, because it encompasses more people, opens up more imaginary spaces and invokes more complex desires.

Finally, with increasing numbers accessing transnational television stations, televisual atmosphere is facilitated. While externally produced materials are brought to the Arab world, this new environment also allows for transregional programming flows and audience groupings across states, according to content interests. As Callard (1997a) argues,

> Over the last seven years the Middle East has moved from a situation of very limited access to television which was virtually all government controlled, to a market where there is a vast number of channels to choose between, often more than that of many European countries.

---

[21] This numerical data was compiled by Canal France International in 1995/96 for a presentation entitled 'Measurement of Satellite TV accesses.'

Erosion of tribal broadcasting by transnational broadcasting

Over the last decade, the effects of Arab transnational broadcasting in the Arab world have become more apparent as the medium gains popularity. Transnational broadcasting bypasses the three most important communication barriers in the Arab world: illiteracy, geopolitical borders and government content control. With most Arab countries suffering high illiteracy rates, transnational channels providing Arabic language programming have a greater appeal to audiences than foreign programs, print media and the internet.

The use of the new media technologies of satellite broadcasting that can overcome geographic obstacles has broken down geopolitical and other topographic obstacles between different Arab states. Meanwhile, governments simply do not have the capability to censor satellite broadcasts originating outside their countries and cannot dictate what local audiences watch, except through prohibiting satellite viewing. As a result of access to uncensored programming that in most cases adheres to global production standards, audiences are becoming more discerning. Moreover, transnational television has contributed to pluralization, with increased diversity of media institution owners and the effective end to the Arab state monopoly in ownership of electronic media outlets. This marks the first time in Arab media history that a real opportunity exists for Arab audiences to choose from a large variety of Arabic and international television channels.

The coming together of government objectives, technological developments, intra-regional relations and popular responses constitutes the next phenomenon to be explored (Sakr 2001).

In the face of these controls on both ownership and content, transnational broadcasting have offered a means of bypassing national restrictions and importantly, influencing the output of state monopoly broadcasters by forcing them to face unwanted competition.

As the chief state censors, Arab information ministers had to face the possibility that foreign broadcasters would regale local viewers with news of, and commentaries on, local affairs that information ministries were responsible for hushing up (Sakr 2001). During his tenure as Jordan's Information Minister, Nasser Judeh captured the potential of satellite transmission in the phrase "offshore democracy."[22] While state officials fumed, intellectuals basked in the limelight state television had denied them. Satellite channels appeared to provide people outside government with a unique platform from which to communicate with policy makers and the wider public. For the first time, commentators felt they could have their say "without governments breathing over their shoulders," as put by Saad Eddin Ibrahim, a well known Egyptian civil rights activist.[23]

Beyond crossing geopolitical borders and overcoming limitations, restrictions and censorship structures of Arab state regimes and language barriers, the

---

[22] The author was told that the Minister used this phrase in private conversation.
[23] Interview with the Egyptian sociology professor and civil rights campaigner, Saad Eddin Ibrahim, Cairo, 6 September 1998.

emergence of the Arab transnational broadcasting has eroded the existing tribal media on several levels.

First, it is the first time in the history of broadcasting in the region that audiences have the luxury of selecting news from a menu of news networks, such as MBC, ANN, Abu Dhabi TV and al-Jazeera. More importantly however, this is the first time Arab audiences are exposed to news events with minimum interference or interpretation of news events by the regime or station manager, who in the past was a government official (Marghalani and Boyd 1998). Increasingly, such channels are providing direct and live coverage events from the field.

This is also the first time that Arab audiences are exposed to newscasts covering a variety of events around the globe, the Arab world and most importantly, events related to internal Arab issues, conflicts and demonstrations that have been ignored or played down by state owned television. Arab transnational broadcasting has begun to play an effective role in conveying news and information of general and specific interest, commenting on events, providing opinion and perspectives, reinforcing social norms and cultural awareness through the dissemination of information about culture and society, providing specialized data for commercial promotion and services and, finally, entertaining (Rugh 2001).

Second, Arab audiences are being exposed not only to news, but also to other programs of documentary format and talk shows, particularly on issues and topics which were (and often still are) deemed taboo by state regimes because of their political and security sensitivities.

This was demonstrated by such documentary programs broadcast by al-Jazeera such *The Lebanon War* or *Top Secret,* revealing the good relations the Jordanian royal family enjoyed with Israel—a taboo topic in Jordan. Moreover, the audience's free access to participate in talk shows and other open programs live via telephone, fax or less usually, the internet, is a dramatic development in the history of the broadcast media in the Arab world. Thus, satellite news broadcasters have facilitated freedom of expression (however relative and limited to those who can afford it) to Arab screens (Amin 1999).

On the third level, transnational broadcasting provided a variety and quantity of entertainment programs that was not available in the era of the tribal broadcasting. I suggest this has actually strengthened the status of television in Arab homes and made it more attractive to all family members. I would also add that entertainment programs have become not only more attractive to viewers, but also more open in the sense of traditional Arab values, as evident on such Lebanese entertainment programs that make heavy use of sexual references in language, dress and behavior—and other permissive content programs like *Ya Leil Ya 'Ein* on LBCI, which enjoys high ratings among Arab audiences.

From the above, it clear that the first direction of the process: eroding tribal broadcasting by Arab transnational broadcasters has been on the level of content. Not surprisingly, many studies indicate that satellite broadcasted programming is of a higher quality than that found on national television (Fahmy 1997).

The second direction of erosion is in the management of television channels. Satellite channel management differs from that of state owned channels.

The former cannot afford to ignore the competition for ratings or the competition between the channels. This is reflected on several levels. The first refers to the change in the basic concept of television management. Station managers plan media strategies according to one purpose: to attract a larger audience and thereby achieve higher ratings for advertisers. This new trend has eroded the basic approach of tribal channel management, which saw the state regime as the guide for media strategy. In this way the erosion of tribal media is reflected in the re-direction of media strategies towards advertisers (through audience ratings) from state regimes. Moreover, targeting audiences *ipso facto* has a bi-directional approach, as opposed to the singularity of direction implied by tribal broadcasting.

Yet despite the advent of satellite television, the swift increase in number of channels, growing mass media privatization and commercialization, terrestrial state television in the Arab world has not disappeared. Today one finds two major trends in these stations as a result of new communication technologies. First, terrestrial state television has lost a substantial degree of its power and allure as the state shifted its attention and resources to transnational satellite television in order to compete in this new medium.

Yet terrestrial state television has maintained an important role not always fulfilled by transnational television, namely covering issues of local importance, fulfilling a local media need. This function is important for both practical and symbolic reasons.

Conclusion

Our findings and discussion suggest several main conclusions in regard to this relatively new media form in the Arab world: The emergence of Arab transnational television in the Arab world has significantly eroded the media structure that existed relatively unchanged for more than forty years, maintained by ruling elites.

Enduring illiteracy, especially among women and in rural areas and the urban concentration of print media have meant that in many states print media rarely moved beyond an urban, predominantly male, educated readership. But television is constructing a national public space that addresses men and women, old and young, educated and poorly educated, urban and rural (Sreberny 2001).

Transnational television is unique in its ability to provide relatively freer information flows and thus the invasion of media content in the Arab world. This trend has many implications, especially for audiences, where new television broadcasting is binding populations into regional audiences in a way that no medium had truly done before, with the exception of Nasser and *Sawt al-Arab*.

In this regard, in the next chapter, I shall introduce different players in this new medium, following with an outline of subsequent state regime regulations taken to control transnational Arab television.

Chapter Four
Arab Satellite TV Stations: Main Players and Classifications

This chapter examines Arab transnational television channels that are Arab speaking or Arab-owned or run, transmitted inside or outside the Arab world and/or to Arab diasporas. I shall introduce the main Arab satellite television stations and players in detail, including structural information about each station, the establishment process and history, ownership, management, location and network correspondents and offices. I shall also introduce station contents, programs and main audiences. In the second part of the chapter, satellite television shall be classified according to different categories, providing a map of Arab transnational television. I shall conclude with a discussion about future trends of Arab transnational television.

Middle East Broadcasting Center (MBC)

On September 18, 1991, Saudi Arabia launched the first Arab satellite television station, MBC, a privately owned network based in London (Ghareeb & Mansour 2000). The station, owned by Saudi royal family members, has been revolutionary in terms of its use of satellite facilities and in regards to content, as I have noted earlier in this book. Unlike content broadcast by state terrestrial television stations, with its emphasis on local news and entertainment and its role as an organ of the state, MBC broadcasts content aimed at all Arab countries, covering pan-Arab issues, including news (for a pan-Arab audience), entertainment and sport.

While the financial support MBC received from King Fahd in its early years will remain a matter of conjecture, the extent of the King's logistical support is a matter record. Despite the official ban on satellite dishes in Saudi Arabia, there was no attempt to hide MBC's large Saudi following.

The evidence of MBC's support from King Fahd was so strong it gave rise to the joke that Fahd himself had chosen the initials MBC to stand for 'My Broadcasting Company' (Alterman 1998; 21). Given the focus of other Saudi satellite companies set up afterwards, it should be noted that MBC launched just in time to cover the beginning of the October 1991 Arab-Israeli peace talks in Madrid and was promoted on the strength of its international news coverage. For most of its early period MBC was considered news-led. The emphasis was on international and regional news however, not on news of politically sensitive developments in Saudi Arabia or other Gulf states (Ayish 1997; 482).

Hundreds of millions of dollars went into the project to emulate CNN. MBC started with $300 million in working capital and an annual budget of $60 million (Marlow 1992). It spent at least $12 million on new headquarters in London while its staff expanded to well over 300. By 1997 the favored guesstimate for its annual outgoings was in the region of $100 million.

MBC was the leader in revolutionizing Arab news coverage in style, content and performance. It was the first to adopt the CNN newscasting style and significantly, was the first to open a Jerusalem bureau, allowing intensive coverage of Palestinian affairs. MBC also opened bureaus in most Arab capitals and major cities in Europe and the U.S. Its news coverage is based on reports and interviews from the field, rather than from polemics or third-hand reports. Just as importantly, MBC has led the charge to cover news previously ignored in the Arab media, such as the coverage of an attempted coup in Algeria in January 1992 and the intensive coverage of the Israeli assassination attempt on a Hamas leader in Amman in 1997.

MBC was also the pacesetter on Arab screens in documentary production and talk show programs. For instance, its seven-part documentary series, *Harb al-Khalij* (The Gulf War) in 1994, bought new facts with a high level of political sensitivity to Arab audiences. Similarly, *Khamsuna 'Aman 'ala al-Sira' al-'Arabi al-Isra'ili* (Fifty Years of the Arab-Israeli Conflict) in 1998 caused significant discomfort for government officials in the region, presenting facts about the behavior of some Arab leaders and countries, accusing them of collaborating with Israel and betraying Arabs. Such documentary series became among the most attractive programs on MBC.

Meanwhile, MBC's debate-based and interactive shows, such as *Arwiqat al-Siyasah* (Political Corridors) and *Hiwar al-Isbu'* (Debate of the Week), bringing intellectuals and politicians together to deal with a spectrum of issues relevant to the Arab world was considered one of the platform programs of MBC. Finally, MBC's entertainment and sport programs have also drawn Arab audiences, their quantity and quality being quite absent on Arab screens before 1995. These programs include *Sabah al-Khayr ya 'Arab* (Good Morning Arabs!), *Sahra Maftuha* (An Open Soiree), *Ibtikarat wa Ikhtira'at* (Creation and Invention), *Sihtak Bi'l-Dunya* (Your Health in this World), *Meshwar* (Journey), *Jawa'iz 'al Hawa* (Live Prizes) and *Ma Yatlubuhu al-Mushahidun* (Audience Requests), *'Ala Masu'liyati* (My Responsibility) presented by Durayd Lahham, the famous Syrian actor, *Anti* (She), a women's-issues based show, the music show *Musicana* and the extremely popular *Mun Sayarbah al-Malyun?* (Who Wants to be a Millionaire?)

Until the emergence of al-Jazeera, MBC was considered the pacesetter on Arab screens in documentary production and interactive shows. And until the emergence of Orbit and ART, MBC's entertainment programs were the most attractive among Arab audiences, predominantly in the Gulf, where the programs were oriented.

The severe financial cuts that followed in 1998 were widely interpreted to reflect an understanding that given King Fahd's advanced age and failing health, his subventions to MBC would not continue indefinitely. These cuts, including around 120 redundancies, were accompanied by a change in management and editorial direction that shifted the emphasis from news to entertainment. The appointment of Ian Ritchie to the post of managing director in April 1998, replacing Hala Omran of Bahrain, set in train a process of putting control over running the station increasingly in the hands of men with experience of commercial media in Britain.

MBC's new evening schedules for autumn 1998 demonstrated a clear decision to compete head-on with the Lebanese satellite channels. This was evident in an upgrading of entertainment, in the form of films, quizzes and game shows and a downgrading of news, reflected in a move to shorten the late evening news and screen it at a later time (Sakr 2001).

In 2001 MBC moved its headquarters to the Dubai Media City, with transmission from Dubai, Cairo and Beirut. This follows other Europe-based Arab satellite televisions immigrating to the Arab world to reduce high station running costs in Europe and also to facilitate the production process.

However, even as MBC was re-orientated as a family entertainment channel, MBC did not give up serious news production entirely. In 2003, it created the all-news and current affairs channel, *al-Arabiya* (The Arab). The channel has since grown rapidly to compete with al-Jazeera and Abu Dhabi TV. The latter underwent massive internal changes in 2004, in part to cope with the new competition, which at this stage, appears to have overshadowed Abu Dhabi TV. However, this raises the question, how will migration to the Arab world where regimes impose (or may impose) limitations upon the media impact upon MBC's broadcasting in coming years?

Al-Arabiya's main programs (current to the time of writing) are: *Bil Mirsad*, a current affairs program; *Nuqtat Nizham* (Point of Order), a hard talk current affairs program, which hosts a guest to comment on a major event, or is a part of that event; *Bil Arabi* (In Arabic), a weekly live talk program focusing on political events; *Min al-Iraq* (From Iraq), covering events in Iraq; *Taht al-Daw'* (Under the Light), an investigative program focusing on current affairs; *'Abr al-Muhit* (Across the Ocean) examines different aspects of Washington's relationship to different Arab countries; *Al-Jawab Al-Shafi* (The Healing Answer), a medical program; *Hiwar ma' Dayf* (Dialogue with a Guest), political and business talk show, covering issues of public interest; *Manarat*, a program that covers scientific and cultural events; *Rawafed*, a cultural program covering noted Arabs; *Muhima Khasa* (Special Mission), investigative current affairs program; *Al-Sulta Al-Rabi'a* (The Fourth Estate), press review program; *Mahatat* (Stations), weekly correspondent's program covering local issues from where they are based in more detail.

Arab Radio and Television (ART)

Satellite broadcasting has been dramatically accelerated by the creation of other two privately owned Arab satellite television broadcasting systems, all of which are owned by Saudi Arabian business interests with links to members of the Saudi royal family.

First, ART in 1993 and in 1994, Orbit TV, owned by two Saudi businessmen, began broadcasting from Italy (ART from Avezzano and Orbit from Rome). Each station has more than one channel and both channels do not place any serious emphasis on news.

ART was founded by Saleh Kamel, a former investor in MBC and another major Saudi investor, Prince al-Walid bin Talal bin 'Abd al-'Aziz. ART began broadcasting as a FTA multi-channel service with five channels to Europe and the Middle East via Arabsat in 1993 from transmission facilities in Fucino, Italy. In 1997 ART changed to a modified subscription-based system. ART currently maintains one FTA promotional channel, but overall the company relies on subscription fees for the bulk of its revenues.

ART is entertainment-focused. Like Orbit, its main competitor, it found an entertainment niche almost absent in Arab terrestrial television programs at the time of its launch. ART produces over 6000 live and recorded shows every year including family dramas, series, plays, sports programs, music videos and documentaries. However, with new entrants into the Arab satellite market, ART and Orbit are finding their main challenge is programming distinguishing them from new competitors, especially as state owned transnational channels focus heavily on entertainment, unable to compete with al-Jazeera, ANN, Abu Dhabi TV and al-Arabiya and other news-based channels due to state regime limitations and censorship.

Another problem facing both Orbit and ART is station running costs from their locations in Italy, which is extremely expensive, compared to the Arab world. A few years after establishment, ART offices were relocated to Cairo. This reduced overall operating costs and bought ART closer to their audiences.

Importantly the station's decision to relocate to Cairo was facilitated by a lack of strong news operations, thus provoking less fear of governmental interference in its operations (Alterman 1998). In any event, the station is perceived as the "most Arab" of the broadcasters that provides a "bouquet" of channels to subscribers—with a greater amount of choice of channels and an emphasis on Arab programs.

In addition to its promotional channel, ART broadcasting began with five channels featuring mostly Arabic-language programming. Today, the ART platform has 49 channels. From these channels, ART produces 14, which are *ART Al-'Alamiyyah 1* (ART Global Middle East), *ART Al-'Alamiyyah 2* (ART Global America), *ART Australia*, *ART Latino*, *ART Teenz*, *ART Movies America*, *ART Aflam* (ART Movies), *ART Hekayat* (Drama), *ART Sport Land 1* and *2*, *ART Manahij* (ART Curriculum), *ART Tarab*, *ART Music* and *Iqra'* (Read).

ART Al-'Alamiyyah 1 (ART Global Middle East) is one of the newer additions to the ART network. The channel provides viewers in Egypt, Levant and

Europe with analytical and social, political, scientific and cultural talk show programs, including popular shows such as *Didd al-Mawjah* (Against The Current) and *Mas'ala ghayr Mahsuma* (Undecided Case).

ART Teenz creates programs for adolescent viewers. The channel has a variety of live and interactive shows including the popular *Utlub wa Ekhtar* (Request and Choose), *Farah wa Marah* (Fun and Games), *Esma'una* (Listen to Us), *Hugo Interactive* and *Koraa 2000* (an interactive football television game).

ART Aflam was the first movie channel dedicated to Arab movies and has exclusive access to the largest single Arabic movie archive (some 3500 titles). It also airs regular live and interactive programs which have become extremely popular, including *Studio el Hawa* (Live Studio), *Skermo, Film Clip, Sa'at Safaa* (The Late Hours) and *Sehraya* (Soiree).

ART Movies America was established to cater for the large demand of Arabs abroad for Arabic movies. The channel shares the much of the same content with *Aflam.*

ART Hekayat (ART Drama) airs dramas from the Arab world. New release dramas, plays and serials are presented in every round of programming along with classic dramas. The channel also features special interaction with its show, *Oscars,* where viewers can vote for their favorite show via telephone, fax, internet and email.

ART Sport Channel 1 and *2* provide coverage of local and international sporting events.

ART Manahij (ART Curriculums) provides educational programming aimed at supplementing the entire Arab secondary educational curriculum with support, training and interactive learning facilities.

ART Tarab broadcasts classical and traditional Arab music; covers important musical/cultural events such as the Beiteddine and Cartage Festivals; provides highlights on local and international operas and modern traditional music. *ART Tarab* also includes special feature programs on leading traditional music icons such as Umm Kalthoum and Fairouz.

ART Music has an exclusive relationship with Rotana Music (also owned by Prince al-Walid bin Talal bin 'Abd al-'Aziz) and as such, features music spanning the Arab world. The channel airs features and interviews with famous artists and is a platform for younger and lesser-known artists to gain inroads into the industry. The channel also has live and interactive talkback, thematic and music related programming including the popular shows *Top 20, Weekend, Studio Mushahadin* (Studio Audience) and *Bass Kermalak* (Only for You).

Iqra' (Read) focuses upon Islam. It offers Islamic entertainment and educational programming, providing a comprehensive overview of religious, cultural, educational, political, social and economic issues related to Islam and Muslims. Highlight programs include *Madarat al-Ahdath* (Around the Issue), a weekly political overview, *Hadeeth al-Sa'a* (Latest Events), a weekly generic talkback show and *Ila Man Yahimmahu al-Amr* (To Whom it May Concern), dealing with critical social concerns.

ART Al-'Alamiyyah 2 (ART Global America) is a mix of popular entertainment programs in the Arab world, incorporating content from across the network including popular talk show programs from *ART Al-'Alamiyyah 1* (ART Global Middle East), local sports events, Arab music, children and adolescent programming from *ART Teenz,* series and dramas from *ART Hekayat* (ART Drama) and popular programs from LBCI, al-Jazeera, MBC and MTV (Lebanon) - the most in popular FTA channels in the Arab world.

ART Australia provides a similar mix to Arab audiences in Australia. The channel includes *ART Aflam* (ART Movies); *ART Music; ART Teenz; ART Hekayat* (ART Drama), international and local sports events. The channel also supplies highlights and programs from the four most popular FTA stations in the Arab world: MBC, LBCI, MTV (Lebanon) and al-Jazeera.

ART Latino is an entertainment channel broadcast to Arabs in Latin America. Much like its other diasporic channels, it combines the most popular content from the entire network including *ART Al-'Alamiyyah 2* (ART Global America), *ART Music, ART Teenz, ART Aflam* (Movies), *ART Hekayat* (ART Drama) and *ART Sport 2,* also providing subscribers with programs from MBC, LBCI, al-Jazeera and MTV (Lebanon).

Orbit TV

Orbit is the third private satellite television station and banquet, created in May 1994. It is wholly owned by the *Mawarid Group,* a multi-billion dollar Saudi business conglomerate controlled by Prince Khalid bin 'Abdullah.

Similar to ART, the station's headquarters are in Italy, although subscription operations are carried out in Cyprus and many of its shows are produced in the Arab world. Like ART, Orbit is a pioneer in extending fee-based satellite broadcasting to the Arab world.

Orbit supplies Arab viewers with entertainment seen as sensitive to traditional, political and religious Arab values. Taking on the role of censor, Orbit broadcasts foreign entertainment to Arab screens while controlling content to ensure audience sensitivities are not offended.

Like ART, Orbit also functions as a 'subcontractor' for foreign channels, providing them with access to Arab audiences. Among Orbit's programming choices are locally adapted versions of ESPN, the Disney Channel, a Super Movies Channel, America Plus Channel and the Star Select package—a package of television channels belonging to Star Select, owned by Rupert Murdoch and broadcasted from Southeast Asia.

In addition to foreign-language channels, Orbit produces five Arabic channels: *Al-Ula* (The First), a 24-hour Arabic-language cinema channel. *Al-Ula* also covers Arabic and International Film Festivals, broadcasting dubbed international films and interviews with Arab and international cinema stars.

Al-Thaniyya (The Second) is a collection of Arabic entertainment programs from around the Arab world. The most famous Orbit-produced show is broadcast on this channel, a daily interview show, *Ala al-Hawa'* (On Air), with Egyptian broadcasting veteran Emad Adeeb. One of its outstanding moments was in January 1996, when *Ala al-Hawa'* was credited with taking a pioneering step towards live debates when it introduced an interview with Israeli Prime Minister

Benjamin Netanyahu, the first time an Israeli politician was interviewed by a Arab television station. *Ala al-Hawa'* also features a call-in segment. *Al-Thaniyya* also has other well-known programs, such as *'al-Sama'* based on viewers calling the presenter, requesting songs and video clips; *Jar al-Qamar* (Neighbor of the Moon) and *'Ishir Ba'd 'Ishir* as indicated through subscriptions as the highest rating entertainment programs on Orbit.

Al-Thalitha (The Third) has a lifestyle focus, with productions made or based in Kuwait, Beirut, Cairo and Dubai. *Al-Thalitha's* most prominent programs are *Leilkum Funn* (Your Night is Art) and *Mubashir* (Live), two talk shows with Arab stars and *Lu'bat Hazh* (Game of Chance), a game show program with direct participation from viewers.

Orbit's fourth channel is *Music Now* broadcasting music from around the world. Orbit's fifth channel is *The Arabic Series Channel*. The channel airs Arabic dramas from all over the Arab world.

Like ART, Orbit's experimentation with news programming has not been successful. When Orbit first went to air, it contracted with the BBC Arabic service to produce news for the station. The agreement failed after tensions flared when the BBC aired stories that the Saudi owners (with close relations to the monarchy) found objectionable, including coverage of the London-based Saudi Arabian dissident Muhammad al-Mas'ari and a *Panorama* report exploring capital punishment in the kingdom.

Al-Jazeera

In 1995, Qatar made initiatives to introduce the first Arab all-news and public affairs satellite channel. The idea for the channel seems to have emerged after the fiasco between Orbit and the BBC, with al-Jazeera employing the BBC staff from Orbit. The channel was established in al-Doha, following an initiative of the Qatari Foreign Minister Jassem al-'Ali through a loan of $150 million from the government. Al-Jazeera went to the air under the statement of *Al-Ra'iy wal ra'iy al-akhar* (One opinion and the other opinion), as stated by the Qatari Foreign Minister. The station's motto was radical for its time. It aimed to provide space for every opinion in a then cloistered tribal media environment, as has been discussed earlier in this book.

Al-Jazeera stunned Arab governments and audiences by broadcasting open political debates, including interactive debates with live phone-ins, forming a new forum for freedom of expression in the region. Al-Jazeera is still leading the region in this direction and is gaining popularity every day (Ajami 2001).

Initially some Arab states and a number of Arab journalists questioned al-Jazeera's role and "presumed hidden agenda" in serving communicational purposes of "American globalization." These accusations have trickled down, but have not disappeared completely. The Egyptian press is exemplary, with its constant accusations of al-Jazeera collaborating with the CIA and Israel (Zednik 2001).

Nevertheless, its popularity among Arabs appears to be increasing. According to a 1999 interview with al-Jazeera's general manager, it was claimed that

70% of Arabs with satellite television rely on al-Jazeera for news, documentaries and politically related programs. Informal conversations with Arab journalists and marketing executives working for other Arab news channels consistently indicate to al-Jazeera being the most watched news network in the Arab world.

Besides al-Jazeera's hourly newscasts based on a CNN news format, covering hot points in the Arab world and beyond, the channel is considered the most credible information resource in the Arab world, due its news updates and efficiency of reaching events directly and in most cases live. Al-Jazeera is also infamous for its important and provocative programs, chiefly its flagship programs, *al-Ittijah al-Mu'akas* (The Opposite Direction) and *al-Ra'iy al-Akhar* (The Other Opinion), both debate programs and heated ones at that. The programs also cause provocation by airing unusual topics or opinions. Al-Jazeera also has several critical political documentary programs, which further add to its credibility, including *al-Harb al-Lubnaniyya* (The Lebanon War).

Al-Jazeera also shifted the visual media in the Arab world into a new era, with CNN news formats, breaking live pictures, highly professional anchors and presenters and slick programming layouts.

Al-Jazeera was the first Arab television station to have achieved global fame and is certainly the most well-known internationally, particularly though its politically provocative (to both Arab state regimes and the U.S.) news and debate programs.

Lebanese Broadcasting Corporation (LBCI)

In 1996, LBCI was established by Pierre Daher and other businessmen with close connections with the outlawed Lebanese Forces, a mostly Maronite Christian militia in Lebanon, established during the Lebanese War. LBCI became the first private satellite television station to operate from within the Arab world (Kraidy 1998). Unlike the other Arab satellite television stations, LBCI was originally a private terrestrial television station operating from Lebanon, which upgraded to satellite to compete with other transnational television channels for Arab screens, in the region and abroad.

As Alterman (1998) argues, if al-Jazeera indicates that news can be entertainment, LBCI indicates that entertainment can be news. Unlike the heavy coverage of news in al-Jazeera, LBCI's formula is social talk shows, light and provocative entertainment based on variety shows and a bit of scandal in search for an audience. LBCI presenters are often attractive young (white) women in revealing clothing. The station's approach is perhaps best typified by several programs, such as *al-Leil Leiltak* (The Night is Yours), whose description reads, "A program that receives a celebrity not to be interviewed as usual, but to be surrounded by four girls who ask him unusual, funny and embarrassing questions." *Ya Leil Ya 'Ein*, a musical game show hosted by Arab stars, is flocked with semi-nude female dancers, quite possibly the most popular entertainment program in the Arab world.

LBCI's more sexually provocative programs exist alongside serious news and Anglo-European-oriented entertainment. Alongside its own news and entertainment programming, LBCI rebroadcasts *CNN International* and *ABC News* daily. It also shows vintage American programs and South American Telenovelas and Hollywood films.

Kalam el-Nas (Talk of the People), *Hiwar al-'Umur* (Life Discussions)— replaced with *al-Youm al-Thamin* (The Eighth Day) are the most popular talk shows of LBCI. *Ya Leil Ya 'Ein* and *Super Star*, replacing *Studio Funn* (Art Studio) are the most popular entertainment programs on Arab screens (the latter also being an important platform for upcoming Arab singers). Finally, *Kif w'Laysh* (How and Why) is the most popular children program on LBCI.

Although LBCI's manner of building audiences in the Arab world is quite unusual, it follows a successful Western provocative-shock model, which is quite appropriate considering the channel's very French-American orientation. LBCI has emerged as a sort of amalgam of Arab and Anglo-European cultures and perhaps a harbinger of what Arab television would look like as a purely commercial venture.

By following a principal of providing "light" entertainment with sexual overtones, LBCI has become the leader of transnational Arab television, especially in terms of profitability. The private-funding/pure commercial formula, which is new in pan-Arab broadcasting, is the only formula that can secure relative independence. However, this formula is problematic in terms of long term viability: what appears racy on Arab screens appears relatively mundane on European channels. Arguably, if more explicit channels were widely available, LBCI might not be able to compete in providing titillating entertainment and there formula could collapse (Alterman 1998). The spread of digital broadcasting technology—and its attendant ability to fit increasingly more broadcasting channels on a single satellite has created many competitors to LBCI, especially from Lebanon, such as Lebanese MTV and Future Television.

But in disagreement with Alterman (1998) I suggest that LBCI will remain popular but may become more sexually explicit. LBCI has a crucial advantage over foreign, more sexually explicit channels, as it broadcasts in Arabic. The trend of Arab satellite television is increasingly towards audience engagement, Arab viewers are seeking programs where they can understand and engage with their surroundings. Thus, I would suggest LBCI's biggest challenge is from other Lebanese stations going transnational, with the same appeal: in Arabic, racy and entertaining.

When its satellite operations began in 1996, comprising two channels, one FTA and the other available by subscription, LBCI had been in the terrestrial broadcasting field for a decade. LBCSat, relying mainly on ART's production and satellite transmission facilities at Avezzano in Italy, considered itself "not really a Lebanese station" and therefore exempt from the requirement of Law 382/94 that 40% of programming should be locally produced.[24] LBCI's flamboyant and uninhibited programs contrasted sharply with those of ART.

---

[24] Interview with Pierre Daher, Beirut, 26 March 1998.

Arab News Network (ANN)

ANN hopes to establish itself as a regional news channel akin to CNN. Going to air in July 1997 and based in London, ANN is managed and operated by Sawmar al-Assad, the nephew of Syrian president Hafiz al-Assad. ANN claims to "address social, economic and political issues" in the Arab world and not shy away from discussing "social ills" in individual countries and "tell the Arab people that their voices will be heard." ANN is considered to have very professional staff, turning out well informed and accurate news broadcasts. It also has very successful news and political talk shows programs, which open its air to different Arab intellectuals and politicians.

When the Syrian president relieved his brother Rif'at of his position as Syrian vice-president in the spring of 1998, some Arabic publications suggested that ANN, operated by Rif'at's son, was a primary cause of the dismissal (Alterman 1998). This is clearly indicative of the importance given to transnational Arab news production on the pan-Arab political playing field. In ANN's case, it is the ownership of this station that has been so provocative to the Syrian regime.

ANN may be perceived as a political weapon in the hands of Rif'at against his brother Hafez al-Assad, the late Syrian President (and now against Bashar al-Assad, Hafez al-Assad's son, who became president after Assad's death), rather than an orthodox news outlet. Indeed, ANN's financing is quite ambiguous, as there is no visible investor. Some sources close to Sawmar al-Assad previously informed *al-Hayat,* a London-based Arabic newspaper that the station was funded through Rif'at. According to other sources ANN's money comes from Saudis close to Crown Prince Abdullah, to serve Saudi interests in the region and outside.

According to other rumors, perhaps less believable, PLO head Yasser Arafat is one of the financial supporters for ANN, especially since the al-Aqsa Intifada, using the station to further Palestinian interests. Importantly, ANN is one of the satellite channels, which covers the Intifada intensively. In some cases, it does appear to follow official Palestinian interests closely.

However, it may well be that ANN is merely a business venture that will soon be sold off to the highest bidder seeking a turnkey operation that can be used as a prestigious franchise.

ANN's management screened no advertisements in the channel's first six months and refrained from seeking a place on Arabsat, sensing that ANN was likely to be viewed as a Syrian opposition station and consequently refused.[25] Gradually, however, the means of reaching a wider Arab audience materialized, accompanied by shifts in editorial coverage. These shifts were limited in scope since ANN, being licensed as a U.K.-based station by the Independent Television Commission (ITC), was bound by the ITC's code of impartiality. Nevertheless, whereas ANN either ignored Syrian government news in its early months or reported it frostily, a softening of this approach was noted after the station started 24-hour broadcasting in 1997 and expanded during 1998.

---

[25] Interview with Qassem Mazraani, ANN editor-in-chief, London, 7 February 1998.

When, in early 1998, ANN suddenly found $40 million to rent a 12-year lease on the brand new Hot Bird 4 Satellite, rumors circulated to the effect that Crown Prince Abdullah was helping to foot the bill.[26] Given the media ventures of so many other Saudi princes, this explanation had credibility. Abdullah's involvement would allow him to influence ANN's editorial stance, boost ANN's ability to challenge the popularity of Qatar's al-Jazeera.

A few months after the move from Hot Bird 2 to Hot Bird 4, ANN gained the promise of a place on Arabsat 3A, which was eventually launched in February 1999.[27] The links ANN established during this period went some way to helping it survive in late 1999, when Rif'at al-Assad's private port in Latakia was demolished by the Syrian government on the grounds that it was used for smuggling and Rif'at's own funds started to dry up.[28]

Nile TV *Egyptian satellite Co. Nilesat (Nilesat)*

Nilesat consists of the Egyptian Space Channel, Nile TV and the digital Nile thematic channels which came later into being on the Egyptian channel.

Egypt began satellite broadcasting quite early. The channel that later came to be known as ESC 1 was started primarily as a means of feeding Egyptian soldiers an alternative media diet to the one offered by Iraq. Its launch involved an agreement between the ERTU and the secretariat of the Saudi-based and Saudi-dominated Arab Satellite Communications Organization (Arabsat) for the three year lease, at a cost of $2 million per year, of an unused transponder on Arabsat.[29] It also involved the installation of downlinks and cable connections in Saudi Arabia and the emirate of Sharjah in the U.A.E.[30] With these arrangements, Egypt became the first Arab country to use Arabsat for a dedicated television channel carrying varied programs, including news and current affairs, films and entertainment, sports and educational and religious material.

Despite the early start, only in 1998 did Egypt begin to be an important regional player with the launching of the Egyptian satellite, *Nilesat 101* on April 28 of that year. *Nilesat 101* provides services in various fields, especially in education, media and culture. The second satellite, *Nilesat 102*, with 149 satellite television channels was launched in August 2000, is to start new services that deal with webcasting and datacasting.

---

[26] Interview with Paul Hitti, ANN executive director, London, 28 February 1998.

[27] *ArabAd* 8/10 (October 1998), p 38.

[28] www.arabicnews.com, 16 November 1999.

[29] Hussein Amin, 1992. "The development of Space net and its impact" in R. Weisenborn (ed.), *Media in the Midst of War: The Gulf War from Cairo to the Global Village*. Cairo, p. 17.

[30] Hussein Amin and Douglas Boyd, 1994. "The development of direct broadcast television to and within the Middle East" *Journal of South Asian and Middle East Studies*. XVIII/2, Winter, p. 42.

Nilesat Co. has also its own channels—more than 25 different magazine-style channels covering entertainment, education, health, education and business.[31]

Al-Manar

Al-Manar is a unique phenomenon in the Arab world and considered one of the big channels in terms of news and current affairs coverage. The uniqueness of al-Manar is in its aims, offering a neo-Islamic, pan-Arab message to Arab viewers, although run by an Islamic minority in the Arab world, Shiites. Its uniqueness is also based in the role al-Manar played and still plays to some extent, in fighting Israel. This was done through having close links to guerrilla groups (including Hizbollah combatants) and being the first to broadcast news of operations against Israel (usually also broadcasting Hizbollah tapes of the event); offering morale lifting propaganda and brutal, visual footage of Israeli troops in Lebanon.

The station's political-ideological broadcasting agenda is concerned with both struggling against the "Zionist enemy" and ensuring contemporary (Shiite) Islamic programming. Unlike the vast majority of the other Arab satellite television stations, al-Manar has only a very small portion of foreign programs within its schedule. The vast majority of the station programs is produced by al-Manar and fulfills its definition as

A Lebanese TV station that aims to preserve the Islamic values and to enhance the civilized role of the Arab and Islamic Community. Al-Manar is the first Arab establishment to stage an effective psychological warfare against the Zionist enemy.

Until Israel's withdrawal from Lebanon in 2000, al-Manar principally focused upon using this medium as an integral part of its "struggle to liberate Lebanon from Israeli forces—including Israel's principle supporter, the USA," as discussed above. After Israel withdrew from Lebanon, the station continued its "media battle" against Israel in the framework of the Palestinian conflict with Israel, which escalated with the beginning of the September 2000 Intifada.

Al-Manar, which broadcasts 24 hours a day, is not a commercial television station. It has no (real) advertisements (except those selling Islamic goods produced or supported by Hizbollah) and is a FTA channel.

A large part of al-Manar's programs are live and based on dialogue with viewers. As al-Manar notes in its website,

Al-Manar focuses on live talk shows and dialogue programs in which it makes sure to bring out different thoughts and beliefs, in addition to the participation of the viewers in the dialogues.

Thus al-Manar quite freely provides audiences with access (and engagement) to wide-ranging critical debates, covering Israel, the U.S. and Arab re-

---

[31] For the full list of the channels see appendix # 5.

gimes. This is quite clear through the kinds of guests invited, the kinds of programs produced and al-Manar's anchors.

Like the other critical transnational Arab stations, while it has own political-ideological agenda, it is open up to certain redlines: Syria, Iran and Hizbollah itself. They are positively represented by the station, avoiding any kind of direct or indirect criticism as the main partners and supporters of Hizbollah.

Despite the high portion of talk shows and the hourly newscasts, al-Manar is not an all-news and current affairs station like al-Jazeera. Rather, beyond times of intense conflict, the station operates in a family format, offering children's programs, documentaries and entertainment shows for adults. However, as a station with an Islamic framework, al-Manar does not broadcast entertainment shows that it believes contradict the spirit of Islam. Much of its entertainment programs are social and historic dramas and series that have a reference to Islamic history and heritage, or the political and military conflict with Israel.

Apart from its hourly newscast, the main programs on al-Manar are the talk shows, *Hadith al-Sa'ah* (Talk of the Hour), *Malafat* (Political Files), *Maztha Ba'd?* (What Next?). Al-Manar's religious programs include *al-Din wal Hayat* (Religion and Life) and *Nidaa' al-Salah* (Prayer Call). Documentary series include *Beit al-'Anqabout* (The Spider's Web) and *Irhabiyoun* (Terrorists).

Governmental and other private Satellite TV channels

Besides the above main regional television players, most Arab countries have begun their own state owned satellite channels to place themselves on the map of the new regional media environment. Updated to September 2002, Arab state regime run/owned satellite channels on Nilesat and Arabsat are: *Egypt 1* and *2, Bahrain, Qatar, Sharjah, Abu Dhabi, Dubai, Saudi 1* and *2, Iraqi, Oman, Sudan, Libya, Kuwait, Morocco, Mauritania, Yemen, Syria, Lebanon, Jordan, Palestine, Masqat, Tunis, Algeria* and *Djibouti.*[32]

There are also around 30 private Arab satellite television channels, which are marginal actors. They include *Nile News, al-Mustaqilah, al-Majd, Dubai Sport, al-Andalus* and others. With the successful launching of Nilesat 102 in August 2000, the supply of digital channels increased yet again and, by the autumn of that year, plans for a private Egyptian satellite channel, backed by businessmen and called al-Mihwar, were well advanced.[33]

In terms of Lebanese channels (their importance shall be discussed in the conclusion of this chapter), apart from LBCI and al-Manar, the next well-known Lebanese satellite station is *al-Mustaqbal* (Future Television) belonging to the Lebanese Prime Minister Rafiq al-Hariri. There is also NBN, which also began as terrestrial television belonging to Amal, the Shiite party, headed by Nabih Birri, the speaker of the Lebanese parliament. Another three Lebanese terrestrial television stations have also upgraded to satellite channels: *New TV, MTV Lebanon* (now closed, with a case pending in the Lebanese courts) and *Tele-Liban,* the official Lebanese television station.

---

[32] For the full list of the Governmental TV stations see appendix # 4.

[33] *Al-Ahram Hebdo*, 20-26 September 2000.

Main players

The quantitative survey, conducted by PARC through face-to-face interviews with 3453 Saudis and Arab expatriates, indicated that al-Jazeera and LBCI were equally popular, but at different times of the evening. Al-Jazeera ratings were higher than those for MBC from around 21:45 onwards.[34] In study 551 respondents were asked to associate statements with specific satellite channels. Nearly three-quarters of those questioned (73.7%) agreed that the statement "People often talk about the arguments raised by its programs" applied to al-Jazeera. Two-thirds agreed that al-Jazeera had a "professional team of program presenters" and was "outspoken and even-handed" (65.9 and 65.3% respectively) and 82.4% said it presented "daring programs about hot Arab issues."[35]

Because of technical limitations on al-Jazeera's availability in 1997, the first full year of real open competition among the major Arab channels was in 1998. In that year, the pioneer channels faced competition from al-Jazeera at a time when LBCI and Future Television were banned by their own government from broadcasting political news. Despite the proliferation of satellite channels, al-Jazeera filled a new need for relatively unbiased, critical, well-covered news from an Arab perspective.

Classification of satellite TV stations in the Arab world

In December 2003, there were 104 satellite television stations in Arabic. 21 broadcast through analog and 83 through digital, distributing on seven satellites. The main three satellites used by Arab transnational television stations are *Arabsat 2/A* and *3/A*, *Nilesat 101* and *102* and *Eutelsat W2*, *W4* and *Hotbird 1,2,3,4,5*. *Arabsat* is owned by the Arab Satellite Communications Organization, a company owned by twenty-one Arab states (Khoury 1994) and was launched in 1985 to send live coverage of the annual pilgrimage to Mecca. This satellite has its headquarters in Saudi Arabia, which owns more the one third of this satellite (Bulloch 1995). It is in full use today with 39 analog television stations and 81 digital television stations in Arabic. *Nilesat 101*, primarily owned by the Egyptian Radio & Television Union (ERTU), was launched in April 1998 and began service in June 1998. It has 149 stations, all digital. Unlike *Arabsat*, *Nilesat*, as I have discussed previously, has its own satellite television stations alongside providing services to other stations in the Arab world. *Eutelsat* and *Hotbird* is the main European satellite banquet, which serves satellite television stations in Europe, Western Asia and North Africa.

Satellite television stations in the Arab world can be classified according to six criteria: *(1) Ownership, (2) Content, (3) Location, (4) Business model, (5) Platform broadcasting and (6) Satellite banquets.*

---

[34] *ArabAd* 8/11 (December 1998), p 187.
[35] Ibid., p 186.

(1) Ownership

There are five categories of satellite television ownership in the Arab world: state, semi-private, content, political party and religious.

State television stations are owned by states and controlled by ruling regimes (resembling terrestrial stations). These stations are nothing more than extensions of the state owned terrestrial television stations, in terms of news and entertainment. Characteristically, these stations do not differ from the state's official terrestrial television stations, where laws regarding censorship and freedom of expression are imposed. There is little technological difference between terrestrial and transnational state regime television in terms of technical effects and allowing direct contact with viewers. Transnational state TV is used as a propaganda organ much in the same way as its terrestrial counterpart. However, transnational television allows Arab state regimes to place themselves on the "media map," representing themselves.

In other words, the approach to advertising on Egypt's numerous satellite channels in the late 1990s provided yet more evidence that income from the channels themselves was not the chief motive behind them. They were linked instead to the ruling elite's determination to present an image of Egypt as a cohesive community to viewers at home and abroad.[36] The many components of the satellite project conceived and implemented in Cairo—from Nilesat itself to various television programs—were geared to a particular official view of Egypt's role in the region and internationally, its ability to provide a counterweight to Saudi Arabia and its future economic development (Sakr 2001).

Saleh Kamel's Dallah's Albaraka business group, with interests ranging from Islamic banking and manufacturing to trade, shipping, farming and tourism, had assets estimated at $7 billion by 1998.[37] Prince al-Walid bin Talal bin 'Abd al-Aziz's fortune by that time was in the region of $13 billion, amassed from land deals and construction work in Saudi Arabia and timely investments in companies such as Citicorp and Saks Fifth Avenue. The prince seemed ready to subsidize the Arab Media Corporation, owner of ART, from the profits of his other businesses.

From ART's staggered launch, between 1994 and 1996, to the end of the 1990s, there was no evidence that it had made any money. On the contrary, some industry estimates suggested it was losing $168 million per year.[38] In 1998, the same year that the two shareholders ploughed in another $250 million to cover the cost of adding four more channels, advertising revenue was probably less than $26.5 million.

Prince al-Walid's motives in absorbing such losses could only be gleaned from his wider preoccupation with the media business as a powerful investment tool.

---

[36] This is the phrase used in an article, "Egypt in the 21st century: Transition to an information-based community" on the official website run by the State Information Service.

[37] *Middle East Economic Digest*, 1998, 23 January, p. 6.

[38] Sherin Moody, 1998. "Pay television in the Middle East." Paper presented to the ARTICLE 19 conference on satellite broadcasting in the Middle East and North Africa (Cairo, February), p. 5.

Semi-private stations refer to stations that strive to be profitable by means of advertising, such as MBC, or by subscriber fees, such as ART and Orbit. The term *semi-private* refers to ownership that is apparently private, yet in reality through structural or family connections, is owned by business people usually from or close to ruling Gulf regimes.

The most famous Arab station from this category is MBC, born in the beginning of the 1990s and is owned by a member of the Saudi royal family. Orbit and ART are also owned by Saudi interests.

Under the 1992 Basic Law, which is effectively Saudi Arabia's written constitution, there is nothing to prevent members of the ruling family from playing as prominent a role in the media, as they do in government. On the contrary, the media are viewed more or less as a tool of government and, internally, Saudi radio and television are run by the Ministry of Information.

While these stations are private enterprises, they are similar to state regime media in terms of following the same 'rules' as dictated by Arab governments regarding content, especially political and religious sensibilities (Sakr 2001). Such stations tend to be most sensitive about news emerging from Arab states where the owners have close relations to and subsequently lesser (although still clearly existing) sensitivities towards other Arab regimes.

Al-Jazeera deserves attention as a special case of semi-private station. Although categorized as semiprivate, it is difficult to classify al-Jazeera because if its unique status and inception's circumstances.

Al-Jazeera is not private, established as it was with financial aid of a Qatari government loan. It is not *state owned* in the sense that it is not owned by the state of Qatar nor oriented or directed by its media policy. It also does not belong to any political party or group, although it is an extremely politicized station with a critical liberal-democratic pan-Arab focus. There are expectations that al-Jazeera will eventually become a privately funded station, using its brand name to establish other channels more attractive to advertisers.

Private commercial television stations are similar to semi-private stations in regards to the commercial incentive for their creation. However they are not owned (outright) by political parties or states.

While private commercial television stations are independent of direct governmental control, they are also affected by the game rules in terms of censorship and sensitivity to news. Moreover, these stations rely on advertisements or subscriptions, as the case of the Showtime company—a cable company that has no independent stations of its own but broadcasts a large variety of Arabic and international satellite television channels.

The vast majority of these independent private television stations exist in Lebanon, where there is a history of commercial media and just as importantly, political and social openness.

Satellite television stations owned by a political party or personality: Like other stations, they offer a variety of programming not necessary related to the political ideology or personality they represent. However, these stations do try represent their ideologies through their news broadcasts, whether indirectly, such as *al-Mustaqbal* (Future Television), belonging to the Lebanese Prime

Minister Rafiq al-Hariri or ANN, which belongs to Rif'at al-Assad, the brother of the late Syrian president Hafiz al-Assad, or directly like the case of al-Manar.

Except for stations transmitted from Lebanon, this kind of satellite television station is found only outside the Arab world, due to the fundamental restriction of nearly every Arab regime to allow television stations owned by political parties, groups and personalities (terrestrial or satellite stations) to operate within their juridical boundaries.

At present, ANN is the only television station from this category, which broadcasts from outside Lebanon, being transmitted from London.

Religious television stations: There are several satellite television channels owned by religious groups/institutions created to evangelize religion on Arab screens. These stations do not solicit money from viewers. Besides al-Manar, there is *Monajah* (Prayer) and *Iqra'* (Read) which are owned by members of the Saudi monarchy. There are also four Christian stations. Tele-Lumiere is the most well known.

(2) Classification by content

Here we refer to television station content: whether the station has a variety of programs or concentrates on one field, such as news/current affairs, entertainment, sport, religion, health, children, education etc. There are two categories of satellite television in the Arab world:

General television stations refer to those with a variety of programming: news, entertainment, sports, music, dramas and etc. These stations differ little from existing terrestrial stations in this regard, although formats are slicker and more appealing to audiences. All state owned television stations previously mentioned and most of the semi-private stations are of this type. General stations characterize the typical television station model in the Arab world.

Thematic television stations concentrate on one theme or subject of interest, such as news, entertainment, drama sports, etc. Stations belonging to this category include al-Jazeera (the first Arabic news and public affairs satellite channel) and ANN. Other examples of this category are most of the 14 ART television channels which each concentrate on field: *ART Teenz, ART Movies America, ART Aflam* (ART Movies), *ART Hekayat* (Drama), *ART Sport Land 1 and 2, ART Manahij* (ART Curriculum), *ART Tarab, ART Music* and *Iqra'* (Read).

The last important example is ERTU (The Egyptian Radio and Television Union) which though Nilesat, delivers 24 thematic open channels, including Nile News, Nile Family, Nile Varieties, Nile Drama, Nile Sport, an Nile Culture. From the 104 Arab transnational stations 66 are general stations and 38 are thematic ones.

(3) Classification by location

In the context of the Arab world, the location of media organizations is extremely important, impacting upon media content and operation.

Arab broadcasters are severely restricted if they are based within most Arab countries, due to strict and inflexible broadcasting regulations. Those broadcasters operating within an Arab state must take into account many political and religious interests when selecting content in order to survive.

Nevertheless, even for stations located beyond the Arab world, ownership or funding structure may also impact on media content. The London-based MBC station, owned by members of the Saudi royal family and other businessmen close to the monarchy, is heavily influenced by Saudi Arabia's leadership.

But the location of a satellite television station inside an Arab country does not definitely mean the government will intervene, as is the case of the Lebanese LBCI station, which enjoys a freedom of operation greater than any other domestic satellite television channel in the Arab world. The U.A.E. and Qatar are also examples of where news-focused satellite television stations can flourish, provided they do not impose in internal affairs of the state, a point I will come to later.

Table 4.1: Classifications according to ownership and location

Ownership	Total	Based inside Arab world	Based outside the Arab world
State TV stations	33	33	-
Semi-private	37	32	2
Commercial TV Stations	30	12	18
Political party/Other	4	3	1
Total	104	83	21

(4) Classification by business model

Stations can also be classified according to business model, which falls into two categories: pay and FTA television, or open and encrypted channels. In the Arab world both pay and FTA channels broadcast, with advertising revenues the more prevalent plan.

Whereas satellite television in the United States and Western Europe has developed almost entirely along the pay route, indications are that the Arab world may be a holdout for FTA broadcasting, albeit alongside pay television (Alterman 1998). This is partly because much of the regional audience cannot afford expenditures of hundreds of dollars a year for programming and because individuals and governments are more willing to sustain losses on their broadcasting operations in the region. From the 104 Arab transnational stations 82 are FTA stations while 22 are pay television.

Pay TV refers to television stations available to consumers who pay monthly or annual fees. Orbit was the regional pioneer in sending encrypted signals over the airwaves and then requiring the purchase of a proprietary decoder box and 'smart card' to ensure payment of monthly fees and pay-per-view charges. ART was a later entry to the field, as were global players Star TV (sold as an add-on to Orbit in the Middle East) and Showtime. Meanwhile, LBCI reportedly plans a premium pay channel in addition to its FTA offerings. Monthly fees for pay channels are steep: $50 a month and upwards, with additional channels available for higher monthly fees (TBS 1999). The pricing puts pay-TV services out of the reach of most Arab viewers, especially those from moderate income countries like Egypt and Jordan. The viewers it does draw, however, are those who would be among the most attractive to advertisers: the wealthiest and most consumer-oriented.

Free to air TV refers to those satellite television stations that can be watched without any kind of fees or other regular payments. These stations' main income is from advertising. According to a recent study, total spending on regional satellite television advertising is currently $90 million, with some 70% of that split between MBC, LBCI (the Lebanese Broadcasting Corporation) and Future Television (Forrester 1998).[39] But access to these channels still requires a signal decoder and other equipment, costs that limit their access to poorer socioeconomic groups.

In May 2001, MBC abruptly changed to encrypted mode on Nilesat as ratings rose for some of its programs, such as *Mun Sayarbah al-Malyun?* (Who Wants to be a Millionaire?). In this way, MBC created an additional source of revenue from subscriber fees in addition to advertisements. This step illustrates the two different income strategies of broadcasting. While Nilesat programmers believe that the future trend is most likely toward subscriber fees, Arabsat personnel envision the continuing pattern of FTA television (TBS 2000). Irrespective of which trend will be more dominant, limited financial resources hint that either way will be a bumpy ride. Proponents of subscriber fees claim that quality programming cannot be sustained by the funds generated by advertising alone and viewers therefore must pay for premium programs. However, as it presently stands, there is not enough evidence that either mode for creating revenues is sufficient for acquiring enough premium programs to distinguish their respective program mix (Fakhreddine 2000).

In reply to: would suggest that the prevalence of state owned or state supported (semi-private satellite TV) leads to the nullification of Fakhreddine's argument. The prevalence of government support for satellite television and the accompanying direct or indirect subsidization implies that neither commercial route to viability is promising, especially as four subsidized (directly or indirectly) channels hold integral positions on Arab screens—al-Arabiya, Abu Dhabi TV, al-Jazeera, ANN and al-Manar. These kinds of stations, which are neither entirely private nor governmental serve to offer viewers high quality presentation and content unaffordable on private television and impossible on state run television. Their presence, I suggest, will always skew the development of both FTA and subscription based channels.

---

[39] Chris Forrester, 1998. "Satellite Strength: Middle East Broadcasts from on High," *Middle East Broadcast and Satellites, March.*

(5) Classification by bouquet broadcasting

Satellite bouquet resembles cable television packages and refers to a package of television channels a company offers to consumers in their homes in exchange for a monthly or annual fee. Some of these bouquets, such as Orbit and ART, produce their own television channels in addition to those offered to their consumers. Other bouquets, like Showtime, do not produce their own channels. In the Arab world, where pay-TV bouquets first emerged in the early 1990s, there are six main satellite television broadcasting bouquets: ART, Orbit, Star Select, Showtime/Gulf DTH, Dubai Space and Nilesat.

STAR select is provided by the STAR Broadcasting Center is located at Clearwater Bay, Sai Kung in Hong Kong. Established in 1991, it is one of the world's most advanced uplink and transmission centers and is engineered to transmit more than a hundred different services to a variety of satellites through advanced digital technology. The STAR Select bouquet is comprised of STAR Movies, STAR World, Fox Sports, National Geographic Channel, Adventure 1, Fox Kids, Sky News, CNBC Europe, UK TV Granada, Channel [V], The History Channel and Fox News.

Star select operates in Syria, Iran, Jordan, Cyprus and Lebanon, Bahrain, Kuwait, Oman, Qatar, Saudi Arabia, U.A.E., Algeria, Egypt, Morocco and Tunisia. It seems that Star select does not have deep penetration into the Arab world, as subscription is expensive and the package is in English.

Showtime/Gulf DTH bouquet Showtime was launched in 1996 to compete with Orbit. It is closely aligned with 1st Net, the region's other satellite package from ART. Gulf DTH, Showtime's parent company whose ownership is divided between Viacom and Kuwaiti Investment Properties Co. (KIPCO) is a digital satellite pay-TV bouquet. Showtime offers an EPG service similar to other satellite television bouquets, but only in English. Showtime covers most of the Arab world. The bouquet carries around 50 satellite television channels in Arabic and other languages, especially English and claims some 180,000 subscribers.[40]

Nilesat: Besides Nilesat's 110 digital TV channels, it provides additional services such as data transmission, high speed internet and multicasting applications. It operates more than 28 satellite television channels.

EDTV (Emirates-Dubai Television) is headquartered in Dubai. The company was established as Dubai Space Imaging (DSI) in November 1997 as a result of a joint venture between Space Imaging Inc. of Denver, Colorado and a group of U.A.E. investors. In November 1999, the company changed its name and logo to become Space Imaging Middle East (LLC), the regional affiliate of Space Imaging Inc. The Company began commercial operations in February 1998, with a temporary satellite ground station to receive Landsat and IRS images in Dubai. This satellite banquet includes more than ten digital channels from Arabsat and thematic and general television channels, including EDTV Sport, EDTV Drama, EDTV Business and EDTV1.

---

[40] Showtime "Viacom in the Middle East" *Transnational Broadcasting Studies.* 2000, No. 5

There are also many small companies that service cable and satellite television in the Arab world, as I have noted earlier. The most important are al-Awa'el, Firstnet and Pehla.

(6) Classification according to satellite platforms

Satellite broadcasting in the Arab world is carried out through the use of mainly three satellite platforms.[41] Only two of them, Arabsat and Nilesat, are owned by Arab companies and governments. Some use analog broadcasting and the other use digital broadcasting. The following is a list of satellite platforms used by Arabic television channels:

Arabsat 2A/3A/2B has 39 analog channels and 80 digital channels. In 1967 the Arab Ministers of Information and Culture adopted the principle of establishing a satellite communications network to integrate the cultural and social activities of the League of Arab States. Nine years later, on April 14, 1976, the Arab Satellite Communication Organization (ARABSAT) was established by the member states of the Arab League with a broader goal: to serve the needs of telecommunication, information, culture and education sectors. ARABSAT was given a mandate to design, configure and operate a satellite system, as well as to define and deliver a portfolio of satellite-based, public and private telecommunications services to Arab states, in accordance with international standards.

2. Nilesat 101 has one analog Arabic channel and 71 digital channels. Nilesat 102 has its own 25 channels and another 120 are leased.[42]

3. Eutelsat: Headquartered in Paris, Eutelsat manages a satellite infrastructure for a measured audience of 98 million cable and satellite homes. Eutelsat transmits television channels as a part of platforms for specific languages such as Arabic. Eutelsat W2 and Hot Bird 1-5 have nine analog Arabic channels and 29 digital Arabic channels. The fourth and fifth Hot Birds, boosted by digital technology, went into position in February and October 1998 respectively. This expansion was part of a program that took Eutelsat capacity from four satellites at the start of 1990, broadcasting a total of 18 channels, to 13 spacecrafts carrying nearly 200 transponders by the end of 1998.[43]

Conclusion

There are several important trends emerging from the new era of pan-Arab television, as well as structural issues that must be discussed.

Importantly, despite the rapid development and popularity of satellite television in the Arab world, development has not emerged through any progressive pan-Arab policy supporting the media as a fourth estate, or a move towards encouraging civil society or democracy.

---

[41] All of the data in this section based on the www.lyngsat.com.
[42] For the full list of the channels see appendix # 5.
[43] *Eutelsat News* 36, 1998. December, pp. 1-2.

Rather, it appears that a mixture of Arab domestic politics in individual states and technology has allowed the formation of satellite television, in particular, news-based channels.

The first important aspect of Arab domestic politics is Lebanon's media environment. Historically, each major sectarian group in Lebanon has been served by its 'own' channel, normally patronized by an important figure within the sect (thus, Rafiq al-Hariri's al-Mustaqbal channel for Sunni Muslims, Hizbollah's al-Manar for Shiites, Pierre Daher's LBC for Maronites and so on). These channels have developed according to their own dynamic to attract different audience groups possibly unrelated to their original viewership. Due to the relative freedom of establishing private channels in Lebanon, despite its size, this country has been entirely over-represented in terms of pan-Arab satellite broadcasting.

The second important aspect of Arab domestic politics has been the interesting nature of the smaller, wealthy Gulf regimes, which have served to put themselves on the regional political Arab map through satellite television, extending their influence far beyond their tiny borders. In another way, this has assisted the formation of critical news networks. Broadcasting from tiny countries that do not have major influence in either intra-Gulf affairs or pan-Arab affairs allows critical news stations to overlook local/domestic news without losing much credibility on the pan-Arab screen.

The third important aspect of Arab domestic politics which has assisted the emergence of critical news channels has been domestic conflicts, perhaps aligned to more influential Arab countries or financial revenue. This, with the right money and technology, ANN was established arguably as a tool of inter-Syrian struggles for influence and power and simultaneously, a credible and critical news outlet.

All these factors have only become of significance as technology allows broadcasting to go beyond borders and straight on to Arab screens.

As running costs become of more significance, there is apparently a trend in satellite television stations to forgo their locations in Europe and return home. This appears to have several implications: There may be a future trend of increased censorship upon satellite television stations. However, it seems most of the satellite stations returning to the Arab world are not entirely concerned with serious news. There may be a two-tired system of censorship, chiefly from Cairo, whereby those with the money (and generating that money into the Egyptian economy) will have some restricted privileges in terms of broadcasting news, while local stations will be obligated to the same censorship restrictions they have always worked under.

Nevertheless, it appears clear the issue of returning back to the Arab world will not affect the serious news stations. These stations have positioned themselves into structures whereby their positions are 'safe': either in Qatar or the U.A.E., or broadcast from abroad (ANN), with no possibility of return to the Arab world.

As the structure of domestic politics combined with technology has allowed satellite television to develop into its present day form, as opposed to clear pan-

Arab policy in this direction, this has also skewed the development of the natural challenge between FTA and subscription in the Arab world.

While ART and Orbit are currently forging a private-subscriptions path, the remainder of Arab channels broadcast FTA. Yet as most channels appearing on Arab screens are directly or indirectly subsidized by Arab governments, there is little room for purely commercial stations seeking to air a high quality product, thus our discussion on LBCI as the possible future of satellite television, although this seems unlikely in the short term future. For the longer term, the transnational stations with the strongest branding may well increase their efforts towards commercial revenue.

The novelty of Arab satellite television, mainly serious news-based channels in the Arab world is still apparent. We are witnessing a time when, only a few years ago, Arab intellectuals could not decipher al-Jazeera's 'code': Was it anti-Arab in being critical? Did it reflect American influence? Satellite television in the Arab world, principally news-based television is working to break Arab media binaries (although it may well be biased, pro or anti-Arab/American/etc.): critical: pro-U.S.; uncritical: pro-Arab, although compromised.

Chapter Five
Regulation and Control of the Transnational Media

When Egyptian President Hosni Mubarak peeked into the al-Jazeera studios during a visit to al-Doha, Qatar, he asked, "All this noise comes from this matchbox?" (Zednik 2002).

This chapter shall discuss different reactions and policies used by Arab state regimes to deal with new Arab transnational satellite broadcasting, chiefly political, cultural, religious and news-based programs and channels. I discuss state regime attempts to control audience access; attempts to control transnational channels; and the creation of 'alternative' state run satellite television channels.

Trends of censorship in the Arab world

Traditionally, Arab state regimes have enjoyed a variety of media policies used to regulate the operation of terrestrial radio and television. While Kuwait, Lebanon and Jordan traditionally have had fairly flexible media regulations, others such as Saudi Arabia and Syria have authorized a wide degree of action to suppress the media (Karam 1999).

Although each Arab state has its own particular media regulations concerning the traditional media (print media and terrestrial radio and television), they enjoy common features. In each case, regulations are premised upon limiting the free flow of information and critical public discourse—i.e., the state acting as the authorizer of information flowing in from beyond state borders and limiting internal flows of information. The media is regulated in a manner that makes its operation as the fourth estate impossible (ibid 1999). Thus in every Arab state, whether *de facto* or *de jure*, censorship is widely imposed (Alterman 1998). Censorship in most Arab states is imposed over religious-moral matters; issues pertaining to the security of the state; issues pertaining to critical political analysis of the state regime and other state regimes at varying times; local, regional or international news relating to the individual interests of the state regime. Thus despite many Arab state regimes enshrining media regulations embodying a liberal-democratic spirit, the implications (or lack thereof) of these regulations lead to a large degree of informal and indirect censorship (Rinnawi forthcoming). Again, in each Arab state, the media imposes on *itself* a large degree of self-censorship. This is either in accordance with informal agreement with the state or because the media group involved concludes self-censorship system is the only way to survive (El-'Aa'idi 1999). In all Arab states, all electronic media are directly or indirectly owned or controlled by the state regime, or state regimes have authority (de facto or de jure) to indirectly or directly control broadcasting and programming.

Consequently, until the 1990s and the beginning of transnational broadcasting on a pan-Arab scale, most Arab state regimes were relatively very successful in regulating the electronic media within their borders and controlling population access broadcasting within and beyond state regime borders.

Challenges to Arab state control

The rise of transnational Arab satellite broadcasting has been the largest and most pervasive media challenge in contemporary history to state regime dominance. This challenge has taken place on several levels: geographically, with satellites covering the Arab world; economic and commercial interests; technological complications in preventing audience access and transmission; and the real desire of Arab audiences to access (Arab) satellite television, subverting state attempts to prevent their access. This has also created a further challenge of increasing state-delegitimization as an accurate or credible source of information, which has placed pressure on states to react through the creation of 'alternative' state sponsored television.

The background of change

Prior to any discussion regarding reactions Arab state regimes have had to transnational Arab broadcasting, it is worthwhile to discuss intertwined pressures upon Arab states, which have affected the development, operation, orientation and functioning of this media. These pressures have been both individual and collective, which have bought to bear upon the ways they have dealt with Arab satellite television broadcasting, particularly of news-based channels. We may broadly separate these influences into Anglo-European pressures towards economic liberalization, including privatization; domestic economic and commercial pressures; domestic pressure towards democratic change, inter-Arab rivalries and their impact upon the development of Arab satellite television broadcasting; and finally, technological pressures.

With the end of the Cold War, the Anglo-European sphere of influence over developing nations has become both wider and far more intense. This has impacted upon the process of privatization of the media industry in various Arab states. In Jordan, Kuwait, Morocco and other Arab countries, the media (both in terms of content and technology) is undergoing a process of commercialization from the state (Boyd 1999). Nevertheless, Anglo-European pressure has not bought to bear in any significant way upon the process of creating a free Arab press. This has been an entirely indigenous process. Separation from the state in the Arab world has not bought to bear on real *privatization*. Where processes of commercialization take place, censorship and control continues—whether through legislated or *de facto* regulation. As I note in my chapter on classification, two of the most prominent news-based stations, al-Jazeera, al-Arabiya and Abu Dhabi TV are actually government sponsored or owned.

Domestic (inter-Arab) pressures however, have had some impact upon the nature of programming in the Arab world. With the inception of pan-Arab dailies published in Europe and sent back to the Arab world, such as *al-Hayat* and *al-Sharq al-Awsat* and others, pressure towards democratization and openness have mounted. More significantly have been internal pressures in individual Arab states, mostly articulated through Islamic opposition movements towards greater democracy, such as in Egypt and Jordan. These movements have had their impact on the state owned press—mainly increasing Islamic rhetoric. However, the space it has offered for increased dialogue has been irregular—occasionally increasing censorship controls and occasionally offering space for debate.

Openness towards the rest of the world, on both the economic-market stage and socio-culturally, have also exposed Arab screens to North American and British media especially in the Gulf, though increasing imports of Anglo-European, especially American television programs (Fayad 1993). On one level, this has allowed (Arab) Anglo-European style entertainment programs to flourish on state run television (terrestrial and transnational). Yet it has also offered more opportunities for regulation to prevent Anglo-European impacts upon Arab-Islamic culture—politically and socially.

Inter-Arab rivalries have also impacted upon the development—and reaction to—Arab satellite television broadcasting. As I have mentioned earlier, the politics of smaller Gulf States, chiefly Qatar and the U.A.E. have allowed for the development of critical news-based satellite television stations as a means of exerting influence in the Arab world. The lack of Arab state regime unity regarding the nature of regulations which should be imposed over Arab satellite television broadcasting has meant that unified action towards critical news-based stations has proven almost impossible—in a meeting of Arab Ministers of respective Information of Ministries of the Gulf Regional Council, a unified decision was taken to call for a boycott of al-Jazeera—on government, popular and economic levels—including a call to boycott products advertised on al-Jazeera. Interestingly, the unified stance could take place because Qatar does not have a Ministry of Information. It is yet unknown what the impact of this decision shall be, beyond a substantial lack of advertising revenue for the channel (al-Jazeera.net 2002).

Meanwhile, the advent of Arab satellite television has created its own inter-Arab state rivalry. While rivalry alone has not created freer conditions for satellite television broadcasting, the *nature* of competition has become crucial. Larger, traditionally influential Arab states, such as Saudi Arabia and Egypt compete for viewers and pan-Arab influence, thus Saudi Arabia attempts through its different broadcasting companies to control the Arab satellite broadcasting atmosphere, while Egyptian acts similarly through the launching of Nilesat. Nevertheless, neither offers a break from state control over content. On the other hand, Abu Dhabi, an emirate of the U.A.E., creates Abu Dhabi TV with a similar format to al-Jazeera.

Technological pressures have also taken their toll. The pan-Arab reach of Arab satellite television broadcasting has allowed unprecedented access to alternative news and entertainment programs. The pan-Arab rhetoric exercised by most state regimes serves as an important foil towards opposing these channels. How does a regime that claims to have pan-Arab interests at heart dismiss or openly oppose a pan-Arab station? Moreover, the very act of comparison: between news programs on satellite television stations, particularly al-Jazeera and between entertainment programs, such as those on LBCI and those on state run television suggest there is no return for Arab viewers, which have consistently overcome state-produced obstacles to access of satellite television.

Regulation of satellite broadcasting

Regulation strategies towards population access

In order to discuss regulation policies towards transnational media in the Arab world, Thomas Owen's (1999) six-point continuum of government policies concerning South Asian countries is useful for our discussion on challenges to audience access as a reaction of state regimes to Arab satellite television broadcasting. These typologies are: *Active suppression, Latent suppression, Prudent inaction, Controlled access, Complacent suppression, and Liberal access* (Owen 1999).

Active suppression: With the establishment of Arab satellite broadcasting, severe restrictions upon ownership of satellite dish antennas or cable access was actively enforced as the first reaction in parts of the Gulf, preventing their population access to satellite broadcasting. In the beginning of the 1990's, Saudi Arabia was the first to react this way. Subscription-based television packages were also limited: some people were allowed to subscribe, others were not (Sreberny 2001). This policy was also in practice in Jordan, Syria and Morocco, prior to Arab transnational broadcasters, when the governments of these countries practiced an active banning policy against the reception of the satellite broadcasting especially in the early years of 1990 and principally during the first Gulf War in 1991,[44] when those with access to satellite dishes attempted to watch CNN and the BBC (Alterman 1998).

This can be seen with the Algerian government's attempts to clamp down on all forms of media activity under the Sate of Emergency it declared in 1992. A decree issued in April 1992, dealing specifically with broadcasting frequencies and the distribution of television by cable, attempted to impose some order on the proliferation of small, localized cable networks which most Algerians relied on to receive satellite transmission.

Despite this, 1992 saw a major increase in satellite connections around the country, as people sought out alternative sources of information about Algeria's internal conflict. As the violence escalated, satellite television came to be used

---

[44] Private interview with Adib Abu-'Ulwan 2002.

not only for information about the crisis but also as a means of escaping from it, through films, drama and music provided by the Egyptian Space Channel and MBC (Sakr 2001). After the 1992 coup, the government tried to regulate the spread of satellite access but by then it was too late. As the violent conflict between Islamist extremists and government forces escalated and censorship was tightened, French-speaking Algerians turned *en masse* to the news and analysis available by satellite.

In Syria, satellite access spread quickly, despite initial government disapproval. Under Syria's State of Emergency Law, still in force at the end of the century after nearly 40 years and a raft of other repressive legislation, Damascus has had all judicial avenues to keep a tight grip on all media activity. In 1994, in the same year that Saudi Arabia and Iran officially banned satellite dishes, there were signs Syria might also put the squeeze on satellite television.

Mahmoud al-Zoubi, Prime Minister from 1987 until 2000 (when he was removed, charged with corruption and then committed suicide), announced in November 1994 that the authorities planned to retransmit suitable foreign satellite programming by cable to viewers in Syria. This would have allowed the screening and censorship of all incoming material. He warned Syrians that there would be "no future" for those installing satellite receiving equipment without a license.[45]

Latent suppression: Egypt, Sudan, Kuwait among other Arab states inconsistently or irregularly enforced policies (stated or not) against the ownership of satellite dish antennae or cable access. This was practiced mainly from the beginning to the mid-1990's.

During the early years of satellite broadcasting, the high costs associated with purchasing the right equipment to access satellite television appeared to exclude the vast majority of Arab screens. This in part explains the irregular or ill-enforced policies in Egypt, Sudan and Algeria. Moreover, according to an Arab official the financial cost of implementing these polices are so high that it is quite difficult for governments to implement.[46]

Meanwhile, in Egypt, the government effectively put its weight behind the MultiChoice marketing drive by imposing a ban on imported decoders other than those authorized by the ERTU. The ban, which also included a ban on advertisements for decoders, was announced by the Council of Ministers in July 1995 on the grounds that Law No 13 of 1979 entrusted the ERTU alone with all matters to do with radio and television transmission so as to "preserve and safeguard society's values, ethics and traditions."[47]

Various explanations were later suggested for the decoder ban. Some said it was an attempt to halt the circulation of decoders able to pick up the Turkish subscription channel Cine 5, known for its late night erotic programming.[48] Oth-

---

[45] BBC, *Summary of World Broadcasts*, 21 November 1994.
[46] Private interview with Adib Abu-'Ulwan 2002.
[47] Egyptian radio report from Cairo on 17 July 1995, reported in BBC, *Summary of World Broadcasts*, 19 July 1995.
[48] Baskerville Communications Corporation, *Middle East Television* (Shrub Oak: NY, 1996), p 42.

ers saw it as a move to prime the market for the impending arrival of digital services from Nilesat, which was ordered in 1995 and originally due for launching in 1997.[49] Yet another possible reason was reaction to competition from new arrivals on the pay-TV market, with both ART and Orbit starting up in 1994.[50] Whatever its motivation, the ban kept Orbit's Scientific Atlanta decoder officially off the market. In other words the authorities alternately accelerated and slowed the intensification of transnational link-ups resulting from the existence of satellite and cable channels.

Complacent suppression implies a lack of laws concerning access to satellite and cable television due to government disinterest or negligence. This existed in most Arab countries, chiefly at the beginning of the 1990's, when officials were convinced that equipment to access transnational media was beyond the reach of most people. While in the early 1990's, Saudi Arabia prevented the use of satellite dishes, most Arab countries still had not formulated a response. While some of Arab state regimes attempted to limit satellite transmission, this has becoming virtually impossible with the increasingly cheaper price and smaller size of dishes.[51]

Controlled access implies access to some satellite and cable channels, subject to government regulation or industry self regulation of content. This has been used in some Arab states, with the multi-channel, multipoint distribution system (MMDS). The MMDS was used in Jordan and Qatar, which allowed satellite dishes. MMDS is relatively cheap delivery system and allows a central (state) authority the power to filter out programming it does not approve, controlling the choices its audience is allowed to make. MMDS has also been used to block terrestrial retransmission of foreign programming at prime time, especially applied against MBC (Sreberny 2001). At the end of the 1990s, most of the Arab countries gave permission to private satellite companies to operate within their borders.

In 1994, Tunisia attempted to ban the import and installation of satellite dishes, replacing the outright ban in 1995 with a licensing regime.[52] This required that dishes be reserved solely for individual use, be registered with the Ministry of Interior and installed by an approved technician. An annual tax on dishes was introduced, payable to the local authority, with fines imposed for non-compliance. Not all applications for dish installation would be approved, with the result that clandestine dish ownership became widespread.[53] In consequence, the proportion of Tunisian households enjoying satellite access may well have been higher in 1997 than the 3.4% reported by Eutelsat for the year (Sakr 2001).

---

[49] James Whittington, 'Egypt seeks to lead Arab media world', *Financial Times*, 22 November 1995.
[50] Napoli, Amin and Napoli: 'Privatization of the Egyptian media', p 56.
[51] However relatively easy access to satellite dishes does not imply that transmission is open to all of population segments.
[52] Law No. 95-71 of 24 July 1995, Articles 3 and 5.
[53] ARTICLE 19, *Surveillance and Repression: Freedom of Expression in Tunisia* (London, 1998), pp 47-51.

In 1992, Morocco's Office National de Postes et Tele-communications attempted to regulate access to satellite television by imposing an annual tax on individuals for the use of a satellite dish. The tax, payable in a single installment, was fixed at Dh 5000 ($515), approximately three times the minimum monthly wage in Morocco at that time.

Two years later, however, the tax was abolished, after the Constitutional Court ruled in August 1994 that the 1992 decree imposing the tax was unconstitutional because parliament had not been consulted. In the intervening period many Moroccans had dismantled their dishes, disgruntled at being taxed for a service freely available over the airwaves and not provided by the Moroccan government.

A few months before the Constitutional Court ruling, opposition parties in parliament had pushed for an amendment to the 1958 Press Law that would authorize the Ministry of Information to jam satellite television programs deemed immoral. This effort proved no more successful than the short lived tax. It evoked an outcry from the local freedom of information lobby and was dropped when the impossibility of mounting the necessary jamming operation was realized.

My investigation reveals that *liberal access:* access to all satellite and cable channels without any regulation or with explicit legal rights is non-existent in any Arab country. Even in Lebanon, considered the most liberal country in the Arab world has not allowed free access to satellite broadcasting with explicit legal rights (Kraidy 1998). However, with time, or under pressure of attempting to enforce difficult laws regulating satellite dish ownership, may yet make an about-face.

The U.A.E. government, for instance, far from considering a ban, made much of its open skies approach. The Information Minister (and president's son), Sheikh Abdullah bin Zayed al-Nahayan, told the Gulf Newspapers Conference in Abu Dhabi in March 1998,

> Here in the UAE, we have adopted an open skies policy because we believe in the free flow of information. We believe also that any attempt to place constraints on the free flow of information is futile.

Al-Nahayan also stressed the importance of information for development, arguing that the best way to deal with incoming material conflicting with traditional Gulf values and beliefs was to ensure that "our own domestic media are of such quality that they can provide an attractive alternative view."[54]

Nevertheless, even these statements must be viewed with some scepticism. Local U.A.E. media is extremely reticent in reporting on issues sensitive to the country and satellite news stations based in the U.A.E. also tread carefully.

---

[54] The text of Shaikh Abdullah's speech was reproduced in *ArabAd* 8/4 (April 1998), pp 36-7.

Regulation strategies towards Arab transnational broadcasters

Concern among Arab countries towards the growing number of transnational broadcasting channels have caused policy and regulation responses, either proactively or reactively. The mode of state control over television broadcasting varies from country to country depending upon its regulatory history, national policy and availability of resources

In analyzing the situation in the Arab world since the early 1990s until now, this study is influenced by two typologies derived from similar studies focusing upon South East Asia. Rubin (1993) presents five patterns of media control in Asian countries: *direct control* through state monopoly of the media; control by *licensing and self-censorship*; *emergency regulations* and *national security legislation*; *pressure on the media* without control; and *violence against journalists*. Chan (1994a) offers four national responses to the advent of satellite television in Asia: *virtual suppression, suppressive openness, illegal openness* and *regulated openness*. While both individually are comprehensive, the Arab world presents inter-state relationship systems and mechanisms which impact upon regulation of Arab satellite media, as well as global pressures.

Thus, it appears that Arab state regimes have provided the following spectrum of action towards controlling Arab satellite broadcasting: Control of Arab satellite broadcasting through ownership; formal regulation, modifications in media regulations to allow commercial interests; State regime pressure on senior personnel; pressure through advertising; self-censorship in the new Arab media; pressure through state owned media outlets; pressure through pan-Arab institutions; limitations and pressure from foreign states on transnational media directly and indirectly; providing competitive alternative media content and finally the Qatari case, unique in its own right.

Control of Arab satellite broadcasting through ownership

As I have noted earlier, there are two main patterns of ownership: direct ownership by the state and indirect ownership through the ruling elite, such as royal family members or other relatives of the regime.

State ownership (directly or indirectly) appears to be the primary form of control over Arab satellite broadcasting. Around 60% of Arab satellite channels are owned directly by Arab state regimes (see Classification chapter). Another 30% are semi-private: owned by Arab state regime family members like MBC, Orbit, ART and ANN. Thus around 90% of Arab transnational channels are under Arab state regime control, allowing relatively easy regulation/control.

In Lebanon, business ownership must be in local hands or joint ventures and this also applies to the media industry. But the licensing of commercial broadcasters, a politically sensitive matter, reflects the importance of patronage by powerful political figures.

Jordan, Kuwait and the U.A.E. permit foreign direct investment, although the process is said to be highly bureaucratic and believed to require political and local business connections to cut through (Khazan 1993). Thus, in one form or another, all countries maintain strict control over investment in the media industry, especially television. While the media may be in increasingly private hands, it appears that control has not lessened, rather they have changed form.

Thus while the location of several important satellite channels are not in the Arab world, they can be controlled de facto through their owners. According to personal discussions with senior personnel from an Egypt TV 1, pressure is applied in covert ways.

So far, the investigation into the Saudi channels has confirmed the commonly held view of a ubiquitous al-Saud ruling family presence and extensive control. But the question of motivation seems to elicit a less uniform response. Acknowledging the unprecedented concentration of media ownership in the hands of members of the Saudi ruling family is not the same as saying the king and princes acted in concert. It is clearly important that investors were able to draw on existing political and economic power to establish a major media operation.

In pursuit of their objectives, investors from Saudi Arabia left the confines of the kingdom, bearing testimony to the fact that harsh censorship laws and the self-appointed but government-financed religious police (*mutawwaeen*) had created an environment intolerant of public entertainment or debate. They did so using the billion of dollars at the disposal of ruling family members and their business partners.

Nevertheless, the following example of ART, which I suggest is not limited to that channel, shows how ownership can control content. In all ART channels editorial staff freely admitted to a high degree of self-censorship.[55] As already noted in reference to Egypt, producers commissioned by ART were required to conform to guidelines very similar to those issued by Saudi Arabia's domestic terrestrial television in 1982. Associates of Saleh Kamel, the main investor into ART, say he made a deliberate business decision to reject the idea of producing news bulletins or a news channel, calculating that it would either damage his relations with Arab governments in the many countries where Dallah Albaraka has interests or create a means by which the same governments would ask him for favors.

Formal regulation

Governments in the Arab world have actually tightened their control over the media in the era of satellite television, rather than the reverse. Egypt's draconian Press Law of 1995, only slightly modified in 1996, remains in force. Jordan's 1998 Press and Publications Law reinstated restrictions that caused an international outcry when they were first applied in 1997. Further revisions to the law under King Abdullah have softened it somewhat, but the clauses removed from the press law are still to be found in the Penal Code (Sakr 2000).

At the end of 1996 and beginning of 1997, Lebanon's Ministry of Information and Council of Ministers instituted a new law, which permitted broadcast-

---

[55] *Ibid.*

ing news and political programs via satellite. This apparently progressive law introduced pre-censorship of news bulletins and political programs intended for these satellite transmissions, to prevent news or political items affecting state security, fomenting sectarian sedition or undermining public order (Kraidy 1998).

Furthermore, when examining the case of what has become commonly recognized as a 'media free zone,' the Jordanian case stands out. Upon learning that MBC and Orbit were planning to move their headquarters to cheaper locations in 1999, King Abdullah promised incentives and freedom of expression to any Arab or other media company establishing a base in Amman. In January 2000, the draft law governing Jordan's proposed free zone was released. However, serious doubts arose as to whether the media free zone could in reality exist, as local restrictions and regulations were being applied (Sakr 2000).

Another example of the contradictions in establishing a media free zone in the Arab world can be seen in Egypt. Egypt's Information Minister Safwat al-Sherif announced in January 2000 that private Egyptian companies would be allowed to broadcast by satellite from a free zone linked to a film studio complex, Media Production City, just outside Cairo. In making the announcement, however, he stressed that the Ministry of Information reserved the right to censor both news and entertainment broadcast by private channels.[56] The basis for such censorship is laid out in the 33 prohibitions contained in the Code of Ethics observed throughout the ERTU. These prohibitions forbid criticism of state officials, the national system, traditional values and religious beliefs (ibid 2000).

As for the media free zone bill approved by the Lebanese government in February 2000, this charged the zone's management board with drafting an 'honor agreement' requiring companies operating in the zone to respect the ethics, public morals, habits and customs of Lebanese society.[57] Most people saw this as a thinly veiled injunction to avoid criticism of Syria.

In another case, the Moroccan Communication Minister, Larbi Messari, announced that the government was preparing to submit a draft law to parliament allowing the creation of private television channels and radio stations and reducing government censorship.[58] However, a government clampdown on the media before the year was through raised doubts about this promise.

In the meantime, by creating an illusion of instant fundamental change and freedom, the proliferation of Arab satellite channels arguably retarded the development process by deflecting pressure on governments to reform their domestic media laws.

Attempts at regulation

Until Lebanon's Audiovisual Media Law authorized a few influential personalities to set up private television stations in competition with the state

---

[56] http://www.arabicnews.com, January 19, 2000.
[57] *Middle East Economic Survey,* 14 February 2000.
[58] *www.arabicnews.com,* 3 July 2000.

broadcaster in the mid-1990s, examples of licensed non-government broadcasting in the Arab world were virtually non-existent.

Modifications in media regulations to allow commercial interests

Egypt has newly allowed independent television channels to broadcast from its territory. The first fully independent television channel in Egypt, *Dream TV* was established from commercial incentives through Egyptian businessmen to promote their products. As a result of the pressure from those business interests groups, the Egyptian political leadership allowed modifications in media regulations to allow Dream TV's establishment as an independent channel.

Saudi Arabia, which in terms of terrestrial broadcasting, follows an extremely strict literal Islamic ethos, has allowed ART and Orbit (owned by different members of the monarchy and businessmen close the regime) to broadcast subscription-based cable television into Saudi borders. This completely contradicts the nature of terrestrial television. It is quite apparent, that given the opportunity, other countries would follow suite.

For example, one satellite channel in Saudi Arabia was launched in May 1994, just weeks after Decree #128 of March 10 banned the use, manufacture or import of satellite dishes and outlawed the delivery of television satellite feeds to subscribers in the Saudi kingdom. The Ministry of Interior was charged with enforcing the ban, which it did selectively (Sakr 2001).

In fact the main result of the so-called ban on dishes was not their removal from the market but a steep rise in their price. Nevertheless, the Orbit-BBC news service provided enough coverage of Saudi dissident activities for the authorities in the kingdom to make a special point of confiscating Orbit decoders.

This and other examples presented here shows the limited explanatory value of saying simply that the three major Saudi-owned satellite ventures were set up under the auspices of members of the Saudi ruling family. The power relations underlying these satellite ventures were complex from the outset because they reflected the shifting alliances known collectively, at any given moment, as the Saudi state. Different branches of the extended Saudi ruling family may have diverging interests *vis à vis* each other, even if they have a shared overall interest in safeguarding the supremacy of the ruling family as a whole.

Satellite technology provided a new arena in which state and non-state actors in Saudi Arabia could collaborate and compete. It is in the tension between the interests of individuals, the monarchy and the state that the story of 'Saudi space' is played out.

In Lebanon, under Law 382/94, no individual or family was allowed to hold more than 10% in a television company. Licenses could only be granted to Lebanese joint stock companies, owned by Lebanese nationals, who were not permitted to hold stock in more than one broadcasting company. Stations applying for a license had to commit themselves to covering the whole country and broadcasting for a minimum of 4000 hours per year, ensuring that 40% of their programming was locally produced. Insofar as Lebanon's satellite channels could claim they had bases outside the country, it seems they were not subject to these regulations.

For example, Prince al-Walid bin Talal bin 'Abd al-'Aziz, the Saudi prince with a 30% shareholding in ART, told an advertising journal in an interview published in 1999 that ART, through its parent company Arab Media Corporation, had a 50% share in LBC's satellite arm, LBCSat (LBCI). In the same interview he also referred to his share in the terrestrial station, Murr TV, one of LBC's competitors on the domestic Lebanese scene.[59]

State regime pressure on senior personnel

From the 1950s and even until now (despite transparent Syrian hegemony over Lebanon), Beirut was haven for Arab dissidents who freely attacked Arab regimes in its newspapers (Mackey 1987), widely read in the Arab-speaking world. As a result, Lebanese newspapers were banned in certain Arab countries experiencing political unrest and Arab governments frequently pressured Lebanese authorities to restrain the Lebanese press (Abu Laban, 1966, Boulos 1996).

This strategy relies upon a political and economic policy of punishment and reward towards satellite television stations to compel them to work according to the common code of censorship of the region. This pressure works on two levels: the state level, where pressure is directed to other state leadership to restrain the satellite channels operating within the jurisdiction areas. The second level is to direct the pressure directly to the transnational electronic media institution itself, compelling it to practice self-censorship.

While struggles for broadcasting diversity were under way in Egypt, Jordan and Morocco, diverse forms of Palestinian broadcasting were coming under sustained attack from the Palestinian police and security forces. When the al-Quds Educational Channel started airing sessions of the Legislative Council in early 1997, its broadcasts were jammed by the authorities.

In May that year, the man behind the channel, Daoud Kuttab, was arrested and detained without charge for a week. The arrest was reported to have taken place on the direct orders of Yasser Arafat, who objected to references made during a televised Legislative Council session to a company allegedly owned by his wife.[60] Broadcasting of the council sessions was suspended, as the political climate made critical reporting of internal Palestinian affairs ever more sensitive.[61] Many temporary closures were forced on television stations from 1996. Those affected included al-Watan TV, Nawras TV and al-Nasr TV.[62] Fragmentation of non-government television in the West Bank and Gaza, with many small operators barely surviving from day to day, lessened the sector's ability to pose a serious challenge to the region's dominant model of television as government mouthpiece (Nossek & Rinnawi 2003).

---

[59] *ArabAd* 9/1 (January 1999), p 14.
[60] *Middle East International*, 30 May 1997, p 9.
[61] *Palestine Report*, 30 May 1997, p 6.
[62] See, for example, *Palestine Report*, 25 October 1996, p 9; *Middle East. International*, 23 February 2000, p 11; press release by LAW, the Palestinian Human Rights group, 30 May 2000.

In Lebanon, authorities are under new wave of pressure to control pan-Arab broadcasts emanating from Lebanese stations. Postwar Lebanese authorities are highly dependent on Arab countries, politically and financially. Politically, Lebanon is fully aligned with Syrian foreign policy, which enjoys "transparent hegemony over Lebanese affairs" (Harik 1994). Financially, Lebanon's reconstruction efforts are dependent on investment and aid from oil rich Gulf countries such as Kuwait and Saudi Arabia. These considerations pressure Lebanese government officials to restrict satellite broadcasts, where programs may be offensive to Arab leaders (Kraidy 1998).

In March 1997, LBCI broadcasted an interview with an eminent Lebanese legal expert during its national newscast, where he severely criticized repressive information policies in the Arab world and government censorship of news and political programs broadcast via satellite.

Immediately, LBCI was contacted by government officials who requested the interview not be broadcast via satellite. LBCI executives agreed to comply with government instructions and then discovered government forces had stormed the one of the earth stations and disconnected the channel from Arabsat 2A (*Et maintenant* 1997)

Another ambivalent editorial stance revealed by Maggie Farah, a presenter with Future Television, in an interview with a Lebanese magazine. She declared that she had "absolute freedom" in her position, but conceded that the link between Future Television and al-Hariri meant she would be unlikely to host Selim al-Hoss, the then-current Prime Minister, on her show.[63]

The case of al-Jazeera is also instructive. Al-Jazeera staff claims the Qatari foreign ministry has received more than 400 complaints. When the network aired a program probing Algeria's War, the government in Algiers cut the signal (Zednik 2002). In 1996, Tunisia, Morocco and Libya recalled their ambassadors from al-Doha in protest of al-Jazeera coverage, reinstating them once their point was made (ibid).

This is not to say, however, that the editorial policies of specific institutions cannot be scrutinized for evidence of attitudes to neutrality and professionalism, as demonstrated in their approach to covering news. In the case of Arab satellite channels, contrasts between al-Jazeera and its competitors on this single issue throw their respective editorial policies into sharp relief. When al-Jazeera reported news and views governments preferred not to hear, blame was invariably heaped on al-Jazeera for performing the role of messenger.

In contrast, editorial policy at the Egyptian Space Channel and the Lebanese Future International was based firmly on the belief that satellite channels in particular have a duty to tell 'good' rather than 'bad' news. The rationale for such an approach lies in the channels' relationship to those responsible for maintaining a certain image of Egypt or Lebanon abroad, especially among potential foreign investors.

In the view of Sane Mansour, the head of ESC who joined it in 1995, terrestrial and satellite television have distinct roles. Whereas terrestrial channels may be given some leeway to bring attention to local matters of concern, airing com-

---

[63] *ArabAd* 10/1 (January 2000), pp 28-9.

plaints if necessary, it is incumbent of the Egyptian satellite channels, ESC 1 and 2 and Nile TV, to be ambassadors for Egypt.[64] This means being 'choosy' about the appearance of people and buildings and certainly not screening documentaries of the warts and all variety. Nadir Munla, chairman of Future TV, shared a similar vision during Rafiq al-Hariri's premiership in the 1990s. Given al-Hariri's dual role as Prime Minister of Lebanon and prime mover behind Future, Mr. Munla saw it as Future's duty to promote Lebanon to Gulf investors, to "tell people that life is back."[65] "Life" in this context was taken to mean fun and entertainment, not searching interviews with Lebanese politicians or taking a critical, investigative stance towards a multitude of issues affecting that country. Al-Hariri's cabinet put programs in the latter category out of bounds for Lebanese satellite channels at the start of 1998.

Splits over the acceptability of washing a nation's linen in public were repeatedly exposed by al-Jazeera's news and current affairs coverage once this became accessible to a wide audience from November 1997. Al-Jazeera's management departed from regional norms when they adopted a news agenda determined by criteria such as newsworthiness and set out to beat CNN and BBC World at their own game by obtaining exclusives and scoops. Government-controlled media in the region responded by echoing government suspicion that this novel approach to Arabic language news reflected ill will from their Qatari counterparts. Nevertheless, al-Jazeera, much like its counterparts in the U.A.E., treads sensitively over local issues, although it has become increasingly open in its coverage of Qatari news.

The politics of advertising

The financing of satellite channels is a major factor in deciding their editorial dependence or independence and thus their ability to benefit the public at large. Financial independence requires adequate funding from diverse sources.

Even without the mass of legal and political obstacles, non-government television ventures face serious problems of funding. These could be attributed in large part to wide-ranging government controls over advertising budgets and state bodies' self-serving resistance to the gathering of credible statistics on television viewing habits. Financial independence is the *sine qua non* of editorial independence. State broadcasters in the Arab world have long been saved from grappling with this equation by local distaste for television license fees. Dependence on license fees makes broadcasters accountable to fee payers. While government broadcasters and satellite stations allied to government figures, could dip into state budgets or their sponsors' financial reserves, any independent competitor must swim against the tide to establish a steady flow of advertising revenue or other business related income.

Despite increases in the ownership of television set in some countries during the first half of the 1990s, levels measured in terms of individual viewers rather than households remained far below other regions. Moreover, if compa-

---

[64] Interview, Cairo, 15 August 1998.
[65] Interview, Beirut, 26 March 1998.

nies are seen to be advertising on a channel that may be popular with audiences but is unpopular with governments, their contracts with government departments may be jeopardized.

Yet this ranking is reflected in two stations' advertising results. While PARC estimated MBC's advertising revenue in 1999 at $91.5 million, its equivalent estimate for al-Jazeera was $8 million—a figure not disputed by well informed al-Jazeera staff. The disparity can be attributed to several factors, including MBC's assured position as a general channel providing entertainment as well as news to wealthy viewers in Saudi Arabia and other rich Gulf states. Al-Jazeera, by contrast, as a news and current affairs channel, has a more targeted appeal and attracted audiences of less interest to advertisers. However, it must be noted that the low advertising figures at al-Jazeera were undoubtedly influenced (according to both marketers and al-Jazeera staff) by the reticence of companies to advertise on a channel causing so much ire, particularly towards other Gulf states, the major Arab market bloc, as I will discuss later.

All FTA Arab transnational channels except those directly owned by the state rely on advertising quotas. The advertising business in the Arab world tends to be more political than in other parts of the world. Regional companies and multinationals alike avoid ruffling the feathers of their host governments.

Despite its ranking as the region's most-viewed news network and second most watched pan-Arab station, al-Jazeera generated only $15 million in advertising revenue in 2000. In contrast, MBC garnered $76 million in revenue in 1998, while the Arab world's most watched entertainment channel, LBCI, took in about $93 million, according to the pan-Arab Research Center in Dubai (Zednik 2002).

Al-Jazeera is an inhospitable place for advertisers who dislike divisive issues. While other Arab stations earn about 90% of their revenue from advertising, commercials account for only about 40% of al-Jazeera's revenues (Zednik 2002). Al-Jazeera's manager, Jasem al-Ali notes Saudi Arabian companies have tried to influence al-Jazeera's coverage by cutting advertising budgets for the station or threatening to do so. Pepsico and General Electric canceled advertising campaigns on al-Jazeera worth a combined $3 million, according to al-Ali (ibid).

It is clear that if Arab stations (not state owned) are caused to fail financially, they may be compelled to turn to Arab governments or private funders, with their own agendas (Ghareeb & Mansour 2000).

Nevertheless governments have withstood repeated exposure to the type of news broadcast by al-Jazeera, which made few concessions to sensitive egos worried about tarnished images or ridicule. Instead of learning to live with uncensored Arabic-language news, whether good or bad, several veteran Arab government ministers and their allies were as vocal in their criticism of al-Jazeera years after its creation—as they were at the beginning. Despite the spread of satellite television, those in power in countries from Egypt, Jordan and Morocco to Kuwait and Saudi Arabia were just as willing to prevent journalists from going about their business in 2000 as they were in 1990.

Self-censorship in the new Arab media

Until the emergence of the satellite broadcasting, the Arab media was fighting two kinds of censorship: conservative political powers originating from governments and communal blocks and socio-religious elites quasi-representing social value systems. In the era of transnational media, where development has been accompanied with commercialization, another source of censorship has emerged: that of new market powers seeking to avoid any kind of serious, critical and qualitative media coverage in order to continue broadcasting without controversy and to attract investment (usually through advertising) of products or services owned, or having relations with individual states (Ghareeb & Mansour 2000).

Pressure through State owned media outlets

Attacks on Arab transnational televisions were not only communicated directly through the regime. State media outlets have also been used to place pressure on Arab transnational broadcasters. In 1998 for instance, Egypt's state media ran a campaign against al-Jazeera's "superficial" programs, denouncing the station's "sinister salad of sex, religion and politics" topped with "sensationalist seasoning." (ibid).

Pressure through pan-Arab institutions

Pressure or sanctions can be directed to transnational television channels through pan-Arab institutions to restrain critical content offending other Arab state regimes.

The case of al-Jazeera can explain how this policy works. The Satellite Channels Coordinating Committee in the Arab States Broadcasting Union (ASBU) took a collective stand against al-Jazeera after controversial political programs which attracted attention across the Arab world during 1998 (Sakr 2000). It soon emerged that the Satellite Channels Coordinating Committee within the (ASBU) had isolated al-Jazeera as the only satellite channel ready to break with censorship taboos. Committee members insisted that al-Jazeera should abide by the "code of honor of the Arab media" before it would be accepted into the ASBU club.[66]

Physical pressure: Closing offices, arresting correspondents

Al-Jazeera is the main focus of this section, where most of physical pressure was inflicted upon this satellite television station, although MBC's al-Arabiya has also been a high-profile victim through its coverage on Iraq.

Al-Jazeera has been rebuked by the Libyan and Tunisian governments in 1999 for providing opposition leaders from those countries significant airtime.

---

[66] http://www.news.bbc.co.uk, January 7, 1999; Financial Times March 13, 1999.

Kuwait and Saudi Arabia, for their part, have complained about al-Jazeera's extensive reporting on the misery of Iraqis, then living under sanctions. Saudi Arabia has implemented an off-again, on-again bar on al-Jazeera from its territory (Ajami 2001), which appears to be taking the shape of a permanent ban, especially after the kingdom created its own news channel in 2003, al-Ikhbariya (The News).

In May 2001, Ramallah, Palestinian Preventative Security Forces closed down the offices of al-Jazeera without prior notice. The apparent reason for this was a critical report made by an al-Jazeera correspondent in Ramallah about the administrative performance of the PA, accusing it of abusing power and corruption. Al-Jazeera also upset Palestinian authorities also with a preview for a March 2001 documentary exploring the role of Palestinian guerillas as players in Lebanon's 1975-1990 War. Security personnel entered the Palestine bureau and demanded that images insulting to Arafat be removed. Al-Jazeera refused and continued to air the footage (ibid).

In November 1998 the Jordanian Ministry of Information, through the Press and Publications Department, cancelled al-Jazeera's press accreditation in protest of a panel debate screened from al-Doha. A Syrian guest in the program claimed Jordan was established for Israel's benefit. He then accused it of colluding with Israel to deprive Syria of water resources.[67] These two cases are a small part of a long series of actions against al-Jazeera. Similar action has been taken by Syria, Egypt and Algeria.

In a similar case with a different ending, on October 26, 2001, Egypt's Minister of Information Safwat al-Sharif, angered by what he perceived as one-sided coverage of Egypt's role towards the al-Aqsa Intifada threatened to close down al-Jazeera facilities in Cairo. Later the Minister reconsidered. It appeared that his reconsideration was based upon how this reaction would destroy the credibility of Egypt's Media Free Zone (with its promise of no political censorship) in the eyes of potential foreign clients, Arab or non-Arab. Meanwhile, Egyptian commentators at the semi-official al-Ahram (the largest and most influential of the semi-official Egyptian newspapers) also turned their pens against the campaign (Schleifer 2000).

On November 3, 2002, Kuwait closed down its al-Jazeera there after claiming that the channel did not accurately report particular events in the country. Al-Jazeera was not the only Arab satellite station, which had action taken against it from Arab states. A month after Jordanian action against al-Jazeera, police there injured and detained MBC's correspondent Saad Selawi as he tried to film the scene where an armed bank robbery had taken place the previous day.[68]

In 2002, Abu Dhabi's TV offices in East Jerusalem were forcibly closed down and their staff's press accreditation revoked, after authorities claimed the station was inciting the Arab world against Israel.

---

[67] BBC Summary of World Broadcasts, ME/3377 MED/6, November 6, 1998.

[68] Jordan Times, October 13, 1999.

Limitations and pressure from foreign states on transnational media directly and indirectly

Here I refer to pressures used by foreign countries whose interests are endangered by satellite televisions. This may be through pressure on the owners and the managers of the stations directly; sanctions on the stations including an advertisements boycott and others.

For instance, in one incident in April 1997, Rachid Ghannouchi, a Tunisian opposition figure living in London, was suddenly cut off while contributing by telephone to the regular al-Jazeera program *Al-Sharia w'al-Hayat* (Sharia [Islamic Law] and Life). Later investigation of the event suggested that the Qatar authorities had intervened after Tunisian government officials made urgent telephone protests to the Qatari embassy in London while the program was still on air.[69]

In 2001—2002, Washington initially treated al-Jazeera as if it were the Taliban's Ministry of Information. It continues to discredit al-Jazeera in Iraq. Even though the channel's critiques of U.S. policy in Afghanistan largely reflected viewer attitudes, the U.S. State Department lambasted al-Jazeera for its "inflammatory rhetoric." The then-Secretary of State Colin Powell went so far as to demand that the channel's editorial chiefs tone down its guest commentaries. Over the years, State Department officials have visited Qatar to discuss al-Jazeera's reporting. But reflective of al-Jazeera's influence, even as the State Department was (and continues to) pressure al-Jazeera to limit its anti-American content, it was offering (and continues to offer) the station its own officials for interviews.

Colin Powell, Donald Rumsfeld and Condoleezza Rice have all appeared on al-Jazeera, as did Christopher Ross, a former American ambassador to Syria who speaks fluent Arabic. The Americans were not alone. British Prime Minister Tony Blair also made his case for "dismantling the network of international terrorism" directly to al-Jazeera viewers (Zednik 2002).

While North American and British officials had access to al-Jazeera's (not insignificant) audience, there was simultaneously another process to pressure the station. Colin Powell initially expressed concern about its inflammatory rhetoric to the Qatari Emir during their October 3, 2001 meeting. Six weeks later, on November 13, a pair of 500-pound U.S. bombs destroyed al-Jazeera's Kabul bureau.

Indicative of the pressure foreign states have applied, in April 2002, 'Abd al-Bari 'Atwan, the editor-in-chief of the London-based *al-Quds al-'Arabi,* went on al-Jazeera, accusing critical Arab news-stations, including the station he appeared on, of softening their guests appearing on television, excluding previous voices.

Concerns about the implications of Lebanese president Rafiq al-Hariri's links with the Saudi leadership appeared to be vindicated in late 1997 when he quickly responded to complaints from unnamed officials in the Gulf about po-

---

[69] ARTICLE 19, *Surveillance and Repression: Freedom of Expression in Tunisia* (London, 1998), pp 48-9.

litical programs carried by Lebanon's two satellite channels. The complaints coincided with a spate of controversial programs, or promotional advertisements for programs, on LBC and Murr TV, involving one interview with Beirut MP Najah Wakim about corruption and another with the exiled General Michel Aoun.

Al-Hariri's Information Minister at the time, Bassem al-Sabaa, told Radio Lebanon in December 1997 that the broadcasts had brought an adverse reaction from "some Arab information ministers, especially in the Gulf."[70] In January 1998, the Lebanese government, using its powers under Law 531, banned LBCI and Future International from transmitting news. The ban remained in force for more than nine months. Pierre Daher, LBC's executive director, denounced the ban as having been instigated by al-Hariri at King Fahd's request. He said the action had been taken because LBCI was on the verge of overtaking MBC as the most watched television newscaster in Saudi Arabia.[71] This allegation was corroborated by the only viewing figures available. The *TV Update* for November 1997 released by the Pan-Arab Research Center in Dubai put LBCI and MBC neck and neck in terms of their share of the audience in Saudi Arabia. Unlike LBCI, Future Television did not protest against the ban, describing it instead as a means of safeguarding continued Gulf investment in Lebanon.[72]

This message was reiterated many times in exchanges between Qatari representatives and the leaders of other Arab states, who took personal offence at al-Jazeera's output. In some cases this was translated into a ban on al-Jazeera newsgathering activities in the country concerned.

As in Jordan, however, experienced media professionals saw al-Jazeera's output from a different perspective. Mohammed Gohar, managing director of Video Cairo, commented that audiences were simply unused to hearing such debates in Arabic. "They'll listen to it on CNN," he told the *Middle East Times* in 1998, "but when you put it in Arabic, that's something else."[73] Two years later, however, the Egyptian authorities had still not become inured to al-Jazeera's editorial style.

When the Egyptian president, Hosni Mubarak, hosted summit meetings in Egypt in October 2000, to try to end Israeli-Palestinian clashes, al-Jazeera provided a forum for those opposed to the summit meetings to air their views. Opposition commentators and Palestinian Islamists criticized the Egyptian leadership for not being tough enough with their Israeli counterparts. This was too much for Safwat al-Sharif. He accused al-Jazeera of focusing its broadcasts "only on attacks against Egypt and its president" and called on it to stop, threatening to cease all co-operations with the channel. By this he meant forbidding it from having studios or correspondents in Egypt or broadcasting from Egypt by satellite.[74]

---

[70] BBC, *Summary of World Broadcasts*, 15 December 1997.
[71] Interview, 26 March 1998.
[72] Interview with Nadim Munla, 26 March 1998.
[73] *Middle East Times*, 22 November 1998.
[74] *Middle East Times*, 26 October 2000.

While members of the Egyptian government felt they were being targeted by al-Jazeera, Kuwaiti ministers apparently felt the same. They objected strongly to the channel's coverage of the U.S. and British bombing of Iraq at the end of 1998, seeing it as biased in Iraq's favor. In mid-1999 al-Jazeera was banned for six weeks from reporting from Kuwait after an Iraqi (apparently living in Norway) called up a live caller show to vent his anger about the presence of Western forces in Kuwait. The caller criticized the Kuwaiti Emir for "embracing atheists and allowing foreign armies to enter Kuwait."[75]

Visiting Kuwait some months after the incident, the Qatari Emir was reported in the Kuwaiti daily *al-Watan* as defending al-Jazeera's output. In his view the problem had stemmed from hostility between Iraq and Kuwait, not from the existence of al-Jazeera. The Emir, Sheikh Hamad, said that if al-Jazeera did not shed light on contentious issues, other media would. He reassured the Kuwaitis that al-Jazeera had not been set up to spite them and pointed out that Qatar had not banned Kuwaiti newspapers when they criticized the Qatari government.[76]

Instead of taking advantage of al-Jazeera to air their own views, however, many officials in the region preferred to boycott it. When the Kuwaiti Ministry of Information withdrew work permits and press accreditation of al-Jazeera staff in mid-1999, it also urged Kuwaitis not to appear on any al-Jazeera programs produced outside Kuwait.[77] After the channel hosted two leading members of the Palestinian Islamic Resistance Movement, Hamas, in 1998, the secretary-general of the Palestinian Authority (PA), Tayyeb 'Abd al-Rahim, requested PA representatives to refrain from taking part in televised exchanges with Hamas leaders abroad. Nabil Amr, information adviser to Yasser Arafat, consequently refused to take part with Mohammed Nazzal, a senior member of Hamas' political bureau in an edition of the al-Jazeera program *Akthar min Ra'i* (More than One Opinion).[78] A similar stand was taken by the Moroccan government. It objected to interviews on al-Jazeera with representatives of the Polisario Front fighting for independence in territory claimed by Morocco.[79] It also complained that al-Jazeera had omitted to cover a visit to Washington by the Moroccan king.[80]

In another incident, Israel in 2002 pressured the U.S. to pressure Egypt to pressure a transnational Egyptian channel not to air the series, *Faris Bila Jawwad* (Knight without a Horse), claiming the program was anti-Semitic. The series is based on the book discussing the Zionist Protocols.

---

[75] As reported in *MidEast Mirror*, 21 June 1999, p 16.
[76] *MidEast Mirror*, 10 February 2000, p 19.
[77] *MidEast Mirror*, 21 June 1999, p 15.
[78] BBC, *Summary of World Broadcasts*, 6 May 1998, quoting a report in the Amman daily *Al-Majd* of 4 May 1998.
[79] Reuters report from Rabat, 17 May 1998.
[80] *Middle East International*, 28 July 2000, p 18.

Providing alternative media content

60% of all transnational stations are directly state owned. These stations were created after initial semi-independent transnational channels were created. As I have discussed earlier, it clearly appears that the creation of these channels was intended to provide competitive alternative media content to balance the effects of Arab transnational television. In this direction Naomi Sakr (2000) argues that Arab states attempts to preempt the liberalizing impact of satellite television leads to the establishment of the Arab satellite televisions by the Arab countries. Indeed it was these very survival instincts that encouraged the Egyptian government and Saudi ruling family to initiate the first Arab satellite stations: Egyptian Space Channel (ESC) and MBC, to meet the challenge created by alternative sources of news and propaganda about Iraq's invasion of Kuwait in 1990 and the subsequent Gulf War.[81]

Sreberny (2001) mentions two main strategies which were taken in order to minimize the effect of the large amounts of foreign, especially American, programming coming to the Arab world: First, a regional strategy of making Arab language programming suitable for Arab Islamic values.

The second strategy is thus to produce programming targeted at the national audience (Sreberny 2001). The second strategy is reflected in government policy of some Arab countries, in particular Syria, Saudi Arabia and Egypt, which aims to encourage production of programming, documentary as well as entertainment, which not only targets national audience, but is also oriented to the socio-cultural and political 'game rules' dominant in the Arab world.

Conclusion

As I noted earlier, the rise of transnational Arab satellite broadcasting has been the largest and most pervasive media challenge in contemporary history to state regime dominance. In many ways however, this challenge has largely been a product of indigenous mechanisms which have allowed transnational television to emerge and subsequent audience demand (and persistence) to access these channels, despite government attempts to prevent or thwart access.

Transnational Arab satellite broadcasting has been a product of four factors: Gulf money for investment; the right technology to (initially) circumvent border-based restrictions, offering state regimes a *fait accompli*; the politics of small, wealthy Gulf states and inter-Arab rivalry, preventing a unified policy.

Moreover, state regimes initially made an important mistake regarding their initial media policies towards transnational satellite television: assuming that it was simply a more powerful form of domestic television. In other words, that it was a mass medium aiming to control the national population in the same way that domestic television was designed to do.

The subsequent policies of Arab state regimes have varied from one state to another. In many cases, they have initially begun with attempts to ban ownership

---

[81] The ESC is based in Cairo as part of the state owned Egyptian Radio and Television Union (ERTU). MBC, based in London, is owned by a brother-in-law of King Fahd.

of satellite dishes and moving onto MMDS. Yet with the development of new technology, battles have taken two different directions: increasingly on the political field: withdrawing ambassadors, inciting local press and so forth and physically: arresting journalists, closing down offices and in the Lebanese case—storming and disconnecting satellites from transmission.

The latter seems to be the most effective form of controlling what should appear on Arab screens, although physical policies of control are the most difficult to perpetuate over long periods of time.

It seems clear therefore, that the most successful policy each state has developed, is mass state ownership—or mass state control, whereby there is an understanding (whether legislated into policy or not) that states have the final say on broadcast content.

Indeed, it is apparent that Arab regimes intend on controlling the media, despite the difficulties this entails through new technology. While there appears to be a trend to simultaneously allowing more commercialization of stations (i.e., not in direct state hands), there is increasing pressure on channels to screen 'safe' material.

Nevertheless: there is an apparent gap between the consistent attempts (in what ever form) of state regimes to control broadcasting and content actually aired. This gap appears to be a result of three other important mechanisms or dynamics surrounding Arab media. First, there is a clear conflict between political interest and ratings. Al-Jazeera is the second most watched channel on Arab screens, for an important reason: it offers audience engagement in critical political and current affairs shows, which viewers have overwhelmingly responded to. Other stations, including ART and LBCI cannot ignore this trend. Thus it appears they will continue airing politically (somewhat) provocative shows, in order to maintain ratings and through this, a part of their credibility.

Second, inter-Arab rivalry, which I have discussed previously, is a crucial factor. Al-Jazeera's case is exemplary. The station critiques all Arab states (with the exception of Qatar, which in most Arab eyes, is hardly a significant player, although the reverse may well be true), thus serving as a useful platform for Arab leaders to derive legitimacy in their struggles with other Arab states.

This leads to my third point, being that from the time al-Jazeera (in terms of news) and LBCI (in terms of entertainment) appeared on Arab screens, a process of comparison and state delegitimization has occurred, whereby Arab viewers turn to non-state sources (al-Jazeera, ANN and others) for information, not state run programs. I suggest the process of delegitimization created a space for such channels those Arab leaders now cannot easily remove without widespread opposition.

Finally we may understand the declaration of one of Arab media policy maker that "the new media technology has made the battle impossible to wage."[82] Already existent strategies, media regulations and control policies are not sufficient to deal with new broadcasting technologies.

---

[82] According to Al-Umran, a member of the Ministry of Radio and Television in Bahrain See Al-Umran, Hala 1996. "MMDS-the Cultural alternative to DTH". In *Middle East Broadcast and Satellite*. September 1996.

Ultimately, freedom of expression, not only transnational television technology as such, is crucial to media development. Satellite broadcasting provides a platform for greater freedom, but how the platform is used depends on laws, policies and habits. Satellite technology may have drawn attention to the dearth of uncensored media in the Arab world, but it has no intrinsic powers to change this situation (Sakr 2001) except for several unique (and therefore inimitable situations).

Chapter Six
Mc-Arabism through Transnational Arab News: the Case of al-Jazeera

Al-Jazeera has risen to prominence in the past three years in light of its handling of social and political issues in the Arab world, where audiences were used to monolithic media performances. In as much as al-Jazeera has won the hearts and minds of millions of viewers, it has also incurred the anger of numerous Arab governments, British and American government officials, their supporters in academia and the press for its critical coverage of mostly political issues.

This chapter serves to introduce al-Jazeera as the primary context for the emergence of McArabism. I provide a more detailed introduction to al-Jazeera, conspiracy theories surrounding the station and list all of al-Jazeera's programs (current to time of publication) in order to introduce the notion of the station's uniqueness as a news and current affairs channel, not simply in the Arab world but globally. Through a comparison of CNN, terrestrial Jordanian television and al-Jazeera in eight newscasts, I seek to provide the reader with a broad context for understanding al-Jazeera's importance as a critical Arab transnational channel and thus its impact and importance to Arab audiences. I then outline a broad discussion about McArabism in light of findings of this sample comparative study.

Al-Jazeera: Background

In 1994, Sheikh Hamad bin Khalifa al-Thani, the crown prince of Qatar, pulled off a palace coup, taking over the government from his father, vacationing in Europe at the time. The young ruler promptly announced a new order of things and set out to challenge Saudi Arabian primacy in the Gulf. He hoped to underline his independence and give his small principality a voice in the world.

When the Emir, Sheikh Hamad bin Khalifa al-Thani, gained power in 1995, the Ministry of Information post was left vacant. In line with Qatar's policy of reform, the Ministry was abolished altogether in 1998. As a result of these modifications, al-Jazeera has had completely different broadcasting patterns, unique in the Arab world.

In 1995, Qatar made initiatives to introduce the first Arab all-news and public affairs satellite channel. Al-Jazeera began broadcasting in October 1996 with a six-hour transmission that ran around the clock by February 1999.

The changing attitude of the Qatari government to the electronic media, which allowed the establishment of al-Jazeera may be explained by economic interest—whereby critical and often provocative journalism attracts high ratings and thus advertising.

The first news of the channel's creation came with an Emir's decree issued on 8 February 1996. Under that decree the state owned venture was capitalized at QR 500 million ($137 million).[83] Start-up was scheduled for 1 November 1996, with broadcasting initially limited to six hours a day. The man put in charge of al-Jazeera was Sheikh Hamad bin Thamir al-Thani, who was still being referred to as under-secretary at the Ministry of Information and Culture at the time of al-Jazeera's launch. The Ministry's actual abolition did not take place until February 1997.

Sheikh Hamad bin Thamir al-Thani made it clear that al-Jazeera would deal predominantly with news and current affairs, establishing a network of correspondents around the world. But the government deliberately distanced itself from the operation by keeping the al-Jazeera logo devoid of any mention of Qatar.[84]

Soon after the Emir ascended to the throne, an Arabic television joint venture between the BBC and Orbit, foundered over the BBC's insistence on editorial independence. The Arab reporters and editors who worked on this failed venture were subsequently hired to run al-Jazeera.

Al-Jazeera enjoys a unique ownership and policy structure. Funding is via the Qatari government and policy is dictated by upper-level staff, not the Qatari government (the only Arab state which does not have a Ministry of Information).

Al-Jazeera and Qatari politics

While al-Jazeera, as discussed previously, does not attract advertising comparative to its viewership, this trend may change in the future. In the long term, there may be plans to turn al-Jazeera into an entirely private enterprise. It may be that the Qatari government allowed the establishment of al-Jazeera as a tool of inter-Arab rivalry, as discussed previously. It may be that the Qatari government allowed the establishment of a critical news-based channel in order to deflect criticism regarding its open-trade relationship with Israel and to 'save face.'

Al-Jazeera can only leave one topic untouched: internal Qatari politics. But as I have noted earlier, it is becoming increasingly open, relatively speaking, on this issue. This has worked well for al-Jazeera and the Qatari government. Al-Jazeera has worked as the fourth estate in the *Arab world*, its target group, but has left Qatar (its founder and principle financer) untouched. The station has given Qatar eminence and influence far beyond its territorial size, resources or

---

[83] BBC, *Summary of World Broadcasts*, 31 October 1996.
[84] Interview with Mohammad Jassem al-Ali, 27 May 1998.

population. A controversial Arab state in its own right (American army bases, strong economic relations with Israel), the Qatari government funds and watches the uncomfortable critical spotlights al-Jazeera focuses all over the Arab world—from afar.

Critics of the experiment claimed that the Emirate was giving itself the freedom to tackle topics that were sensitive in other Arab countries while keeping controversial aspects of domestic politics off-limits. The Foreign Minister, Sheikh Hamad bin Jassem bin Jabr al-Thani, refuted this criticism in a press interview in October 1999, citing instances in which he and Qatari government policies had come under attack, including on al-Jazeera. Judging from the amount of criticism, he said "you would think that [Qatar's] population numbered 50 million rather than half a million."[85]

Indeed, the Emir's willingness to provide media outlets for local complaints served to reinforce al-Jazeera as a means of asserting Qatar's independence from less receptive Gulf regimes. This was demonstrated when local radio aired grievances about allowances paid to members of the al-Thani family, which one caller described as a "big emotional and financial weight on the nation and its people."[86] The talk show host, 'Abd al-'Aziz Mohammed, said the debate proved there were no more red lines for the Qatari media. However, the breaking of taboos was not proof of the absence of media manipulation at the highest level of the Qatari government.

Al-Jazeera's red lines are clearly seen through the satirical internet publication, *The Arab Times*, which enjoys flogging Arab state regimes and their politics (in Arabic). In one 'article,' *The Arab Times* puts up a picture of al-Jazeera host Faysal al-Qassem, with a list of questions which serve as the context for the debate on *al-Ittijah al-Mu'akas* (The Opposite Direction), as al-Jazeera does on its own website.

Chapter 6
This set of questions asks,

Why has Sheikh Hamad betrayed his father [in making a palace coup]?

Has Sheikh Hamad returned the millions of dollars, which he says his father stole?

Why Sheikh Hamad restricted the movement of his children from his first wives?

How true are the claims that Qatar's Foreign Minister is an alcoholic and a gambler?

But on the other side . . .

Isn't it the right of Sheikh Hamad to be the ruler because he is so fat?

---

[85] *Al-Hayat* website, 2 October 1999.
[86] Associated Press report from al-Doha, 19 June 1999.

Isn't it true that Sheikh Hamad's first wife, Banana, is better than his latest wife, Cucumber?

All of these questions await your fabricated and pre-prepared participation on the following number . . .

On a more serious note was a book written by Jamal Ismail (2001) titled *Ben Laden, al-Jazeera and I*. Ismail was al-Jazeera's correspondent from Afghanistan during the U.S.-led war on the country. In the book, Ismail alleges that al-Jazeera used its reports to further Qatari interests. He cites several examples of this, including a time in 1998 when Ismail was asked by al-Jazeera to conduct an interview with Dr. Ayman al-Zhawahiry, an Islamist from Egypt.

Dr. al-Zhawahiry previously lived in Egypt but had escaped to Afghanistan after facing persecution in Egypt. Ismail claimed that al-Jazeera wanted to conduct the interview with him because they wanted strong reactions from various Arab states, primarily Egypt. The conflict between Egypt and Qatar dates back to 1995, when Sheikh Hamad bin Khalifa, carried out a place coup against his father, Sheikh Khalifa bin Hamad al-Thani (referred to as Sheikh Hamad and Sheikh Khalifa).

Following this, the father once again unsuccessfully attempted to regain his power from the hands of his son. Qatar representatives contend that Egypt supported Sheikh Khalifa against his son and that Egyptian generals present in Qatar were involved in the attempt to undermine the new regime. Jamal claims that the reason for al-Jazeera's insistence on conducting the interview with Dr. al-Zhawahiry was primarily a tactic against Egypt, providing an individual with the chance to have his say against the country. Ismail noted,

> The making of a televised interview with Dr. al Zhawahiry will have a greater harmful effect on the Egyptian government than any other media campaign, which the Qatari state can make through other mass media.

At another time, Ismail conducted an interview with Usama Bin Laden in December 1998, as an exclusive for al-Jazeera. Ismail finds it peculiar that al-Jazeera in fact rather than featuring the report right away, dragged their feet in the matter. Ismail claims that the editor-in-chief, Salah Najem (who Ismail claims was assigned to the position as a part of a deal between the Qatari and Egyptian governments after reconciling their differences) threatened to resign if the report was broadcast on al-Jazeera because Ismail allowed Bin Laden freedom in the interview rather than limiting him. Ismail claims that Salah Najem explained as follows:

> I [Salah Najem] do not want to provide with Bin Laden with a mouthpiece because it will provide ammunition for those wanting to close down the Qatari station.

Regarding the deal between the Qatari and Egyptian governments, Ismail notes that at al-Jazeera's inception, many of its correspondents were Egyptian, who had transferred from the Arabic BBC. When the Egyptian regime felt it was constantly being attacked by al-Jazeera, they asked their Egyptian citizens to resign their positions and in fact they did do this.

One of these employees at the time was Salah Najem. When the relations improved between the two countries once again, Najem was asked to return. Ismail also claims that when he realized that al-Jazeera had no intention of running his piece with Bin Laden, he began to insist and follow the reasons closely. At that time he spoke with al-Jazeera's General Manager Muhammad Jassem al-Ali, asking for an explanation. Al-Ali apparently explained to Ismail that the real reason for not airing the piece on al-Jazeera was external pressures on the Qatari government at that time, due to the high level of Arabic antagonism against the attacks of America on Iraq (December 1998).

Al-Jazeera did not want to air the piece at the time because they feared it would only cause a rise in the already existing antagonism against the United States. Furthermore, Ismail learned that al-Jazeera provided a copy of both interviews to the Egyptian and American Embassies.

Another instance took place between Ismail and al-Jazeera, where al-Jazeera again delayed the airing of a piece. On February 13, 1999, the-then Deputy Minister of the Taliban regime in Afghanistan told Ismail that Bin Laden had fled Afghanistan to an unknown destination. The Deputy Minister requested that this fact be publicized in al-Jazeera as an exclusive. Ismail claims al-Jazeera didn't seize the opportunity and air the piece directly. Rather, the channel stalled and asked for excessive details about the source of Ismail's information, citing as an excuse the need to be certain of the facts.

Ismail began to feel that the close questioning of al-Jazeera's editor-in-chief might have been for espionage. Ismail was informed at this time that if he wished to continue to work with al-Jazeera or to improve his current standing, he should cooperate with their tactics much more. At this point, Ismail contacted MBC and provided them with the news. Four hours later, al-Jazeera aired the news piece but did not cite Ismail as the source.

The Bin Laden interview conducted by Ismail was finally aired June 1999, although only parts of it were shown. Ismail claims that the interview was only aired after he pressured al-Jazeera by informing them that if the interview was not aired the followers of Bin Laden would become angry and take action against al-Jazeera. In other words, Bin Laden's spokespeople threatened al-Jazeera to either air the interview or give them back the tapes; otherwise they would take action against the channel. Ismail admits that he fabricated this story in order to finally force al-Jazeera to air the interview. Ismail claims that airing the interview at this specific time was not by chance. He says it served the U.S. campaign against Bin Laden in the summer of 1999.

Ismail claims that he received a call from the General Manager, Muhammad Jassem al-Ali, asking him not let it become general knowledge of when the interview was actually conducted with Bin Laden. At the same time, he told Ismail that the FBI had called him and asked when exactly the interview took place. At that time, al-Ali informed the FBI of the actual date and asked Ismail to do the same only for the FBI. However, he did not want this knowledge known publicly.

In a third instance, Ismail was contacted and informed by contacts in Afghanistan and Pakistan that American Special Forces were present in Pakistan. Ismail contacted the editor-in-chief that night when he received the information and asked him air the news. Al-Jazeera aired the news, but he was criticized by the Pakistani government. Al-Jazeera experienced a great deal of pressure as a result and Ismail was asked to conduct interviews with Pakistani and Afghani government representatives who would confirm the information, thus removing some of the pressure on al-Jazeera. Ismail was told to carry out these interviews, or his future with al-Jazeera would be affected.

This finally led to Ismail's resignation from al-Jazeera and his deportation from Pakistan, as ordered by the Pakistani government—which Ismail claims occurred following the Pakistani Information Ministry receiving a great deal of correspondence from Arab Ambassadors, including Jordan, Saudi Arabia, Egypt, Kuwait and others. He claims that these Arab states requested his deportation, feeling that his reporting was negatively influencing the relationship between Pakistan and Arab states.

Conspiracy theories and al-Jazeera

Since al-Jazeera's inception, Arab state regimes and their mobilization press have somewhat unimaginatively accused al-Jazeera of being a part of a greater Zionist plot to discredit Arab-state regimes; of al-Jazeera being in the hands of the United States; of al-Jazeera seeking to confuse Arab audiences by showing the truth but telling lies.

The usual chorus emitted from Arab state regimes and their tribal press does not usually warrant examination; for those following Arab politics, this chorus is so regular it may be have been pre-recorded, pre-written and simply issued anew to every body, group, or state threatening or challenging state regimes and more appropriately, their own Orwellian truths, as represented on state terrestrial television.

Nevertheless, the debate around al-Jazeera is not limited to Arab state regimes. Conspiracy theories about al-Jazeera extend to its viewers, intellectuals and even al-Jazeera staff. In this section therefore, I shall list some of the conspiracy theories around al-Jazeera.

1. Al-Jazeera is funded by Zionists

The legitimacy for this conspiracy theory emerges from the fact that one of the investors in al-Jazeera is Jewish. One repeatedly asked question is why would a Jewish man have an interest in investing in al-Jazeera, when it clearly is such a bad investment option, attracting little revenue?

2. Somebody is funding al-Jazeera to allow Israeli normalization in the Arab world

It is no secret that Qatar is one of the most pro-American states in the Arab world. It is moreover the most pro-Israel. Al-Jazeera may be seen as a step to introduce Israeli normalization into the Arab world. While it may first begin with critical reporting of the Occupation, it indeed treats Israel's existence as something normal. Al-Jazeera, much like the Qatari government, does not boycott Israel. It has offices in Ramallah, hires Palestinian citizens of Israel to be reporters and regularly interviews Israeli figures on the channel.

3. Al-Jazeera is supported by the U.S. to further its own geo-political ends

It is not a point of contention that the U.S. strongly influences the Arab world through its resources, being a major purchaser of Arab oil and also a major donor to Arab countries.

The Arab world is indeed perhaps the worst example of a region, which regardless of the system used to control the state (monarchy, democracy, etc), *mediocracy* could best term most states in the region, which systemically practice some of the worst cases of human rights abuses.

In the post-Cold War arena, it is not enough to control Arab states through their regimes, which the U.S. has done consistently through its role as a world superpower. Arab people have increasingly little to lose and perhaps the U.S. is beginning to question whether the regimes in place will be able to control the Arab street forever.

A new map of the Arab world may be indeed called for, something akin to Afghanistanization or Eastern Europeanization; whereby relatively more tolerant and democratic states exist—however, still under the firm thumb of the U.S. to ensure resource control.

Al-Jazeera emerges into this picture, as a channel created by a pro-Israel and pro-American regime. The U.S. is not funding al-Jazeera and had no role to play in its inception.

Indeed, the U.S. is known for being a poor government sponsored propagandist. Its only real move to create something akin to a pro-American Arab media influence has been *Radio Sawa, al-Hurra,* a news station created on the al-Jazeera model, but alas, with little of its credibility or sleek formatting. Both were established after September 11, not before.

In this regard, the U.S. has supported al-Jazeera by not destroying it. The U.S. once sent al-Jazeera a warning by bombing its offices in Afghanistan—apparently by mistake, as it once bombed the Chinese Embassy in Yugoslavia—apparently by mistake. It is fully within the U.S.' power to urge Arab governments to close down al-Jazeera offices in each respective country—end of story.

However, the U.S. has seen al-Jazeera's potential. Indeed, it has worked to delegitimize most Arab states (except Qatar) upon Arab screens. Al-Jazeera shall prove to be useful when the U.S. decides to create a new map of the Arab world—a map with more friendly governments—respecting human rights, democracy and of course, American interests in the region, such as oil and Israel.

Al-Jazeera's success

Despite the conspiracy theories, al-Jazeera is successful and does not speak with one voice. Al-Jazeera's anchors and guests hold views as diverse as the tribal with the urban, pro-Arab, pro-America, Islamist, die-hard secularists, feminists and misogynists. This is either genius or total failure. But although things are working out quite impressively, I do not attribute much of al-Jazeera's success to what takes place within what Egyptian President Hosni Mubarak described as "the match box." Al-Jazeera's number one strength is that there is not another al-Jazeera in Arabic. It remains to be seen whether Arab audiences will turn en mass to al-Jazeera's most credible competitors in the region, al-Arabiya, ANN or Abu Dhabi TV.

In the world of straitjacketed Arab media, al-Jazeera has one of the only free hands. Its talk shows can legitimately claim to showcase the full range of Arab opinion. Al-Jazeera has several documentary programs, which add to its popularity, revealing secrets about important Arab players, chiefly Arab leaders, creating controversy and often government-initiated backlashes against al-Jazeera.

Al-Jazeera is an all-news channel like CNN and uses a similar anchor-reporter format and visually attractive presentation. The station is considered to have the most news-credibility in the Arab world, because of its regular updates and its policy of reaching the news directly and in most cases live. It is famous (or infamous) for its important and provocative programs, mainly its two flag-ship programs, both with regular heated debates, al-Ittijah al-Mu'akas (The Opposite Direction) and al-Ra'iy al-Akhar (The Other Opinion).

As with CNN, it is easy to see al-Jazeera's luster withering away in a time of peace and normalcy. There are steady news updates throughout the day (it is always daytime on al-Jazeera, which announces its coming schedule in Mecca time, Greenwich Mean Time and New York Time.) There is a financial broadcast of the standard variety. Sports (soccer for the most part) have a regular report. Oddly for a passionately pan-Arab channel, the station broadcasts dubbed programs bought from old American libraries: a wildlife documentary, a history of French Art.

Al-Jazeera is not a star-driven channel. The station works on the BBC pattern: reporter driven, with a succession of reporters and anchors drawn from different Arab countries (Ajami 2001). Concerning its journalism policy, al-Jazeera provides Arab news from an Arab perspective, with journalists who hail from Mauritania to Iraq—no single nation dominates. It also has bureaus in almost all Arab countries, including one in the West Bank (Zednik 2002).

Al-Jazeera's success has not been restricted to the small screen. It manifests itself more obviously on other people's screens. Al-Jazeera's influence reminds one of the popular Egyptian singer 'Abd al-Halim Hafez: hated by rivals but copied by many of them. MBC, for instance, had to abolish what insiders considered internal red lines since the advent of the newcomer. A whole new set of programs which look like typical inventions of al-Jazeera has been introduced to most, if not all Arab satellite channels. Abu Dhabi TV suddenly appeared from nowhere to counter challenge al-Jazeera's effect, as did Arab News Network (ANN) in a bandwagon fashion. Al-Arabiya (the news network created by MBC) and al-Hurra, sponsored by Washington have also leapt into the scene.

Al-Jazeera now reaches viewers in more than 20 Arab countries, mostly through private satellite dishes, tremendously popular in the Arab world. Al-Jazeera claims a global audience of 35 million Arabic-speaking viewers.

Al-Jazeera programs: Live Broadcasts

Akthar min Ra'iy (More than One Opinion), hosted by Sammy Hadad. Broadcast on Fridays, repeated Saturday and Sunday. Open-discussion talk show treating the latest 'hot' news topics, whether political, economic, social, or otherwise. The show involves three or more participants from various areas of specialty.

Al-Ittijah Al-Mu'akis (The Opposite Direction), hosted by Faysal al-Qasem. Weekly show broadcast on Tuesdays, repeated Wednesdays and Thursdays. Open-discussion talk show dealing with the latest news topics. The audience is encouraged to participate via phone, fax and e-mail. Two guests (from appropriate specialties) with opposing opinions debate each other through the show. Program known to decend into screaming matches between the two antagonists.

Bila Hudoud (Without Borders), hosted by Ahmad Mansour. Broadcast on Wednesdays, repeated Thursdays and Fridays. Open-discussion talk show focusing on current affairs (political, social, economic or academic). Show invites a guest specialising in particular area of concern. Invites audience participation.

Taht al-Hisar (Under Siege), various hosts. No time frame (days or air time). Live discussion show discussing the current events in Palestine and the Israeli Occupation of the 1967 Palestinian territories.

Hiwar Fi al-Riyada (Discussions on Sport), hosted by Aymad Jada. Broadcast on Saturdays, repeated Sundays and Mondays. Open-discussion show that invites audience participation, with one or more guests from the world of sport, discussing both Arab and international sports.

Hiwar Maftouh (Open Discussion), hosted by Ghassan Bin Jadow. Monthly discussion show, broadcast on Saturdays, repeated Sundays and Mondays (live only once a month). Several guests are invited, usually political leaders, intellectuals, and decision and policy makers. Invites audience participation. Show seeks to shed light on significant events, showing all aspects of the issues, distinguishing sides, history and final outcome to be expected.

Su'al Fi al-Riyada (Questions about Sport), hosted by Ayman Jada. Broadcast on Saturdays, repeated Sundays and Mondays. Answers questions in the field of sport.

Al-Shari'a wal Hayat (Islamic Law and Life), hosted by Maher Abdullah. Broadcast on Sundays, repeated Mondays and Tuesdays. Invites audience participation. Open-discussion show dealing with various topics from an Islamic perspective. Primarily depends on the prominent Egyptian Islamic scholar, Sheikh Yousef Al-Qaradawy. Occasionally Islamic figures from different fields are invited from Arab and Islamic countries.

Qadaya al-Sa'a (The Issue of the Hour), hosted by Malek Al-Triky. Weekly show involving the reading of captions of latest news from newspapers and current affairs publications.

Min Washington (From Washington), hosted by Hafez Al-Mirazy. Weekly show presenting relevant current affairs from the U.S. The show debates international developments from the perspective of the media professionals, intellectuals and decision makers in the U.S.

Mawaqi' al-Hadath (The Scene), hosted by Hasan 'Abd al-Ghani. No time frame (days or air time). Tracks current affairs and significant events through a live open debate involving prominent figures, intellectuals and concerned individuals. The show aims to bring to light the subject in question, its various opposing sides and expected end result.

Manbar al-Jazeera (Al-Jazeera Pulpit), hosted by Jumana Namour. Broadcast on Thursdays, repeated Fridays. Open and free arena geared towards understanding the opinions and stands of ordinary Arabs. Subjects and ideas are presented which are of significance to the Arab world in order to learn what the stand of ordinary Arabs are to them.

Lil Nisaa'i Faqat (For Women Only), hosted by Muntaha al-Rahmi. Broadcast on Mondays, repeated Tuesdays and Wednesdays. The show discusses issues related to woman from various perspectives. The program uses recorded film captions, summaries, reports and guests (normally women) to discuss the issue at hand.

Al-Jazeera: Recorded Programs

Ishraqat (Shining/Eastern), hosted by Kawthar al-Bashrawi. Weekly cultural program centering on Eastern culture, presenting a recorded segment, usually clips from movies, plays, poetry readings or dancing. Guests are invited to discuss issues revolving around arts and culture.

Baramij Mutafareka (Program Variety) hosted by different news anchors. No set time. Topics tend to revolve around important current affairs, presented usually through one or two episodes.

Taht al-Majhar (Under the Microscope), hosted by different news anchors. A documentary program that closely investigates a social, humanitarian, or political issue. Through this program, al-Jazeera presents reports and documentation of its news reporters from the site of the story, which is given the opportunity to discuss issues in depth.

Al-Jarima al-Siyasiyya (The Political Crime), various presenters. No set time. An investigative journalism program that researches and examines actions and events considered outstanding contemporary political crimes with the intention of revealing their secrets.

Al-Kitab (The Book), hosted by Khaled al-Haroub. Weekly. Cultural/educational program which critiques and examines latest publications about issues pertaining to Arabs and Muslims. The show usually invites authors, Arab and non-Arab for discussion and debate, as well as inviting academics who specialize in the particular area covered in the book.

Harb Lubnan (The Lebanese War), hosted by 'Umar al-'Issawi. Weekly. Investigative journalism series examining events of the Lebanese War and its impacts (economic, moral, psychological, etc).

Sirr Lil Ghaya (Highly Confidential), hosted by Yosri Fawda. Monthly. Investigative journalism program, which pursues issues surrounded by secrecy. The program relies upon evidence from documents, recordings, eyewitness accounts, investigators, inspectors and informers.

Shahed 'Ala al-A'ser (Witness to an Era), hosted by Ahmad Mansour. Weekly program involving dialogue between figures playing significant roles in the political Arab world over the last several decades.

Shay' Min al-Tarikh (Something from History), hosted by As'ad Taha. Weekly. A program examining an event or day significant in Arab history, explaining occurrences, important participants and individuals close to the event.

Dayf wa Qadiya (Guest and Issue), hosted by Muhammad Krishan. Weekly. A recorded program centered around an interview with a prominent figure on an important current affair. The show presents an introduction to the subject, an explanation of the various stands in the subject, factors effecting it and finally development of the subject.

Ziyara Khasa (Special Visit) hosted by Sammy Klebe. Weekly. An al-Jazeera correspondent visits an individual who has stood out in making news on a significant issue of the time.

Liqaa' Khas (Special Interview), hosted by various anchors. No set time. Discussion and analysis program that involves inviting outstanding and recognized political figures making the news in order to shed light on regional and international affairs. Al-Jazeera correspondents present the show from the most important Arab capitals.

Liqaa' al-Youm (Interview of the Day), hosted by various anchors. Discussion and analysis program that involves the most recognized political, economic and academic figures, in order to shed some light on the most important regional and international affairs. Al-Jazeera correspondents present the show from the most important Arab capitals and states.

Al-Mashhad al-Thaqafi (A Cultural View), hosted by Tawfiq Taha. Weekly. Show invites recognized and well-known members of the cultural community in order to discuss their works and opinions.

Al-Malaf al-Isbua'i (The Weekly File), hosted by Jamil 'Aazer. Weekly. News reports surrounding the most prominent news issues from an international level with an analytical aspect. The purpose of the show is to bring understanding to the issues by examining causes, effects, possible outcomes and varying sides. Furthermore, consultation takes place involving specialists and those following the events for feedback.

Muraselu al-Jazeera (Al-Jazeera Correspondents), hosted by Muhammad Khair al-Burini. No set time. Feature topics (various: political, cultural, etc) are reported from al-Jazeera correspondents around the world.

Maw'id fi al-Mahjar (Appointment in Diaspora). Weekly. Interviews with prominent Arabs who immigrated outside the Arab world, particularly Anglo-European countries. Program shows the struggle of these individuals in attempting to succeed despite obstacles and establish themselves as recognized members of society.

Qadiya Sakhena (Hot Point) hosted by As'ad Taha. Monthly. Analytical program that follows explosive conflicts around the world in an attempt to understand causes and reasons leading to conflict and its impact. Program also discusses different regional and international stances.

Yaqulu An . . . (It is said that . . .), hosted by As'ad Taha. Bi-weekly. Program documents a social incident that has a political, cultural, religious, or racial dimension, or perhaps a combination of all, which took place in recent history or which continues to take place.

Yawmaha Kanu Hunak (They Were There that Day). Weekly. A program that documents events based on first hand accounts of individuals who were present at important events relevant to the Arab world. The program also uses photographs, recorded documentation and other sources to present a precise recounting of the event.

Methodology

To provide a broad context for understanding al-Jazeera's importance as a critical Arab transnational channel and thus its impact and importance to Arab audiences, I examined the newscasts of al-Jazeera, CNN and the terrestrial Jordan television channel. Al-Jazeera is a transnational media outlet stressing a pan-Arab agenda, Jordan TV is a localized outlet emphasizing more tribal interests and CNN is intended to serve as a kind of control group since it operates according to considerations outside of the conflicting agendas held by the Arab media outlets. We perform a content analysis on samples from each of these three outlets in order to examine any differences between them, particularly between the tribal and transnational agendas.

Eight newscasts are analyzed on each television station on the same day from July 15, 2001 to October 8, 2001 on different days of the week. The newscast samples were taken on 15 July, 17 July, 22 July, 25 July, 28 July, 3 October, 5 October and 8 October. A part of the newscasts were before the September 11 attacks. All these newscasts were during the al-Aqsa Intifada. Analysis and comparison was based on the following parameters:

- News line-up.
- Number of news items in each newscast.
- Total time of each newscast.
- Average item length in each newscast.
- Area of coverage.
- News topic.
- News Format: V.O (Voice-over), C.O (Camera On), interviews and reports.
- Attitudes toward Selected Political Players.
- Language used by anchors and reporters.
- Items and Time given to Israeli-Palestinian conflict.

CNN was chosen as a comparative station to highlight the news and current affairs context al-Jazeera has challenged. CNN has traditionally been important to Arab viewers (particularly prior to al-Jazeera) as a credible source of information for Arabs about the Arab world. Differences highlighted through comparison bring to light the massive transformation in news legitimacy bought to the Arab world by al-Jazeera, with its specific attention on Arab and Islamic perspectives. I selected Jordanian television to highlight the tribal media context of traditional terrestrial Arab state regime stations al-Jazeera has emerged in.

Between Local and Global: Number of news items in each newscast

In general, CNN newscasts are normally shorter than that of al-Jazeera and the Jordanian television. The CNN newscast length is between 15 and 20 minutes while the newscast of al-Jazeera is 30 minutes and the Jordanian newscast is between 30 and 40 minutes.

Average item length in each newscast

Among the three newscasts, the al-Jazeera newscasts had relatively the smallest number of the items. However, more time was given to each item.

67% of al-Jazeera news items were pan-Arab and 73% of total time in the eight newscasts was given to pan-Arab items. This is also evident Ayish's study (2001) where he found that all five Arab satellite television services studied carried a high percentage of news items about pan-Arab developments and issues: 55.5% for Abu Dhabi, 72.3% for al-Jazeera, 43.9% for LBCI, 48.4% for MBC and 57.1% for Syrian Satellite television (SSC). International topics were given fairly normal coverage for a news station, some 33% of total topics on the 8 newscasts. This was also evident in Ayish's study where he found that international news was the highest in LBCI (56%), MBC (51.5%) and Abu Dhabi (44.4%) and was low 19% in al-Jazeera (ibid 2001).

As expected, CNN as a global television channel primarily aired international news (97%), giving 98% of its time to international news. It is interesting to note that CNN was considered for this study, as according to its policy, pan-Arab issues are a part of the global issues the channel covers.

Jordanian television gave 57% of its news items to local issues and was given 64% of the time. Only 24% of the news topics were pan-Arab and given only 18% of the time. 19% of news topics concerned international issues and were given 19% of the time.

The overwhelming majority of pan-Arab news items in the three television channels newscasts were about the al-Aqsa Intifada, which began in September 2000. These news items were normally at the beginning of al-Jazeera's newscasts. Jordanian television and CNN tended to put these issues back in the newscast. Jordanian television generally opened its newscast with local topics normally related to the King or other Arab state leaders.

That the al-Aqsa Intifada was raging during these times and that only al-Jazeera chose to give these items weight by giving them primary importance in the newscast is interesting: Ayish argues in his findings (2001) that the coverage of the events in Palestine reflect satellite television services interest in conveying newsworthy events to their viewers, but also to underscore their keenness to bring the suffering of Palestinians under Israeli occupation to the attention of Arab audiences (as a tool for legitimacy on Arab screens). It has been noted that the role of Arab world satellite television services in promoting Palestinian resistance to Israeli occupation has been instrumental in keeping the Palestinian uprising alive (Khairi 2000). This is consistent with the findings of previous studies about an enduring negative Israeli image in Arab world television (Alterman 1998).

The study shows that Jordan television had the largest number of news items (102) in the eight newscasts of the sample with 217.16 min., followed by al-Jazeera (86) with 201.53 min and CNN (74) respectively. Jordan television follows a format in which the largest number of news items is included in the news lineup, with a very short duration for each item. Al-Jazeera in the other hand presented less stories but gave more time in presenting them.

For the three television services, political news was the most dominant topic, scoring 48% on CNN, 54% on Jordan television and 72% on al-Jazeera. This trend is also evident in the level of the time given for the political news, comparing with the time given for other news topics. Al-Jazeera has the greatest *degree of time* devoted to political news - 66%, while on Jordanian television it is 60.8% and 52.6% on CNN. As Ayish (2001) argues in his study, these finding may be explained by the fact that political news has traditionally been an important news selection criterion used by Arab media gatekeepers, to the extent that news has often been defined mostly in political terms. Economic, military and civil strife followed in terms of percentage: between 5-20%, between 4-8% and between 2-6% respectively.

News Format

Concerning the news format, I chose to deal with the event rather than the item in order to introduce my findings. The difference between *event* and *item* is that event is part of the item where the item has normally more than one event. The events are present in news according to one of four means: *report*, which is done by the television correspondent on regular bases (live or recorded). *Interview* is when the anchor or the correspondent interviews some body during the newscast (live or recorded). *Voice-over* is when the anchor reads the news, while footage is played on-screen. Finally, *camera-on* is where the anchor reads the news without any accompaniments.

Voice-over news events were the dominant format used on Jordanian television - 32%. On al-Jazeera the voice-over format was minimally used—17% and 28% on CNN. While the report format was dominant in newscasts aired by al-Jazeera 29% and on CNN 31%, only 25% of news events on Jordan TV were presented this way.

Concerning al-Jazeera, these findings are also evident in Ayish's study, where he found the station has a high percentage of report format. Ayish argues that similar news services (al-Arabiya, Abu Dhabi TV, al-Jazeera, LBCI, MBC) seem to have adopted new delivery styles drawing on North American and British presentation formats (ibid 2001) such as CNN and the BBC. While al-

Jazeera had correspondents stationed at major Arab world and international cities, from where journalists dispatch reports daily, Jordanian television does not have a single reporter, even inside Jordan.

Interviews were also extensively used at al-Jazeera (23%), less so on Jordanian television (17%) and even less on CNN (14%). Most interviews on al-Jazeera were live (82%) with the majority done in their studios and also for CNN (94%). Most interviews on Jordanian television were not live (more than 95%) and were conducted by telephone. In the best cases, a picture of the person interviewed was screened.

The low percentage of reports on Jordanian television newscasts were offset by a high percentage of voiceovers and on-camera items. This reflects a lack of comprehension of the visual potential of television as a medium of communication at some government-controlled services. As Schleifer (1998) notes in reference to MBC:

> MBC has staffed a growing network of news bureaus with its own growing cadre of Arab TV producer/reporters in Cairo, Brussels, Jerusalem, Tunis, Amman, Paris, and Washington DC. In contrast to the news programming of the national Arab channels, MBC followed the international format in which newsworthiness rather than government press releases determine the lineup and in which news stories-be they field reports or studio voiceovers-are scripted to picture rather than an anchor reading wire copy that at best barely approximates the overall content of the available video.

Attitudes Toward Selected Political Players

The two Arab broadcasters were supportive of pan-Arab and pan-Islamic issues, mainly in instances of confrontations with former colonial powers, America and Israel. Overall, most concern was devoted to Palestinians and to a lesser degree Iraq, at that stage under a 10 year embargo. Al-Jazeera gave more weight to Bin Laden and Taliban sources, rather than U.S. sources, during the last U.S. attacks on Afghanistan. Besides extensive media coverage through newscasts of the two Arab broadcasters of these pan-Arab issues, al-Jazeera covered these events with a clear editorial position. This was expressed by different parameters: besides time given for these issues, the language used by anchors and reporters in describing events or giving reports using superlatives and different sets of terms that tended to be unbalanced on behalf of the Arab or Islamic side. News lineup was also an important parameter.

Pro-Arab and Islamic attitudes were reflected notably in newscasts by al-Jazeera, with 41 items out of a total of 86 overall: 24 on the Intifada, 13 on the Taliban and Ben Laden and the remainder on Iraq and its crisis with the U.S. and one on Hizbollah and its conflict with Israel. Intifada items were normally on the newscast's promo and were the leading or second item. In six of the eight al-Jazeera newscasts, the Intifada was the opening item. In 21 of the 24 items on the Israeli-Palestinian conflict, covert and overt anti-Israeli reporting was evident. Similarly al-Jazeera offered negative, critical treatment for conflicts involving the U.S.

Ayish (2001) argues that this supportive attitude towards Palestinian resistance against Israeli occupation reflects Arab world television's commitment to furthering Palestinian national interests. Although al-Jazeera featured Israeli personalities on their news programs, the way those programs were handled by news anchors reflected a clear disenchantment with Israel's excessive use of force against Palestinian civilians.

While Jordanian television reflected pan-Arab and Islamic attitudes, this was quite subdued compared to al-Jazeera and tended to emerge only when the news item was related to the Intifada or Israeli aggression against Palestinian civilians. Moreover, these attitudes would be expressing the viewpoint of the King or the Jordanian ruling regime. From 25 items on the conflicts between an Arab or Islamic party against Israel or the U.S., 12 items covered the Intifada, eight items focused on Afghanistan, three items were on the Iraqi crisis and two on South Lebanon.

Unlike al-Jazeera, the items on the Intifada were not on the newscast's promo and were not normally among the first items of the newscast. This was usually saved for items covering internal issues, mainly the King. In fact, in seven of the eight newscasts, Jordanian television opened with King Abdullah and regime leaders. For example, on July 17, which saw large escalations in fighting in the Occupied Palestinian territories, the Jordanian newscast opened with a six-minute item covering King Abdullah's inauguration of an industrial area in Jordan. The next item covered Palestine and was three minutes long.

The role of the King is evident in the items dealing with the Intifada. Indeed, it is apparent through the newscasts that the issue of primary importance was the King or the ruling regime's reaction to events, rather than the event itself. For example, in July 22 newscast, the first four items dealing with the Israel-Palestinian conflict covered activities of the King in order to bring peace to the region. The first item covers a meeting between the King and Yasser Arafat, the second covers a phone call between the King and the Egyptian President Hosni Mubarak concerning the crisis, the third covers the King's meeting with the British Foreign Minister regarding the situation and the fourth covers the Jordanian Prime Minister's declaration of the implementation of the Mitchell agreement.

Following this, we may compare the newscast on 28 July on al-Jazeera and Jordanian television, where both aired an item covering the Israeli Supreme Court's decision allowing a fanatic Jewish group to enter the al-Aqsa Mosque square and place the founding stones for building the third Jewish Temple.

First of all, the differences in emphasis are apparent in the news title. Al-Jazeera says, "Israeli supreme court decision to allow a fanatic Jewish group to place a stone foundation for the building of a third Jewish temple in the area surrounding the al-Aqsa Mosque in the old city of Jerusalem." The title itself is descriptive and does not place al-Jazeera at the center of the story, or anywhere else within the story for that matter. On the other hand, the Jordanian television began with the title "Jordan warns about the consequences of Israeli Supreme Court decision permitting a Jewish fanatic group to place a foundation within the gates of al-Aqsa in Eastern Jerusalem." It is clear from this title that Jordanian television is not reporting the story simply as significant news, rather indicating the ruling regime's reaction to it.

The allocation of time for the story is also telling. Al-Jazeera gave a coverage time of three minutes and ten seconds. Jordanian television dedicated 50 seconds.

The story's structure was also important. Al-Jazeera began by presenting pictures of the site in question, while the reporter began his summary. The station then switched to a live interview with Hanan Ashrawy from the Ramallah studio, who stated that the event was an atrocity against the entire Muslim, Arab and Palestinian people. The third segment was an interview with Dr. Jad Izhak, the director of a respected research center in Bethlehem discussing this issue. Dr. Izhak forewarns that the actions discussed could in fact lead to further conflicts and clashes. The fourth segment shows pictures of Israeli soldiers imposing movement restrictions on the Palestinians. The concluding segment sees the al-Jazeera reporter summarizing the issue and its implications.

Compare to Jordanian television: the first part of the item was composed of a declaration from 'Abd al-Ilah al-Khatib, the Jordanian Prime Minister against this step, describing it as a desecration of the sacredness of the al-Aqsa Mosque. The second segment showed the anchor repeating al-Khatib's ideas. Finally; the final segment was a voice over where the anchor stated the ideas of the Foreign Minister while screening his picture.

Moreover, while al-Jazeera focuses on the story, Jordanian television tended to dwell on political and diplomatic activities to resolve the conflict. Only 10 of Jordanian television's 22 items on this topic covered Israeli military activities in the West Bank and Gaza. Meanwhile, Jordanian television tended to be quite neutral concerning the U.S., unlike al-Jazeera.

CNN did cover both Arab and Islamic crises with Israel and the U.S. However, no pan-Arab or Islamic attitudes were present—clearly reflecting CNN's role as a primarily American network. This was also reflected in the number of items about Palestine. From 21 items covering Arab/Islamic conflicts between Israel and the U.S., only five covered the Intifada, the remaining sixteen were about Afghanistan. Additionally, items about Palestine normally did not make it to the promo, nor were they usually among the opening items.

Similar to Jordanian television, CNN coverage of the Palestinian-Israeli conflict tended to focus upon political and diplomatic activities to resolve the issue. Only one of the five items covered Israeli military activities in the West Bank and Gaza. Needless to say, wherever al-Jazeera dished out negative treatment towards the U.S., the opposite was true for CNN.

Language used by anchors and reporters

The language used by anchors and reports to describe events or report them is reflected in superlatives and different sets of terms used in describing events.

In terms of language, al-Jazeera newscasts were the most anti-Israeli and anti-American and the most pro-Arab and Islamic. While Jordanian television tended to settle in the middle, shifting between relative neutrality and pro-Arab and Islamic stances, CNN tended to try for neutrality in covering the Palestinian-Israeli conflict and was pro-American regarding its coverage of the U.S. war on terrorism.

This was evident along several levels. News titles, emphasis in stories, editorial offered by either the anchor or reporter, people chosen for interview and analysis all worked to provide indicators of subjectivity.

For example, the15 July newscast on each of the stations covered confrontations between Palestinians and Israel, although in very different ways. CNN's news item was titled "Restriction on movement imposed in the West Bank as a result of the murder of two settlers." In the same newscast, another news item was titled "Confrontations between the Israelis and Palestinians."

In the first news item, equilibrium is offered: an action is detailed and a result is indicated. The second news item attempts to offer neutrality, although it gives the audience the impression of two equal sides (Israelis and Palestinians) rather than a state occupying army against militias and civilians. Moreover, the background to these confrontations is not presented as an important factor in the ultimate result: Murder of settlers; confrontations.

On the other hand, in the segment presented by Jordanian television, there is an obvious stand taken. The anchor begins with "Seizure of a Palestinian home," informing the audience "an activist from Islamic Jihad was arrested." Finally, the newscast from al-Jazeera is even clearer in realizing its editorial position. The anchor on al-Jazeera begins with "Seizure of a Palestinian home," and continues with another news item, "Israeli settlers burn down a Palestinian house in Hebron." In the third story, al-Jazeera titles its news item "An activist from Islamic Jihad kidnapped."

Arrested or *kidnapped*? The Jordanian station implies a rule of law, recourse before the law, the assumed context of a previous declaration of guilt. Al-Jazeera implies lawlessness, rule by force/power and an arbitrary use of justice.

In the newscast of 17 July, the CNN anchor states, "Deployment of Israeli powers in the West Bank." On Jordanian television, the news item is titled "Funeral march of martyrs from Bethlehem." In al-Jazeera, more detail is given, with a camera-on titled "Heavy shooting of Beit Jala." The reporter then continues with an item, "Four individuals martyred." What CNN called "Israeli powers," the al-Jazeera reporter from the field says, "Israeli tanks placed in the Palestinian territories in preparation for attack."

Moving on the U.S.-led war in Afghanistan, CNN provides a Jordanian-esque version of the news, discussing "Rumsfeld's visit to Saudi Arabia and his planned visit to Egypt and Jordan in order to plan for the campaign of the U.S. against terrorism" and during the same segment another news caption states, "The leader of Uzbekistan declares he will support the U.S. campaign against terrorism."

The Jordanian anchor gives a similar title "US Defense Minister reaches Saudi Arabia." However, on al-Jazeera the anchor states "The head of the Taliban movement gives a speech to the Islamic nation that the purpose of the American crusade is to destroy the Islamic regime in Afghanistan."

On 5 October, CNN discusses "Rumsfeld visits Turkey in order to gain its support in the campaign against terrorism." In another item, the CNN reporter states, "A representative of the former Afghanistan government requests the assistance of the UN in order to destroy the Taliban regime." In the Jordan news segment, there is an interview with the Jordanian Prime Minister who states, "Jordan declares its support in the campaign against terrorism and uprooting it altogether." Al-Jazeera's anchor and reporter discuss "Enormous demonstrations in Islamic states against the participation of Pakistan in the alliance against Afghanistan."

Another example is the newscast of October 8, where CNN broadcasts an interview with Rumsfeld. He declares, "The US insists on the struggle against terrorism in places other than Afghanistan as well." In the case of Jordan, the reporter states, "The Jordan Government spokesperson declares the following: Jordan fully supports the international efforts against terrorism and the destruction of it altogether." Al-Jazeera, on the same day, brings an interview with an Afghani citizen, whose home was destroyed by U.S. strikes, who says, "The attacks on us have been going on for twenty years and no one heard our cries." The al-Jazeera anchor then states "Another night of American strikes against Afghanistan."

It is clear from the research and as shown from the examples listed above that in the case of the language used in relaying the news, the three television stations each act quite differently. Al-Jazeera, when covering Palestine and Afghanistan, is straightforward in its opinions and its stand is clear in both instances. In the case of Jordan television, we notice that in the case of the Palestinian-Israeli conflict, at times they present their opinions clearly and thus their support for the Palestinian people, while at other times they do not present their own stand and simply present detached facts. In the case of CNN, the station shows without a doubt their pro-American stance in the case of Afghanistan, clearly and consistently supporting the U.S. war on terror. However, in the case of the Palestinian issue, we notice that CNN presents the news in an apparently neutral manner.

News lineup

The news lineup is an important parameter of how each station sees the importance of each news item.

Through our research, it is clear that al-Jazeera provided more relevance in its lineup to those items involving Palestinians, or crisis with Israel or America, especially items showing Arabs (Palestinians, Iraqis, Lebanese) or Muslims (Afghanis) as victims of Israeli or American brutality. While Jordanian television showed these items, they were considered secondary to news about the King and regime leaders. CNN also showed these items, although from an American perspective.

If we compare between the newscasts of the three stations we see that the items of each were as follows, according to the title given by each channel for the news item:

25 July, 2001

Item One

Al-Jazeera	Israeli settlers attack Palestinians in Rafah, Gaza
Jordan	King Abdullah leads a meeting of cabinet ministers
CNN	Continued fighting in Macedonia

Item Two

Al-Jazeera	Palestinian—Israeli meeting in Tel Aviv
Jordan	King Abdullah stresses the importance of modifications to Parliamentary elections
CNN	Conviction of Croatian general in the High Supreme Court

Item Three

Al-Jazeera	None of the five candidates for President in Indonesia acquire a 50% vote
Jordan	Israeli assassination of Hamas activist
CNN	America refuses to sign contract to destroy biological weapons, citing international security considerations

Item Four

Al-Jazeera	Renewal of fighting between Albanians and the Macedonian government
Jordan	Carter criticizes Bush's stand towards Israel
CNN	OPEC declares a reduction of its products for the third time in one year

Item Five

Al-Jazeera	Sri Lankan Airport re-opens after its closure following suicide attack
Jordan	Jordanian Prime Minister welcomes an Iraqi leader
CNN	Negotiations between the U.S. and China to solve issues concerning civil rights

Item Six

Al-Jazeera	Croatian general arrives in Holland to stand trial
Jordan	Discussions between Jordanian economic team and the World Bank
CNN	Murder of Indian cabinet member

3 October, 2001

Item One

Al-Jazeera	Six Palestinians martyred in Gaza

Jordan	Discussions between King Abdullah and neighboring Arab countries
CNN	Rumsfeld visits the Middle East and says the White House possesses information on location of Bin Laden

Item Two

Al-Jazeera	Israel says the Palestinian Authority is responsible for the attack on the Eli Sinai settlement
Jordan	Escalation in the Palestinian territories
CNN	NATO forces say they will strengthen their positions to reach the Taliban

Item Three

Al-Jazeera	Two Israelis wounded by Palestinians in Hebron
Jordan	Bush says he will support the establishment of a Palestinian state
CNN	Humanitarian aid for Afghani refugees campaign to begin

Item Four

Al-Jazeera	Sharon cancels meeting scheduled with Palestinian leaders
Jordan	Declaration of Jordanian Prime Minister concerning Islamic—Christian relations in Jordan
CNN	Cooperation between Russia and NATO in campaign against terrorism

Item Five

Al-Jazeera	Hizbollah attacks Israeli forces on Israeli border
Jordan	U.S. provides NATO with list of aids in war against terror
CNN	Bush visits New York for the second time following September 11 to discuss economic projects with financial leaders

Item Six

Al-Jazeera	U.S. Defense Secretary says the U.S. has knowledge of Bin Laden's whereabouts
Jordan	International discussions on conditions in Afghanistan following the Taliban's overthrow
CNN	White House says it has evidence proving Bin Laden responsible for September 11 events

5 October, 2001

Item One

Al-Jazeera	White House rejects Sharon's statement that Washington is lenient with the Palestinians

Jordan	Jordan's Prime Minister condemns events in the U.S., which he describes as criminal and terrorist acts
CNN	Sharon criticizes U.S. moves in asking for assistance from the Arab community in its fight against terrorism

Item Two

Al-Jazeera	Five Palestinians martyred during confrontation with Israeli tanks
Jordan	Jordanian Prime Minister says that the U.S. President Bush's statement supporting the formation of a Palestinian state reassuring
CNN	Rumsfeld visits Turkey following a visit to Uzbekistan to gain support for the war on terror

Item Three

Al-Jazeera	Israeli tanks invade Palestinian territories
Jordan	King Abdullah presents the Iraqi issue to American administrators
CNN	Representative of former Afghani government to the UN requests assistance in overthrowing the Taliban government

Item Four

Al-Jazeera	U.S. Foreign Minister arrives in Uzbekistan
Jordan	Murder of six Palestinians during Israeli attack on Abu Snenah neighborhood in Hebron
CNN	Taliban movement hinders arrival of humanitarian aid to Afghanistan

Item Five

Al-Jazeera	Pakistan and U.K. agree on creation of new Afghani government to replace the Taliban
Jordan	Israeli military escalation in Palestine
CNN	Blair visits Pakistan to discuss eliminating the Taliban and its implications on the region

Item Six

Al-Jazeera	Demonstrations in Islamabad against U.S. attacks on Afghanistan
Jordan	Jordan's Minister of Communication denounces Sharon's declarations against Islam
CNN	Britain signs an agreement to establish international court, the U.S. refuses to sign

8 October, 2001

Item One

Al-Jazeera	New U.S. and U.K. attacks on Afghanistan
Jordan	Talks between King Abdullah and al-Assad for cooperation between the two countries
CNN	Second attack on Afghanistan kills Taliban movement members

Item Two

Al-Jazeera	The Taliban movement warns the U.S. of consequences of its attacks on Afghanistan
Jordan	Jordanian and Syrian Prime Ministers condemn terrorism
CNN	Defense Secretary Rumsfeld says the attacks on Afghanistan is the first step in a U.S. campaign to destroy terrorism

Item Three

Al-Jazeera	White House says the U.S. has the right to attack areas outside Afghanistan
Jordan	The spokesperson of the Jordanian governments confirms the support of Jordan to international efforts against terrorism
CNN	Britain decreases its participation in the attacks against Afghanistan

Item Four

Al-Jazeera	British Defense Secretary says attack on Afghanistan hits 30 targets
Jordan	King Abdullah sends humanitarian assistance to Afghanistan
CNN	Residents in northern Afghanistan welcome U.S. attacks and say they hope to be rid of the Taliban

Item Five

Al-Jazeera	Live broadcast of the attacks on Kabul. (Al-Jazeera was the sole news agency to broadcast live from Afghanistan, while other stations used al-Jazeera footage)
Jordan	Continuation of the American and British attacks on Kabul
CNN	Live broadcast of the press conference of President Bush from the White House

The review of these four samples indicates the following trends. First, in presenting salient news items, al-Jazeera highlights Palestine and pan-Islamic issues, above all to Afghanistan, following September 11. This is also due to al-Jazeera's privileged status as the only news agency allowed in Afghanistan.

In the Jordanian instance, these issues are not given importance according to context, but rather according to event. Moreover, as a terrestrial station, Jordan tends to center upon and opens more with local news. CNN presents more global issues, with emphasis upon the war between Afghanistan and the U.S. following September 11.

Al-Jazeera and McArabism

As stated in the theoretical chapter of this book and based on the above findings and discussion we argue here, al-Jazeera in particular has worked in the direction of creating a new sense of regionalism which I call McArabism.

Al-Jazeera's mandate is clearly Arab-speakers and the Islamic world (where Arabic is often taught as a second or third language). While Jordanian television sees its first mandate as an extension of the Jordanian Ministry of Information, CNN sees its principle role as news for Americans (or American news to the world), al-Jazeera takes its mandate from its viewers: ordinary Arabs. Thus al-Jazeera tends provide background and facts (including maps, talking heads, etc) and then head for *subaltern* events: reporting demonstrations, house demolitions, funerals, etc., which often provides a more emotional, or *popular* (in the German sense of *volk*) perception of events.

In this regard, it has both addressed (through focusing on concerns of the Arab and Muslim world) and created a sense of pan-Arabism: a notion of concern based upon a shared language, history, present and religions. Al-Jazeera's attractive presentation, live interviews, news bought straight from the scene, the engagement it offers viewers through audience participation, high proportion of investigative journalism programs has all worked to create legitimacy as an Arab news and current affairs station.

Moreover, al-Jazeera's legitimacy is strengthened through its keen interest in Palestinian affairs as *news,* as opposed to the terrestrial state regime pattern of treating ruling leader's reactions to events as the focus of concern. In this regard, it has taken the mantle from MBC and has pushed it far further.

Al-Jazeera's legitimacy is strengthened once again through its emphasis on indigenous structures and names—thus Fouad Ajami writes in critique of al-Jazeera,

> Its [al-Jazeera's] reporters in Kabul always note that they are reporting from the Islamic Emirate of Afghanistan—the Taliban's official name for the country. Conversely, Washington's campaign is being waged not against terror, but against "what it calls terror."

While this may infuriate Ajami, it is indicative of the respect al-Jazeera gives to its target group: Arabs and Muslims, who may (or may not) be critical of the U.S.' war on terror, contexted as it is in strategic oil and resource rich locations, who may identify the Taliban as the ruling power in Afghanistan and so on.

Al-Jazeera's legitimacy is important to this discussion. Only with this kind of legitimacy, can Arab audiences move beyond the screen to a sense of engagement and importantly, identification. To understand the general *context* of al-Jazeera's impact, Jordanian television offers Arabs news in their own language. However, as I noted earlier, the mandate of terrestrial Arab state regime outlets are their rulers (conveyed through the Ministry of Information), not the Arab screen it appears on. In this regard, such television does not offer interesting programs, challenging journalism or visual attractiveness. The ruling regime's public relations for so long has relied on a set of borders to keep other news sources out. There is barely any relevance or engagement between the viewer and the screen. In terms of credible television news before al-Jazeera, Arab viewers had to make to with the large American, U.K. and European stations, with two obvious issues emerging: language, not simply as a barrier to understanding, but a barrier to engagement; and mandate—with none of the large foreign satellite television stations having Arab viewers as an area of concern or a real target group. Arabs, to put it succinctly, learnt about themselves through others.

While this may impact on notions of bias or imbalance, which are crucial to later discussions about McArabism, there are two arguments of note here. Al-Jazeera's mandate is the Arab and Muslim world. There are natural imbalances arising from the fact that al-Jazeera will necessarily highlight concerns and news important, primarily to this target group. Israeli victims of suicide bombings, the deaths of American marines are important as *facts* for this station, but not as *stories*.

This is also impacted by access, in terms of Israeli-Palestinian conflict reporting. Violence against journalists and other media professionals in the West Bank and Gaza Strip has long been a point of criticism by media support groups, while the Israeli Press Office's overt hostility towards Arab journalists must also be taken into consideration. Al-Jazeera also beams out of its Ramallah studios, rather than Jerusalem, unlike most major satellite channels in the region, which cumbers fast access into Israel. However, there are also obvious unnatural imbalances—and thus biases in the critical sense of the word, on al-Jazeera.

While it is beyond the scope of this study to provide a critical linguistic analysis of al-Jazeera's reporting style, especially concerning conflicts involving Israel and/or the U.S., it is apparent from the overall presentation of news that al-Jazeera indeed creates an unfair bias in its work through the use of the following:

Time to speak

Al-Jazeera in general is quite happy to allow talent to speak for longer than the usual time other good news and current affairs stations would allow, chiefly in live interviews. In particular, it virtually gives a free floor to prominent Palestinians, whether from the Palestinian Authority, Hamas or Islamic Jihad to speak about events as they see them. This is not a flaw in of itself—clearly Arab audiences are willing to hear such people speak if al-Jazeera has continued to use this policy without change, since its inception. However, Israeli spokespeople and 'antagonistic' parties are not normally provided a free floor, nor a sympathetic host asking simple questions. This is apparent through times of crisis for Palestinians and far less so during relatively normal periods, where al-Jazeera's critical gaze is also focused upon the Palestinian authority.

Who speaks: official voices

Whether due to the sensitivities of Israeli army spokespeople appearing on camera, access to their physical locations or a perceived unimportance, Israeli sources are cited far less frequently than Palestinian sources and when they are cited; they are usually juxtaposed against what Palestinians have said. There are of course, reasons for this, firmly based in journalistic experience: official Israeli army sources can be flexible with numbers of dead and injured, how the dead or injured came to be that way (context) and what the Israeli response was/will be. The Mohammad al-Durra incident is a case in point, where until (and even afterwards) the picture of Mohammad was screened worldwide, showing him being shot in his father's lap, Israeli sources insisted he was caught in crossfire.

Nevertheless, al-Jazeera could to more to include more Israeli voices, to allow their faces to appear more frequently on screen, to allow them more time to speak. It does appear that allowing Israelis to speak on al-Jazeera seems to the individual imperative of al-Jazeera reporters, rather than station policy. Moreover, it seems that in allowing more Israelis to speak, risks a loss of legitimacy to individual al-Jazeera reporters and perhaps to al-Jazeera's coverage of the conflict. However it should be noted that al-Jazeera has become increasingly attentive to bringing on Israeli spokespeople.

Area of focus

Almost unique to a major news and current affairs station covering the Israeli-Palestinian conflict, there is only secondary attention given to internal dynamics within Israel. It is not that events in Israel are not covered: but it *is* given secondary attention and usually juxtaposed against events in the Occupied Palestinian territories. Thus al-Jazeera suffers from an almost complete absence of subaltern (i.e., ordinary) Israeli voices on its screens. While filming a middle class area of Tel Aviv, or even a development town for Eastern Jews in the Galilee is unlikely to create any sort of sympathy or recognition with Arab viewers, who, due to al-Jazeera's focus on Palestine, are most likely to juxtapose Israel's affluence with Palestine's poverty, there does seem to be a need in covering a conflict that does have two sides to actually be present in both of them.

I do not anticipate that al-Jazeera will open an office in Tel Aviv, yet there is much to be said for a station which, out of the interests of good journalism, sends professional reporters to all areas of the globe concerned with Arab affairs and yet does not have one al-Jazeera correspondent permanently stationed inside the Green Line, Israel's internationally recognized borders.

How facts become facts

Gathering facts is a precarious business in the Palestinian-Israeli conflict. While some (certainly not all) Anglo-European journalists tend to head straight for the Israeli Defense Force offices to check with English speakers on Palestinian deaths, occasionally rounded down to the lowest believable figure, available without a name, story or history, al-Jazeera heads for opposite logical source: hospitals and civil society institutions. In of itself, this is good journalistic practice, by-passing problematic practices Anglo-European journalists occasionally whither under—taking the Occupier as the yardstick of facts and events happening in the Occupied Palestinian territories; allowing language to become a barrier to in-depth, human stories about Palestinian victims of the Occupation; allowing previous prejudices (whiteness, ability to speak English, familiarity with North American and European cultures) to overcome good journalistic sense.

However, Palestinian institutions: hospitals, Red Crescent workers, eyewitnesses do make mistakes, although they are the best first point of contact. Some Palestinian officials (notably Saeb Erekat) *do* exaggerate casualties and use overly emotive language; and occasionally it is not possible to know what has happened. Al-Jazeera's reliance or even information gathering from the Israeli side could be more strenuous without it affecting its indigenous nature, or its legitimacy.

Context and Binaries

Although journalists' shouldn't, providing background (as good journalists do) can often be an overt or subtle exercise in creating binaries for the viewer, based in their understanding of their target audience—their contemporary histories, evocative terms, religious/spiritual world view, etc. Individual al-Jazeera journalists have tended to create a background with subtle binaries indicating who are the right and wrong parties, who is most likely to tell the truth and conversely, to lie, who the victims and aggressors are.

In terms of the Palestinian-Israeli conflict and the American-Taliban conflict or Iraq these assumptions are easily built into the audience's own world view, based on their own backgrounds and the fact that the journalist *is one of us*—and indeed, al-Jazeera journalists reporting from Israel-Palestinian conflict are Palestinians who live the circumstances they report..

When Walid al-Omari is reporting and a missile lands close by, this is not scripted (although it will inevitably be included in the final edit). When Jevara Boudeiri in Bethlehem (possibly al-Jazeera's most emotive reporter) gestures to the night sky behind her and assures viewers more bombs/missiles/bullets are not falling (at present) on Bethlehem but these are noises from fireworks in the nearby Israeli settlement of Gilo celebrating Israel's independence day, the viewer tunes in.

When Shirin Abu 'Aqleh is literally marooned in the al-Jazeera office, reporting for 12—18 hours a day because the other journalists cannot leave their houses and receives a fax that soldiers have entered the building and are stationed on the floor beneath her, there is a sense of immediacy, legitimacy and feeling given to al-Jazeera reports. This works to create given binaries: first emphasized through the very circumstances al-Jazeera reporters live and then emphasized through background reports. Quite simply, Israelis (or Americans, or other Anglo-Europeans) cannot ever credibly challenge the binaries al-Jazeera creates.

Indeed, the threats al-Jazeera faces simply add to its legitimacy as a pan-Arab news station. Bombing the al-Jazeera office in Afghanistan (an American "mistake") and threats, jamming and antagonism towards al-Jazeera journalists have added to al-Jazeera's credibility. This in turn has impacted on its own messages about McArabism, widening its influence on Arab screens.

Sensationalism: al-Jazeera

Thus accusations of sensationalism (a common chorus against al-Jazeera) I believe are overly critical. In the context of reporting the Israeli-Palestinian conflict in Anglo-European states, tainted by interest groups, lobby groups, noisy protests and continual op-eds, most editors have decided on *bland* rather than *balanced,* preferring the polite montage of an Israeli soldier shooting (to seemingly nowhere) or the blood remains of a suicide bombing as opposed to the reality Palestinians and Israelis live: Occupation on one hand, a fear of terrorist attacks on the other.

In the context of the Arab world, with terrestrial television stations, as I have indicated repeatedly above, controlled by Ministries of Information, Palestinian suffering (and certainly never Israeli suffering) is not shown in the context of news, but in the context of political strategy. Syria may wish to demonize Israel in light of failed peace talks; a figure from the U.S. administration may be visiting Lebanon in context of the Palestinian issue and so on. As my fieldwork suggests however, the natural order of Arab terrestrial television is to mute the Occupation while emphasizing the particular regime leader's efforts to end it. It is a much analyzed, much commented theme in Arab journalism and politics: never show the Palestinian problem to be bigger than the Leader who claims to speak and act on behalf of Palestinians.

It is in this background that al-Jazeera is often admonished with sensationalism, both compared to Arab and Anglo-European media: reporting live from funerals, sites of conflict, filming dead bodies and the ubiquitous checkpoints dividing up Palestinian territories and lives. Ayish (2001) uses the example of the footage (played and replayed) of the Palestinian child Mohammed Al-Durra being shot to death while lying in the lap of his father, which was sufficient to attract viewers' attention and inflame anti-Israeli sentiments. Ajami (2001) prefers to critique al-Jazeera's "seething" reports from the streets of Baghdad and Afghanistan. He argues moreover, that the second Intifada was a Godsend for al-Jazeera, with attractive visual shots of masked Palestinian boys aiming slingshots and stones at Israeli soldiers, making compelling television.

Yet the question begs, where should good journalists make their reports and entirely in the self-interest of ratings, what should prevent a news and current affairs station from repeating incidents it knows will grab viewers' attention?

Such arguments to do with sensationalism appear to imitate similar critiques regarding indigenous structures with apparent (or assumed) influence in the context of a post/neo-imperialism desire emanating from the Anglo-European world to influence affairs within newly sovereign resource-rich states. It is the indigenous structure, which has now taken the mantle of responsibility and rule that must assume the traditional position of the colonialist police (composed of lo-cals for added legitimacy): it must *reign* in, it must *act responsiby,* it must be *balanced,* of course, within Anglo-European binaries constructed from a history of occupation, colonialism and exploitation of resources of the third world. Physical violence against such structures accompanies these critiques. Thus bal-ance often implies preserving Anglo-European interests (and by extension, Is-raeli interests), an absence of critique, analysis or context to relevant contempo-rary events and the silence of subaltern voices. The bombing of al-Jazeera's offices in Afghanistan simply articulated through violence what academics and intellectuals firmly posited in neo-colonialist thought write.

Thus al-Jazeera is accused, in different methods of articulation, of sensa-tionalism, as it films Israeli soldiers shooting live, when it delivers "seething reports from the streets of Kabul," (Ajami 2001), of reporting from funerals or filming dead bodies, of inciting anti-Israeli and anti-American sentiment.

Indeed, in the period studied, almost in each one of the eight newscasts from al-Jazeera there was at least one live or recorded report showing the brutal-ity of the Israel solders or settlers against the Palestinian population: burning houses, killed leaders and civilians—women and children, destroyed infrastruc-ture, pictures of blood and funeral processions.

According to these critics, the reader would assume it is al-Jazeera staging or stage-managing the Occupation of 1967 Palestinian territories, the daily bombing and embargo against Iraq, of civilian casualties in the U.S.-led war against Afghanistan and so on. Dutifully so: al-Jazeera is expected to play the journalistic version of the colonialist police. There is, on the other hand, a total absence of similar critique regarding the Occupation, the war on terror and the then-embargo on Iraq.

Al-Jazeera is a media outlet. Its target groups are Arabs and Muslims. Were it to report according to the wishes of the latest U.K./U.S./etc administration, it would play perfectly into the role of a neo-colonial police force. But it would not be a media outlet. In this context, in no sense are al-Jazeera's real faults cri-tiqued: faults contexted in good journalistic practices, rather An-glo/European/Israeli interests in the Middle East, chiefly the Arab world.

It is the howling Ajami-esque critique which perhaps, more than anything, demonstrates the impact of al-Jazeera and the willingness of Arab viewers to grant al-Jazeera legitimacy, to engage with their screens and to subvert through viewing, the sovereignty of reigning state regimes, U.S. and U.K. credibility within the region.

In this context, what kind of impact has al-Jazeera and other critical transnational Arab television channels had on Arab publics and what kind of regional identity has al-Jazeera in particular, put forward? In the next chap-ter, I put forward an introductory discussion of impact, both on terrestrial state regime television and on Arab publics. In effect, I argue that a result of both new technology subverting state regime borders and content, above all from critical Arab stations, such as al-Jazeera, *McArabism* has emerged.

Chapter Seven
Pan-Arab Media: Implications and Effects

In January 1996, Orbit TV (a Saudi-owned satellite TV company) was credited with taking a pioneering step towards live debates when it introduced *'Ala al-Hawa* (On Air). The first of its kind in Arab television broadcasting, *'Ala al-Hawa* is a live show where audiences directly engage with guests and freely ask questions or provide commentaries - without censorship or editing.

The successful show attracted attention by featuring guests like the former Israeli Prime Minister Binyamin Netanyahu and Libyan leader Mu'ammar Qadhafi, with viewers calling in from around the world. Following the success of *'Ala al-Hawa and* the establishment of al-Jazeera, most explicit and implicit taboos upon Arab satellite channels have been broken, with the station's politically provocative live programs *al-Ittijah al-Mu'akas* (The Opposite Direction) and *Akthar min Ra'iy* (More than One Opinion), which created a revolution in the basic concepts of television broadcasting in the Arab world.

Meanwhile, the privately-owned LBCI (Lebanon Broadcasting Cooperation International) is consistently pushing the boundaries of acceptable viewing in the Arab world, with MBC often neck-to-neck, challenging traditional, Islamic and conservative attitudes, with its popular program *Ya Leil Ya 'Ein*, displaying a very open, (clichéd) European approach to male-female relationships, such as open flirtatious dancing and quite provocative female dress.

This chapter explores some implications of Arab satellite television. I shall begin with the erosion of state borders as barriers to information, then briefly discuss different ways the emergence of transnational television in the Arab world, particularly al-Jazeera, has impacted upon the media itself. This has been important in altering broadcasting agendas to reflect commercial success rather than nation state building, changing popular broadcasting styles, introducing previously taboo social and political topics and issues, changing the nature of audience participation and providing access to politically or socially marginalized minority groups and audiences.

The chapter will then explore the social and political impact of transnational television on women, Islam and other areas, notions of civil society in the Arab world and the Arab-Israeli conflict. I shall conclude with an examination of a new, participatory Arab regional identity that has emerged through Arab satellite television.

The most immediate impact of the advent of satellite broadcasting in the Arab world in 1991 has been the erosion of state sovereignty and borders as information barriers and the greater accessibility of regional audiences (Sreberny 2001, Alterman 1998, Barkey 1996, Tagliabue 1996),

Previously the broadcasting media was a powerful tool in the hands of Arab regimes and ruling elites to exert influence and control over citizens (Karam 1999, Boyd 1993). Except in Lebanon, all terrestrial television stations in the Arab world belong to the Ministry of Information (ibid). Prior to satellite television, free information flows, especially in the political sphere, were almost non-existent. Arab State regime media control over information has consistently meant providing audiences with an "official" version of the news (al-Hitti 2000). Alternative information flows from beyond the State were extremely limited—often to only to radio, such as *Radio Monte Carlo* and *BBC Arabic.*

Yet the phenomenon media content exchange inside the Arab world is not new. From the 70's and 80's, Egyptian movies and Lebanese-Syrian plays, telenovelas and soap operas have been shown on almost every Arab television. While most terrestrial television stations are extensions of state information ministries, news has also been exchanged between them, although generally on the margins of the receiving station's newscasts (Karam 1999). Yet due to the high degree of state considerations governing national television stations, even program/news item exchanges have been limited, as political alliances and sensitivities shift. Moreover, local news—the main item exchanged between state owned terrestrial television stations—has had little intrinsic journalistic interest, often being local news items.

With the onset of regional Arab satellite television, the trend to exchange content has increased. By 1975, Mowlana observed "multinational corporation has become one of the chief organizers and manufacturers of the international flow of communication." The entrance of transnational media to the Arab world has quantitatively and qualitatively increased this trend (TBS 2000). More importantly, it has lead to new kinds of media content, not exchanged previously, such as news and documentary programs. Thus while the amount of information received has increased, largely due to a "diversity of outlets," (Alterman 1999, Karam 2000), Government control is becoming more informal and indirect.

While diversity has been an offshoot of Arab satellite television, the most important point is the release of information from government's control. Qatar was the first Arab state to cancel the control of the Ministry of Information on the media. In 1994—95, this leads to the establishment of the al-Jazeera channel. In the other states like Jordan, Kuwait and Morocco the Ministry of Information has began to be less evident. Information is now managed according to different interests: business—playing itself out in advertising and market power—ratings. For state owned satellite television, political interests, or a desire for regional importance, are also important. Thus both al-Jazeera and Abu Dhabi TV command high ratings and are supported by their respective governments, seeking a place on the Arab political map.

As I have noted earlier, it has traditionally been the role of small, often marginalized Arab states to take on the vangaurd of provactive, free media.

Without contraints of vying for leadership roles in the Arab world while similtenaously seeking influence in Arab affairs, Lebanon previously and the U.A.E. and Qatar today are producing critical, relatively open political news, whilst providing platforms for critiques of Arab state regimes.

With the erosion of state borders to stop the flow of information, Arab satellite television, with its regional audiences, has previously relied heavily on basing its operations offshore. Production location is secondary to product content. Talented editors, writers, announcers and programmers are sourced from virtually anywhere. The popular entertainment programs for Ramadan produced mainly in Egypt, Syria, Jordan and Dubai and sold to almost all Arab television stations (local or regional) is typical.

Prior to the entrance of Arab transnational television, each Arab state was fitted to its own borders, mainly due to technological restrictions of the terrestrial broadcasting and geopolitically, the lack of interest and relevance of local Arab state programming agendas to other states. In the era of transnational broadcasting, new media technologies have overcome this problem. Arab regional broadcasters are organized and oriented for regional audiences and structure their programming accordingly.

Changing popular broadcasting styles

In government broadcasting, competition from global television networks such as CNN seems to have brought further pressures on government television organizations to modify their news programming contents and techniques (Ayish 1995).

Wide population exposure in the Arab world to transnational channels urges producers in each Arab state to take into considerations other (Arab) audiences from all over the region. As commercial interests and political interests—as some Arab states attempt to influence other Arab audiences, take priority over nation state building, successful programming emerges from experimentation and audience engagement. Thus we see changes in popular broadcasting styles with the introduction of satellite television.

In the pre-satellite Arab world, television producers planned locally, replicating local programming used on other Arab terrestrial television stations. Meanwhile, most television programs were produced locally for local/state (regime) needs, except for Egyptian movies, Syrio-Lebanese soap operas and plays and Arab-Islamic dramas delivered to other Arab states. Satellite channels have eliminated this process to a large extent, uniting many Arab television markets in their pan-Arab coverage.

This has impacted on several levels. Modern Standard Arabic rather than local dialects is used so that pan-Arab audiences can understand what is being said. News and current affairs programs are completely different: conventional camera-on or voiceover news-cast formats has proven a failure compared to the sleek, visually attractive news programs like CNN, whose news layout has had a notable impact on Arab news programs. MBC and al-Jazeera are exemplary, with live broadcasting from different regions, comprehensive, fairly unrestricted, news coverage—that local television in each region often cannot, or does not, report and attractive newscasters. Major satellite channels have also swayed audiences into their fold by giving television entertainment a new meaning.

With this change, many local television channels have found themselves redundant (although not closed down, as a section of the Ministry of Information), while a few others have rejuvenated and repositioned themselves as competitors to the more prominent satellite channels. The Syrian local channel is a good example for this, changing its program agenda in 1997 to more attractive programs of music and light talk shows. A local Egyptian channel has also renovated its programs, bringing attractive programs, focusing on social talk shows and hosting popular Arab stars in order to compete with Orbit and ART in 1996.

Rejuvenation has proven difficult however. Cosmetic makeovers are given to news programs, although content is fairly unchanged (Karam 1999). More entertainment programs may be pumped into broadcasting agendas and less politically dogmatic programs may be aired, such as *Parliament al-Shabab* (Youth Parliament), whereby students ask (trusted) representatives of the Jordanian government questions, live and face to face.

Yet state owned channels simply do not have pan-Arab appeal. It may prove to be more difficult to renovate a brand image of a channel than to revitalize its program mix. Fixing a program mix may simply require that more money be pumped in. Face-lifting a brand image requires that all the marketing mix elements, such as promotional advertising, program content, upgrading, new talent, be activated (Fakhreddine 2000). Thus we see that satellite television stations run by Arab regimes are often comparably similar to their territorial versions. The most prominent example in this sense is the Syrian satellite channel, which is principally similar to the Syrian terrestrial television station in terms of concept and programming. Even broadcasting hours are similar, running the same programs simultaneously. This is also the case of the Saudi satellite television stations, Egypt, Morocco and the U.A.E.

Changing television news formats

In the Arab world, the traditional role of television as a mouthpiece of ruling political and economic elite groups came under pressures as new groups began to stake their claims in this important medium of mass communication. Research in the 1970s and early 1980s showed news on Arab television as highly dominated by government sources and activities to the exclusion of other groups (Ayish, 1989). The dominant paradigm of news as a government information outlet dictated the inclusion of protocol news, personality hype and politically maximizing information in news programs. In technical terms, news formats were characterized by serious and formal delivery methods, usually colored by asymmetrical orientations.

Furthermore, newscasters were appearing most often on camera, reminding viewers of radio newscast they had listened to hours earlier. The visual potential of television news was barely evident and so was the handling of domestic issues falling outside government agenda. In its basic configuration, a newscast was a lineup of either very long items dealing with leadership news or very short items dealing with regional and international developments. Television reports were hardly used as the newscast drew on studio delivery (Sakr, 2000). The launch of commercial television in the Arab world has not only widened viewers' programming choices, but it has also given them access to new formats and styles rarely used in government-monopolized television. Professional rather than political considerations seem to be the driving force behind news work at private stations keen on establishing a foothold in a highly competitive media market. For them, what makes news is a host of values that relate to the event or issue and its significance for the audience.

When academics study CNN they are often attracted by what has come to be known as the "CNN effect."[87] Philip Taylor, for example, remarks that, by "providing a public forum to the traditionally secretive world of diplomacy," CNN appeared during the 1991 Gulf War to be "quite simply changing the rules of international politics."[88]

In comparison with this assertion, CNN's effect on Arab media was just a sideshow. But it was an important sideshow nonetheless. For example, CNN's live international broadcasts from Baghdad during the 1990-91 Gulf crisis marked a turning point not only in establishing the genre of 24-hour satellite television news but in bringing Arab viewers' dissatisfaction with terrestrial television news coverage to a head. In the absence of CNN in Arabic, Arab broadcasters felt compelled to produce a replica. MBC in particular was explicit about wanting an Arabic version of CNN.[89] Sakr (2001), quotes Sami Raffoul, general manager of the Pan-Arab Research Center in Dubai, explaining why stations serving the Arab world would want to follow the CNN formula:

> CNN came on the scene presenting 'pure, untainted, spontaneous' news, with a disclaimer clearly attached to pictures saying they were unedited. They were telling people to see and make their own judgment. The public found this unusual. It was unprecedented for them to be asked to use their own powers of interpretation. It was a turning point.[90]

In the Arab world, CNN found an intense hunger for reliable, up-to-date regional news. This appetite had been growing for at least two generations through

---

[87] This is not to say they necessarily endorse any hyperbole about it, e.g. Piers Robinson, 'World politics and media power: problems of research design', *Media, Culture & Society* 22 (2000), p 228; Dwayne Winseck, 'Gulf war in the global village: CNN, democracy and the information age', in J. Wasko and V. Mosco (eds.), *Democratic Communications in the Information Age* (Toronto, 1992), pp 60-74.

[88] Philip M. Taylor, *War and the Media: Propaganda and Persuasion in the Gulf War*, Manchester, 1992, p 7.

[89] Hussein Amin and Douglas Boyd, 'The development of direct broadcast television to and within the Middle East', *Journal of South Asian and Middle East Studies* XVIII/2, Winter 1994, p. 46.

[90] Interview, Dubai, 20 October 1997

a combination of regional crises related to the Arab-Israeli conflict and super-power involvement and a lack of uncensored information generated locally.

In the decade and a half following the October War of 1973, the practice of sampling a range of foreign radio stations and other different news sources in order to piece together an understanding of current events may have subsided somewhat. During the Gulf War of 1991 it resumed with a vengeance. With the discovery that, through CNN, viewers could see breaking news stories covered on screen, the context for all Arab print and broadcast media changed. Having sampled this impression of spontaneity and immediacy in political and economic news broadcasts, it seems Gulf viewers wanted it in lifestyle programming too.[91] From the beginning, the MBC schedule was publicized as containing not just news, religious programming and television drama but coverage of "fashion, money, sport, health and tourism."[92]

Just as the proliferation of Arab satellite channels was driven by the copycat syndrome, whereby governments felt compelled to respond to the use of the new medium by outsiders and then by each other, the same happened with the model of the 24-hour news channel. Ted Turner, the American who launched CNN in the U.S. in 1980 on the back of Turner Advertising, said that the idea of a 24-hour global news network was "uncharted waters." However, he told an interviewer in 1999, "when I saw we were going to make it, we started spreading all over the world, like a virus."[93]

Similarity between the names of Arab News Network (ANN) and CNN is no coincidence. Qatar's al-Jazeera was set up to specialize in news and current affairs, while Egypt created Nile News as one of the Nile Thematic Channels. In reaching agreement with the BBC for an Arabic news service, it is believed that Orbit originally intended the service to develop into a 24-hour operation.[94] But while models are one thing, actual content is another. The BBC Arabic service was kept to only eight hours per day and was then axed because of disagreements over news stories about Saudi Arabia. Despite this, Orbit's management acknowledged that the rationale for running an Arabic-language all-news channel had not gone away.[95]

Most news staff has been either trained in Europe or North America or has worked for media organizations from these two regions. Their sense of news work draws on it as a highly selective process. To this end, private broadcasters have invested heavily in news development by introducing state-of-the-art technologies and establishing far-flung networks of reporters and correspondents who often do their dispatches on live bases. The visual capabilities of television are highly utilized with rich graphics and video materials as well as sleek delivery formats. A newscast is made up of a series of news intros for reports and

---

[91] Interview with Jihad al-Sibai, deputy vice-president for media, Fortune Promoseven, Dubai, 19 October 1997.

[92] Advertisement in *al-Sharq al-Awsat*, 18 September 1991, quoted in El Emary: 'L'industrie du feuilleton', p 257.

[93] Curtis: 'The mouth of the south'.

[94] *Al-Quds al-Arabi*, quoted in *Mideast Mirror*, 8 January 1996, p 15.

[95] *Gulf Marketing Review*, July 1998, p 35.

news items. Rarely does a news item appear without an accompanying footage. Conversational and friendly news delivery methods are adopted. The head of al-Jazeera notes (Schleifer 2000):

> It is also a question of the content of the news. You often get here someone reading an item about leaders arriving in the country, sitting together—it's not news, they only do it to give them TV time. The view is of leaders sitting together, talking together, and everything is fine, there's no news. But behind the scenes, everything is not fine. They never put that on the screen. People saw something dramatically different in CNN's coverage of the Gulf War. At that time everyone was watching CNN; no one was watching any entertainment then, just the news. There were so many stories in the war; human interest and war stories even took the place of entertainment.

A new generation of television executives and practitioners with solid professional training in North American, British and European media settings has pushed for the opening up of traditionally closed media systems, including news formats and delivery modes. The introduction of these technical features has been viewed as an integral component of a professional broadcast outlook. The use of digital and computer-based technologies in television news production is thus taken as a craft governed by professional standards that bear heavily on both message format and content.

For young viewers in tune with computer-based interactive technologies, the sleek newscast formats seem to be the most appealing. Young viewers seem to be attracted mostly to the conversational nature of news delivery, the use of digital technologies and virtual designs and the timely reporting of events from around the world. In the cases of Abu Dhabi, al-Jazeera, ANN and MBC (before al-Arabiya's establishment), a good number of interviews were conducted live with personalities in the West Bank and some Arab capitals. Al-Jazeera went one step further by showing live footage of clashes in Jerusalem between Palestinian stone throwers and heavily armed Israeli soldiers (Ayish 2001).

Altering broadcasting agendas to reflect commercial success rather than nation state building

"When wealthy Arab audiences vote with their remotes, it makes sense for advertisers to take notice." (Zureikat 1999)

As I have noted previously, media institutions in the Arab world were established with an orientation toward local needs, consumption and nation building, where the state regime apparatus manipulates the media on all levels, in order to ensure state (regime) survival (Karam 1999). Thus, since the creation of new Arab states and until the appearance of Arab transnational media in the 1990s, localism or statism became both the orientation of the media and a social reality.

In other words, the process of the establishment of the nation state and the subsequent need to ensure its survival and strengthen it, characterized the developmental media model created according to the spirit of the Barber's (1992) term "Jihad," denoting a form of "tribal media." This was reflected by the television programs, notably news and documentary shows which place or identify the regime as the homeland (the new Arab state); feeding the audience nation building improvements done by the regime, whilst also encouraging citizens to be more loyal to the current ruling elite and manipulating religion to strengthen the position and the legitimacy of that elite.

For instance, local Jordanian television has produced a documentary called *al-Qimmam al-'Arabiyyah* (The Arab Summits), which forces the viewer to see the summit through King Hussein's eyes. Almost all of the terrestrial state owned televisions in the Arab world present development programs, such as Jordan's *al-Ard al-Tayyibah* (The Fertile Earth) and other 'learn about your homeland' programs alongside religious shows and local documentaries and social dramas.

The creation in the 1960s and 1970s of national media structures in Arab countries worked in part to create a heightened sense of nationhood using the framework of the nation state in the shadow of pan-Arabism. Repressive measures such as censorship were used in combination with state sponsored media as a means to prevent the infiltration of media effects from beyond the state's borders and to create a closed ethno-national media environment. Hence, one of the primary goals of creating a tribal media was to shape a narrow national identity to be oriented towards and controlled by the respective political regimes.

In the Arab world, de-monopolization since the beginning of the 1990's, has been reflected in the expansion of commercial broadcasting satellite channels, from one - MBC (Middle East Broadcasting Company) - in 1991 to more than 50 in 2002. However, commercialization—a process whereby media becomes dependant on market responses for revenue—has mainly been realized through the transformation of the media's financial structure, not through the transformation of the media's ownership (Chan 1994).

Commercialization of the Arab satellite broadcast media is characterized by a swift growth in advertising. In fact, commercial pan-Arab television proved its worth to advertisers, by 2000 mushrooming into a half-billion-dollar industry (at rate card value). It has also been accompanied by a rapid increase in foreign programs such as Mexican soap operas and American movies and an expansion of channels and broadcasting hours with little alternation to programming content or diversity, with most satellite channels imitating the other.

While most pioneering initiatives (in terms of content) have been from private satellite channels, the overwhelming majority of satellite media is state owned, thus although the commercialization of satellite media is still in its infancy, it remains the most popular and powerful television viewing in the region (Ajami 2001).

The commercial nature of the Arab transnational televisions is reflected in programming policy that aims to attract increasing audience numbers, such as creating Arabic versions of famous television game shows, such as *Mun Sayarbah al-Malyun?* (Who Wants to be a Millionaire?) *Greed* on LBCI other musical shows and light entertainment programs like *Super Star and* socio-cultural talk shows live with audience participation, as broadcast from ART (Arab Radio and TV Company) and Orbit TV. Meanwhile, semi-commercial programs and channels have used intensive political and documentary programs and talk shows as their main focus, such as al-Jazeera, al-Arabiya, Abu-Dhabi TV and ANN.

Fee-for-service stations like ART and Orbit have been successful in this regard. Driven by high per-user fees and a superior ability to monitor the viewing habits of their wealthy customers, they have identified a way to remain afloat without subsidies from outside parties. These stations seem destined to have their sights fixed mostly on the Saudi market, where incomes are highest (and individuals are most able to pay the requisite fees) and entertainment alternatives the lowest.

As Arab transnational television becomes more market-oriented, they will engage progressively more with audience choices. If the Turkish experience, from state owned to privately run media s any guide, this Arab medium will find pushing boundaries often proves more successful than keeping within them. On the other hand, as audience choices are balanced with profit targets, which are paramount to the success of commercial satellite channels, the quality of programming and its content shall suffer. This may prove worse than Arab-state regime control of visual media. While the growth of the media market will force outlets to continue to experiment with content to draw more viewers, this may be at the expense of quality.

Dajani, for example, notes the main problem facing satellite broadcasting in Lebanon today (specifically regarding LBCI) is not government interference but giving predominate attention to commercialism at the expense of professionalism . . . rather than public issues, and television is a mélange of various inconsistent programs, policies and structures, predominantly foreign in orientation and barely relevant to the needs Lebanese society or the Arab world (Zureikat 1999, Ajami 2001)

Ajami's description of al-Jazeera is telling,

> The show of al-Jazeera paused for a commercial break. One ad offered a striking counterpoint to the furious anti-Westernism of the call-in program. It was for Hugo Boss "Deep Red" perfume. A willowy Western woman in leather pants strode toward a half-naked young man sprawled on a bed. "Your fragrance, your rules, Hugo Deep Red," the Arabic voiceover intoned. I imagined the young men in Arab-Muslim cities watching this. In the culture where the commercial was made, it was nothing unusual. But on those other shores, this ad threw into the air insinuations about the liberties of the West—the kind of liberties that can never be had by the thwarted youths of the Islamic world.

Introducing Previously Taboo Social and Political Topics and Issues

The history of television in the Arab world reveals a complex relationship to multiple issues of sensitivity to tradition and religion, preserving existing state regimes and nation state building needs, which have spawned firm regulations, restrictions and censorship (Karam 2000; al-Hitti 2000). Nudity, sex, positive portrayals of homosexuals, positive spins on violence and drugs have all been taboo. Nevertheless, the grip of traditional-religious ideologies over television has varied over the Arab world. It has tended to be strongest in Saudi Arabia and weakest in Lebanon.

Satellite television has worked to introduce previously taboo social and political issues. In terms of social issues, satellite television has both introduced socially *permissive* programs and academic programs *deconstructing* social behavior. For instance, *Haysa,* a Lebanese MTV program, virtually enacts an 'Oriental strip tease,' whereby women dance, in suggestive clothing or semi-nude to songs during a competition contest. The widespread popularity of this show is indicated by the diverse advertisements throughout the show - from Coca Cola to local banks.

Satellite television has also worked to introduce programs which analyze controversial social issues within the Arab world, such as discussions on prostitution, polygamy, women's freedoms on an al-Jazeera women's show, *Lil Nisa'i Faqat* (For Women Only) and through religious programs, or as guests on other talk shows or discussions.

Although satellite television has introduced previously taboo social issues, it is worth noting that it still does not certain red lines. For instance, the terrestrial LBC station broadcasts extremely provocative films and advertisements, occasionally featuring almost nude women or sexual scenes. Meanwhile, LBCI—the transnational channel, will not go so far. Indeed, often the same advertisement on LBC is repeated on LBCI, but with less provocative or suggestive speaks and more fully covered women.

MBC, LBCI, MTV, al-Manar, al-Jazeera, al-Arabiya, Abu Dhabi and ANN have regularly broken political taboos through their broadcasting. As recalled previously, these satellite channels are either privately owned, or belong to marginalized Arab states. Al-Manar hosts *Beit al-'Anqabout* (The Spiders Web), MTV *Jadal* (Debate), al-Jazeera host *al-Ittijah al-Mu'akas* (The Opposite Direction), LBCI *Kalam al-Nas* (People's Talk), and ANN *Parliament,* each offering a diet of critical political analysis.

However these programs may be considered *relatively* free or critical. Since the beginning of the latest Intifada in September 2000 and the accompanying increase in poverty, dispossession, destruction and civilian deaths, critiques of the Palestinian leadership has virtually taboo. This was not the case prior to the Intifada, as discussed previously in the chapter on regulation. It is worth noting however, that *critiques* of other Arab state regimes have increased.

Changing the Nature of Audience Participation

Interactive television broadcasting has allowed live audience participation and similarly, audience shaping of broadcasting content. Interactive television broadcasting covers live guests, shows which cover voting, live phone calls, game shows, talk shows and other similar programs. These programs may be political or socio-cultural in nature.

It appears that interactive television of all kinds has increased in terms of broadcasting hours in the Arab world. It seems that the popularity of interactive television is in part caused by its novelty status. Interactive television is genuinely a new form of broadcasting in the Arab world. It cannot be overstated that these programs engage the audience, sidelines Arab state regime power and empowers the audience by providing both a voice for them publicly and by airing views—politically or socially. We may speak of interactive television as a form of ventilation of social and political pressure pervasive in the Arab world: the former through strict cultural mores regarding relationships, combined with poor economic aspiration; and the latter due to the pervasive presence of individual Arab state regimes in the lives of citizens (al-Hitti 2000).

Nevertheless, while audience participation has shaped and influenced broadcasting content, the participating audience is extremely small: limited to those Arabs who can afford to make international calls (where the show asks the viewer to call), limited to those Arabs who have access to the internet (where the show asks for an internet vote), limited to those Arabs who have geographic access to be present in a live audience. African-Arab states are also extremely hidden from audience participation. Moreover, each of these factors systematically works against women, rural populations and youth.

Arabs in diaspora are over represented in interactive programs, as are social and political elites. This is not to say that women, rural populations, youth or people from African-Arab states do not have access to these programs, rather—they are immensely under-represented in the calling population.

This however, does not imply their estrangement from interactive programs. Rather, the popularity and number of similar programs indicate that callers are either speaking somehow on behalf of estranged groups, or are providing ideas that have response among viewing populations. Additionally, it may be noted that Arabs in diaspora and citizens of relatively free Arab state regimes, are more openly critical of internal Arab issues, both social and political.

Access to marginalized groups and audience

Perhaps as a reflection of the way transnational television has leaded to greater democratization are the new opportunities given to marginalized/opposition groups. Different political groups, parties, movements or individuals who find themselves in the opposition to Arab state regimes are invariably denied access to domestic media are dependent on transnational media both to convey their message nationally and internationally and to monitor developments elsewhere within their own country (Thomas 1999).

Historically, as recalled previously, terrestrial Arab television has functioned principally within the Ministry of Information, denying access to all alternative forms of socio-political reality, including political or social opposition groups and even civil society.

With the outset of critical satellite television, such as al-Jazeera, al-Arabiya, ANN, Abu Dhabi TV and the like, political opposition leaders and dissenting intellectuals have been encouraged to access programs and their audiences. This may or may not be emerging from a real commitment to journalistic values, as the fourth estate. However it is clear that such programming, as a clear break from monotonous Arab state regime only views, attracts viewer interest and thus ratings.

There appears to be a clear dynamic between opposition groups, leaders and prominent oppositionist individuals in the Arab world and critical satellite television. Zednik (2002) notes in his article, "Inside al-Jazeera" one method in which Arab state regime failings are highlighted on transnational media: whereby an opposition figure speaks to the satellite channel directly, indicating a problematic issue not dealt with by a particular government. The satellite channel opens an avenue to discuss this problem in a talk show and then invites the relevant government minister and (normally) the oppositionist figure for debate.

So for instance, Al-Ghanouji from Tunis, Laith Shbeilat and Toujan al-Faysal from Jordan, Hassan Tourabi and Sadiq al-Mahdi from Sudan are given access to political and social programs to air their critiques and views of their particular governments and socio-cultural structures. Indeed, al-Faysal was jailed after her comments on al-Jazeera indicating that ministers in the Jordanian government had benefited from the new insurance laws.

While political opposition leaders and individuals have been provided relatively open access to such programs, social commentators are not given similar access. It is not clear whether this is due to a lack of audience interest, professional disinterest, static programming policy, or a fear of crossing social red lines in the Arab world.

Impact of Satellite TV on Islam in the Arab world

Firm regulations, restrictions and censorship have been a cornerstone of television policy in the Arab world, sensitive to the conservative-religious character of Arab societies in general (Karam 2000, al-Hitti 2000). Most Arab State regimes emphasize Islamic values as the basis of society and the basic values of the State. Almost without exception, most Arab countries, chiefly in the Gulf, place a special emphasis on the role of media in manifesting Islamic values and beliefs (TBS 1999).

The exception to this quite possibly is Lebanon, despite it having quite strong guidelines forewarning the broadcasting, publishing or producing of any materials which may be offensive to any sectarian group (Dajani 1999), this is generally interpreted as avoiding targeted slurs towards sectarian groups, rather than activities which may cause offense to any religious sect in general, such as semi-nude women or mixed dancing.

The role of the media in promoting or conserving Arab-Islamic values is consistently maintained when planning for programs in terms of both content and schedule. In terms of content, there are very strict redlines which media content must take into consideration—not causing offence to Arab-Islamic collective Arab moral values, mainly regarding female behavior and sexual relations. Meanwhile, in terms of scheduling, regardless of programming, playing the call to prayer and pausing five times a day, every day, for up to ten minutes characterizes television as broadcast in most of the Arab world.

The role of media in these societies is assumed to reflect peoples' interest in Islam and their needs for such programming. Meanwhile, it seems to attempt to divert people from the non-Arab external satellite channels, which are perceived to feed very different ideas into the minds of the television audiences in this part of the world. Indeed, even programs imported from abroad (whether Mexican soaps, American/Western dramas, films, movies etc) are also altered (and often edited) to fit this system of ethics.

Traditional/religious ideology prevailing in most Arab societies like the Gulf societies consists of traditional and religious elements that are past-oriented. In the case of these societies, past orientedness is combined with sacredness. Consequently, adhering to many traditional patterns of thinking and behaving, merely because these patterns came from the past, permeates many aspects of Arab societies.

However, the strength of traditional/religious ideology upon the social structure varies from one Arab society to another. It tends to be strongest in Saudi Arabia and weakest in Lebanon. The latter is characterized by far weaker degrees of traditional/religious ideological influence. In Lebanese-owned or run television stations sensational news items are accompanied by heavy entertainment programming in which central cultural and religious values are ignored.

Nonetheless, all political authorities in the Arab countries invoke the traditional/religious ideology in their pronouncements and they have all succeeded in making the prevailing religious ideology subservient to their power (Kazan 1993).

However, transnational satellite television by definition need not respect the individual red lines of each Arab state regime. Often based beyond state borders, transnational satellite television focuses on its main goals: advertisers and ratings.

In this light, the new sensational styles used heavily by the new transnational media contradict socio-cultural and religious values of Arab society in general (Ayish 2001), such as semi-nude women on LBCI and the production and transmission of liberal musical programs and game shows on many Arab satellite channels, such as *Sahra* (Soiree) on MBC and *Jar al-'Amar* (Neighbor of the Moon) on Orbit. This sensational entertainment content is most clearly displayed on Lebanese terrestrial and transnational channels as well as on ART and Orbit. An indication of these shows' popularity is the amount of callers and audiences participating in these programs, the discussions and debates they create in public spaces and the nature of the advertisements aired during these programs, such as Saudi Arabian products during the most controversial show, *Ya Leil Ya 'Ein* on LBCI.

Consequently, the most important impact of both foreign and regional media on the Arab societies is the degree of exposure it provides to secular, principally European and North American, values, lifestyles and more importantly, patterns of thought.

Although there has been few 'open' or public reactions against this new kind of programming (most notably the 2004 protests in Bahrain to prevent MBC's Big Brother to filmed in the country, even after altering the household to fit to some—not all—Arab and Islamic mores), it has created widespread public debate among secular and Islamic elites. Even women's magazines and local newspapers, traditional troughs for the gossip stars from such shows enjoy feeding from enjoy criticizing these shows for precisely the values they broadcast. Arab satellite television has taken advantage of the controversy caused by new sensational programming by allowing more space to Islamists and secular elites to debate and discuss these issues through their programming. This includes al-Manar, the Hizbollah station, which regularly airs these issues live, with viewers calling in on al-Deen wal Dunya (Religion and Life).

Thus, sensational programming has also given secular groups more opportunity to discuss previously taboo issues, mainly in the pre-September 11 context of the rising power of Islamists, such as the case of Hamid Nasr Abu Zayd. Abu Zayd, an Egyptian scholar was forced to divorce his wife in Egypt under the pressure of Islamists, who accused him of kufr—renouncing his religion, punishable by death under Islamic law. Abu Zayd subsequently enjoyed a long interview on al-Jazeera about this issue.

Meanwhile, alongside the increasing number of Arab satellite channels appearing, Islamic stations have also appeared, appealing to traditional and neo-conservative Muslims, such as Monajah (Prayer), broadcast from Saudi Arabia and Iqra' (Read), a part of the ART group. These satellite channels offers religiously based programming, encouraging Arab-Muslims to stay within Islamic boundaries and to educate audiences on this basis.

Interestingly, Islam has also emerged in some elements of the media as a unifying force for the region, reflected in news, documentaries, on historical programs on Arabs, such as the series on Salah al-Din al-Ayoubi (Saladin) and other historical series. This is reflected in the popular al-Jazeera program, al-Shari'a wal Hayat (Islamic Law and Life), whereby Sheikh Yusuf al-Qaradawi, a prominent Mufti (Islamic jurisprudential legislator) answers callers' questions live about Islam and daily life. I shall discuss Islam as a unifying element in more detail through the section on the Arab-Israeli conflict and transnational television.

It is impossible to say whether the emphasis on Islam is driven primarily by the fact that the overwhelming majority of Arabs (in the Arab world) are Muslims, or by the dominance of Saudi financing in the transnational Arab media or by a new impetus or cognition of Islam, as reflected by McArabism. Nevertheless, it is important to note that whereas states and elites led the charge for pan-Arabism in the 1950s and 1960s, transnational Islamic movements and their mass followings are much more important actors today and their efforts are being significantly abetted by the new media.

This has been reflected in the changing attitude towards the Palestinian-Israeli conflict, particularly since the beginning of the latest Palestinian Intifada in September 2000, especially demonstrated in the identifying title given to this Intifada—Intifadat al-Aqsa (the Intifada of the al-Aqsa mosque in Jerusalem - the third holiest site in Islam). The idea of preserving an Arab Jerusalem is anxiously conveyed, while Arab television stations have telethons to raise money for Palestine, using a new emotional rhetoric of an Arab Muslim-Christian Jerusalem. Indeed, Palestine's *Islamic context,* encouraged by Palestinian Authority leadership, Hamas and even traditionally secular groups such as the Popular Front for the Liberation of Palestine (PLFP) have encouraged this new focus, at the expense of the *human rights context* of the Palestinian issue (the right of return, self-determination, etc).

This emotional rhetoric is also conveyed through the regular broadcasting of emotional, alternately sad and angry, musical montages showing footage from the 1987 Intifada, the war in South Lebanon and the latest Intifada. The broadcasting of these montages increase whenever emotional tragedies strike in Palestine (such as the death of Mohammad al-Durra in 2000). Importantly, only al-Manar, the Shiite Lebanese television station regularly runs any sort of montage whereby Palestinians possess real *agency,* such as playing militant music or broadcasting scenes of Palestinian women/children/fighters actually fighting back. Regardless of the montage, most Arab satellite television stations will also include some kind of prayer for the liberation of *Jerusalem.*

It remains whether to be seen if there will be any movement to boycott satellite television channels that regularly cross Arab-Islamic cultural red lines. This is unlikely, considering the diversity or specialization of Arab satellite television, which accommodates Arabs of secular, traditional and/or neo-conservative persuasion.

Impact of satellite TV upon civil society

It is widely accepted that a free system of communication networks is an essential component to create, maintain and safeguard a healthy functioning democratic society. The theoretical basis of this discussion regarding the need for free communication networks finds statement in the Habermasian concept of the public sphere, being the space between government and society where private individuals exercise formal and informal control over the state: formal control through the election of governments and informal control though the pressure of public opinion. The media is central to this process, distributing information necessary for citizens to make a formal choice at election time; they facilitate the formation of public opinion by providing an independent forum of debate and they enable the people to shape the conduct of government by articulating their views. The media is thus the principal institution of the public sphere (Curran 1994). Like any set of institutions rooted in a political system, the broadcast media of a country or region reflects the existing distribution of power.

The existing distribution of (television/visual media) power in the Arab world is strongly skewed towards preserving Arab state regimes. Unlike much of the Arab press, which enjoyed at least a formative development as privately owned newspapers that functioned within the context of some sort of journalistic tradition, all Arab terrestrial television: be it prevailing state systems, ruling left or right-wing groups, market or socialist economies, republics or monarchies, are state owned (Boyd 1982). Thus, the building an information society in the Arab world is crucial to civil society. Satellite broadcasting and the internet services, are the two main factors that will aid Arabs in this transition (Zureikat 1999).

In this regard, we can see several different impacts of transnational satellite television in the Arab world contributing to civil society:

One of the most important effects of transnational satellite television is that its new style and content allows the audience to make comparisons between what they see on the screen and what they have in almost all levels of life, particularly socially, politically and materially. For instance, through documentaries, live-reporting from the field, how a demonstration in one locality may change government decisions, changes in government (through election) - even through al-Jazeera reporting on a particular bill in a particular country where ministers debate, make and break coalitions, audiences are exposed to utterly different realities from their own, where the absolute majority of Arabs live under non-democracies: whether monarchies, autocracies, dictatorships or quasi/de facto dictatorships, or are stateless or live as an unrecognized indigenous minority with minimal rights.

The automatic comparison between the broadcasted and reality forces many to rethink the very basic issues of their lives (al-Hitti 2000). This is also produces itself in the social level when exposed to Anglo-European/secular ways of life through different non-Arab programs and movies (although edited for Arab-Islamic audiences). This process urges them to begin thinking of changing their political and social reality. Although there are no specific indicators which show a direct relation between satellite television and political or social change in particular, this seems to intergrate itself with the larger cultural shift taking place in the Arab world today, towards nuclear families, women working outside the home and intergenerational relationships.

Anglo-European styles of broadcasting that have characterized Arab transnational television so far, has had a great effect on Arab viewers in the direction of adopting different styles of political thought and social behavior. This is due to the fact that the discussions and ideas which the viewers receive from television is transformed to daily life meetings discussions in private meetings in cafes, clubs and other social spaces, mostly meeting places for (male) Arabs of all walks of life. The impact of satellite television upon women, although *felt,* is even more difficult to quantify, as Arab women traditionally do not access spaces such as cafes or clubs. Nevertheless, their access to satellite television is in many ways greater to men, through their traditional roles within the household.

Civil society in the Arab world is also given an opportunity of primary importance to develop. That is, new media technologies have provided individuals and marginal groups large podiums allowing them to reach wider audiences and segments of Arab society, such Syrian, Kuwaiti, Iraqi, Saudi opposition groups *and* ethnic minorities, such as the Amazigh and Iraqi and Syrian-based Kurds. This has lead to a degree of opportunity for political liberalism and civil society to flourish through awareness raising and public debate.

However, opportunities for change are limited. The development of civil society clearly, has and will always be limited by political regime-structures that do not allow for real democratic change or civil society development beyond their reach or control. Meanwhile, this may be limited to tiny segments of Arab society. Some researchers argue that the opportunities for democratization emerging from the new media technologies can be utilized by the intellectual elite of Arab society and certainly not the marginalized or poor (Ghareeb and Mansour 2000).

Nevertheless this argument overlooks how satellite television affects all walks of live and how it affects the individual citizen in his or her various roles. With satellite broadcasting there is an element of "social engineering," (TBS 1999) which includes its role as a forum for the exchange of thoughts and ideas between citizens or the different social groups of communities; its function as an integrating influence upon children and young people and its importance as a platform and agent for all kinds of cultural forms and expressions; and its function to advance communities, speed progress and enhance development. This does lead to the enhancement of basic structures developing civil society and builds on the interactive role of different institutions of society.

Indicative of this, the policies of most traditional terrestrial Arab state owned media are based on short-term goals, where messages concentrate on current affairs. Arab audiences watching these stations are more engaged with daily issues and less with tomorrow or the construction of a pan-Arab collective character and culture (al-Hitti 2000). Transnational media, despite its principle interest being profit, functions also an educational agent through the different kinds of programs broadcasted, chiefly its pan-Arab contents, such as pan-Arab news, documentaries, entertainment programs which appeal to pan-Arab audiences, which in time shape a sense of collective identity. I elaborate on this through my discussion on transnational television and a new regional Arab identity.

However, as I argue, Arab transnational television has contributed to a new regional Arab identity and that some of these new social and political ideas transmitted become a part of thought structures, a value and a binary comparison or otherwise engaged with individuals in the Arab world (al-Hitti 2000), apathy may the other result. The abundance of TV channels, its variety, availability and continuous broadcasting hours—especially of political news, may similarly lead to apathy, desensitization or a fixation with escapist programs, given the prominence of entertainment shows and music video clips in transnational broadcasting.

The importance of media to civil society as discussed by Habermas finds its articulation in Arab transnational TV, chiefly critical news stations. While access to this space, or to critique or debate social or political issues is fairly restricted to political and social elites. Although apathy may reign and even while there are no direct indicators for the impact of Arab transnational TV upon social or political change, its contribution to civil society development is vital. Arab transnational TV has functioned to raise awareness about issues previously taboo or unknown to many Arabs beyond specific locations. It has functioned to (re)create or strengthen a pan-Arab identity, which may transform into pan-Arab aspiration (beyond the Palestinian issue). It may well have more important functions in the future.

Impact of satellite TV on the Arab-Israeli conflict

Indeed, before satellite TV, media coverage of the Palestinian-Israeli conflict was simply limited to the policy and personal interests of each leader and regime, where the main focus of the coverage was the 'virtual role' of the regime and the state leader on behalf of the Palestinians, in order to strengthen the leader/regimes popularity as a patriot for the Palestinians and the Arab issues.

The performance of the Israeli Prime Minister Ehud Barak on al-Jazeera before the last Israeli election in January 2001 was a historic act in the Arab media tradition, not only because of uniqueness of the appearance of an Israeli official on an Arab TV screen, but also to the meaning and the timing of this appearance in the context of the Arab-Israeli conflict; the attitude of the Arab media and public to Israelis and finally to the use of the Arab media by Israeli politicians for lobbying for their interests.

Following Barak's appearance on al-Jazeera, a growing number of historical documentaries appeared on Arab television, including interviews with important Israeli figures, made the appearance of Israelis on Arab screens a normal phenomenon. Arab transnational TV has impacted directly and indirectly on the Israeli-Arab conflict.

Israeli officials and politicians can now access Arab homes directly without any mediation, contributing indirectly to lobbying for Arab public opinion. In one sense, this has lead to 'virtual normalization' between Israel and Arab state regimes on symbolic and conceptual levels. In other words, that Israeli leaders have become a part of the Arab media and using this framework to engage in discourse with the Arab media has had its own unique effect.

Meanwhile, the regionalization (or pan-Arab access) of news has had an especially important influence on Arab public opinion towards the Arab-Israeli conflict. Arab television has blasted away the isolation experienced by Israeli politicians and policymakers. No longer content to provide a one-sided perspective on either history or the recent past, Arab producers are finding that including Israeli views increases a show's credibility and viewer interest. Israel is no longer ignored or denied in the Arab media, but increasingly is presented as an important regional actor (Alterman 1999).

Arab satellite television also provides Arab homes with another picture on Israel—the internal picture: domestic issues, politics, social-cultural events and way of life. This has been entirely unprecedented in the Arab media. Thus, Arab transnational TV's not only closely monitor the statements of the Israeli government, but also evince a rather sophisticated understanding of Israeli internal politics and Israeli governmental policy (Alterman 1999).

Arab satellite TV moreover, covers events of the Palestinian-Israeli conflict more effectively than their terrestrial or Israeli counterparts. While due to political or public opinion sensitivities, Israeli TV stations will not report accurately on suicide bombings for instance, or show graphic images of such events, al-

Jazeera, al-Arabiya, al-Manar and Abu Dhabi TV in particular, have no such hesitations. In fact, they often provide more accurate reports of casualties and deaths. In this regard, the high prominence (ironically) once given to Israeli TV as more accurate and factual than its Arab counterparts has fallen by the wayside.

This has not come without cost however. While the Gulf War was the first televised war, bought to audiences by CNN, this stage of the Palestinian-Israeli conflict is the first televised war whereby Arab transnational TV sets the agenda for the Arab audiences—the first comprehensive indigenous coverage of the Palestinian-Israeli conflict.

Alongside including Israeli voices and perspectives, Arab satellite television has covered the Israeli-Palestinian conflict more intensively and without censorship, especially in times of crises with Israel, such as the latest Intifada. Arab satellite television has clearly portrayed Israel's activities against the Palestinians and their suffering in an intensive way, unlike state TV. Using a network of television reporters in broadcasts, reports on Israeli settlement construction, home demolitions and open conflict with Palestinians, Arab viewers are receiving a largely negative picture of Israel. Therefore, despite the fact that Arabs can meet Israeli personalities directly and unmediated through the screen, Arab satellite TV has served to strengthen negative impressions about Israel and its supporters, mainly the U.S.

Thus the findings of Muhammed I. Ayish are no surprise. Ayish's research on the five Arab transnational TVs show that anti-Israel items were reported by all five services with the highest number of negative items reported by SSC (Syrian Satellite Channel), Abu Dhabi (Abu Dhabi Satellite Channel) and al-Jazeera. The United States received mostly negative treatment in news items carried by the five broadcasters. This is clearly due to U.S. support for Israel's position during the al-Aqsa uprising. This supportive attitude towards Palestinian resistance against Israeli occupation reflects the commitment of transnational Arab TV to furthering the Palestinian cause.

Transnational Arab TV has also had a crucial role in freeing coverage of the Palestinian-Israeli conflict from Arab government censorship (Rinnawi 2003). In the past (and continuing today on terrestrial television), the Israeli-Arab conflict was brought to Arab audiences and homes by the Arab state controlled media, which occasionally (or often) exaggerated events (Syria and Iraq usually), or melded and softened these events due to state interests - or as a result of American pressure to these regimes to "soften" reporting.

A positive result of Arab satellite TV coverage of the Palestine-Israel conflict has been the exposure of Arab state regimes—in the vast gap between terrestrial reporting and transnational coverage. Arab leaders have been held up as powerless and silent towards the Occupation—literally viewed live by Arab viewers. Consequently, the conflict's escalation in the last two years and the intensive coverage the conflict has created, based on a relatively free flow of information has strengthened internal pressure on Arab state regimes. This has lead to (perhaps cosmetic) changes in terrestrial coverage of the conflict, so it may at least cover some of the clear gaps between it and transnational coverage, certainly perceived as more credible.

Another change, which I have alluded to previously, is the transformation of the Intifada to the *al-Aqsa* Intifada through transnational Arab TV, finding its center of concern in preserving an Arab Jerusalem. Arab transnational television stations invest time and concern to this issue, both politically and religiously important. I have previously spoken about the way the regional nature of transnational TV has created pan-Arab audiences and later, I shall discuss this in the context of a new Arab regional identity. However what is important to note here, is why al-Aqsa has been focused on and marketed by Arab transnational TV.

The latest Intifada began in the al-Aqsa compound, thus ecouraging pan-Arab identification with the struggle. Meanwhile, Palestinian spokespeople, whether secular or Islamist, have highlighted this issue as a public relations boon, highlighting the Arab nature of this struggle through Jerusalem and thus sociliting concern and strengthening the symbolic position of al-Aqsa to Arab audiences, on a religious and political pan-Arab level. Ayish notes:

> The supportive role of satellite television broadcasters for the Palestinian uprising has been viewed by observers as an important factor accounting for sustaining acts of resistance in the Palestinian territories despite the heavy losses incurred. It has been noted that the 2000 uprising differs from the 1988 uprising in some important features, the most outstanding of which has been the satellite television reporting of the events. In 1988, the Middle East had no satellite television as all world and regional events were reported by government-controlled services on a limited basis. Television broadcasters in 2000 seem to be convinced that in order to attract their viewers' loyalty, they have to be in line with their political expectations about national and regional issues like that of Palestine. When some TV channels were hosting Israeli personalities during the uprising, they came under fire for acting irresponsibly regarding the Arabs' central issue: Palestine.

Ultimately, the impact of transnational Arab TV upon the Arab-Israeli conflict has been both important and in some ways, permanent. Arab regimes will never be able to rely on terrestrial channels to convey their version of the struggle within their own borders. Israeli figures will not disappear from Arab screens and the level of intensive coverage is most likely to continue unabated, despite Israeli soldiers confiscating journalists ID cards, killing or expelling individual journalists, as in the case of closing the Abu Dhabi TV office in Jerusalem.

Unlike most observations arguing that the new transnational media is positive for the Israeli Arab conflict and shall improve the negative image of Israel among Arab audiences, I suggest that this medium strengthens the negative image of Israel and makes the conflict more salient and live through the sensationalism effect in the short term. However, in the long term, a process of normalization has already begun, which once the conflict abates, will continue to work to create a spirit of openness about Israel—both negative and positive, but nevertheless, placing Israel firmly on the Arab political map and consciousness.

Political implications of Arab transnational TV

The slow and skewed socio-economic liberalization of Arab societies, coupled with accelerating advancements in information and communication technologies, seem to have created a new environment conducive to the utilization of television as a powerful force of public opinion formation.

The rise of commercial satellite television alongside government-controlled broadcasting has brought about a new public sphere marked by varied news agendas. More than ever before, previously suppressed political perspectives and orientation have become more visible on Arab world television. Regional broadcasting has created regional news organizations-both in terms of news coverage and delivery-that far surpassed what had previously existed, partly based upon a new generation of television executives and practitioners, with professional training in the United States and Western Europe. They seem to believe in the potential role of Arab world television in the age of globalization and media competition. New television journalism practices drawing on news work as a professional rather than a political domain, have also become more common with the rising popularity of live talk shows, panel discussions and interviews (Ayish 2001).

Perhaps as the Arab world has been experiencing dramatic political developments in the past 50 years, this seems to have created a deep consciousness amongst people in the region of the centrality of politics in shaping their lives (al-Hitti 2000). As television has evolved within government institutions in the Arab world, political news always tops news agendas. Political news has also been the most sensitive point of state run TV.

In contrast to Arab state regime media, Arab transnational TV has generally adopted the American journalism model, whereby news is defined in terms of what is fit to print. According to this definition, politics may not by itself be newsworthy unless it deals with issues that are important, relevant, and timely and with significant consequences for the audience (Ayish 2001). These changes will be discussed and illustrated in the final chapter of this book.

The rise of Arab transnational TV—here in particular critical transnational TV—has had several important political implications to audiences and regimes alike. As previously sensitive or taboo information becomes freely broadcast, there has been a rise in political cynicism, a greater awareness of political issues, and a transformation from political news broadcasts to fit political reality towards audience acceptance of ideas. This rather democratic move is mirrored in the rise of an indigenous critical media, which can no longer be dismissed by Arab state regimes.

An important effect of the Arab transnational TV is the rise of political cynicism within society (al-Hitti 2000). State owned TV aims through its media agenda to sustain the political order and to legitimate its existence, trying to build a 'virtual' reality through its political and news programs, enforcing 'virtual' legitimacy, through neglecting sensitive issues and focusing on the general, defused and uncontroversial issues which do not raise instability or suspicion.

Meanwhile, the transnational TV channels work in the opposite direction, creating deeper gaps of trust between the two essential classes in the Arab world: the ruling and the ruled (al-Hitti 2000), as it attempts to trace and address sensitive political issues (Ghareeb and Mansour 2000).

Consequently, the audience's degree of uncertainty regarding the national, regional and world environments is heightened in this situation, adding to a structure of *dis-trust* already present, whereby audiences watch state run TV to check for 'local versions' and critical transnational TV to check the event. Thus at the death of Hafiz al-Assad in 2000, many Lebanese watched Syrian and Lebanese TV to check the official version of events, but transnational TV to see *what happened*.

Previously, Arab audiences in times of uncertainty, used to resort to foreign media to find out about the true version of events within their countries or region. This was the case during the attack of the Muslim fundamentalists on Mecca in 1979, in the aftermath of Sadat's assassination in 1981 and during the Iraqi occupation of Kuwait in 1990-1991 (Kazan 1993). With the emergence of Arab transnational TV Arab audiences have turned to an indigenous critical source of news to check real (or relatively truer) versions of events.

Rising indigenous critical press has enjoyed a positive effect, whereby previously Arab state regimes, above all those deriving legitimacy from their own versions of pan-Arabism, cannot successfully delegitimize critical indigenous transnational media as plots or conspiracies of Western imperialism.

The rapid expansion of information available to Arabs transmitted by transnational media, besides their function as an alternative source of information, has put an increased premium on their ability to sort through that information and separate the important and meaningful from the scurrilous or irrelevant. The likely effect on politics is unclear. Besides the rapid growth in the amount of information that reaches them, Arab audiences are exposed to new topics, issues and discourse in the political arena previously marginalized in the best case - if not deleted or ignored and not included in the media agenda, considered sensitive issues. Arab audiences will have to evaluate political data and reports with a more critical eye than they have done to date and governments will have to put forward information in a competitive marketplace of ideas in which those ideas will increasingly stand or fall based on their acceptability to the public rather than on governments' ability to compel their acceptance (Alterman 1999).

Conclusions and a new participatory Arab regional identity

Most importantly for this discussion, has been the impact of transnational TV upon a new Arab regional identity. The pioneering steps of transnational Arab TV have impacted strongly on state regimes, eroding their soveriegnty, forcing their positioning within a regional information market place, where most have floundered, despite cosmetic makeovers and entertainment program stacking.

If not yet qualitatively visible, transnational TV has impacted upon the Arab world, creating new visions of Islam; the Palestinian-Israeli conflict; Israel's positioning in the Arab world. It has created new dialouges about women in the Arab world; critiques on various levels of political relationships and is fostering, slowly, moves towards strengthening civil society. Transnational TV, through its role as appealing to a mass market place, with competition firmly in place, is adopting the Turkish model of pushing social boundaries, broadcasting alternative realities of social relations, while also appealing to Muslims concerned with Islam through Islamic programs and specialized channels.

The relationship of transnational TV to Arab audiences is principally of *engagement,* whereby new technologies, combined with individual policies specifically conveying a sense of Arabism of several (critical) transnational channels, such as al-Arabiya, ANN, Abu Dhabi, al-Jazeera and an already existing background of Arab identity, have coalasced on varying levels towards a new regional identity: McArabism.

Chapter Eight
Conclusion

The emergence of Arab transnational television in the Arab world has significantly eroded the media structure that existed relatively unchanged for more than forty years. It has been maintained by Arab state regimes, while the communal nature of television watching in the Arab world makes Arab screens a powerful tool for governmental and private satellite channels respectively. Television is constructing a national public space that addresses men and women, old and young, educated and poorly educated, urban and rural (Sreberny 2001). Meanwhile, transnational television is unique in its ability to provide information unhindered by borders—giving rise to an invasion of media content in the Arab world.

This trend has many implications, especially for the audience, where the new television broadcasting is binding populations into regional audiences in a way that no medium had truly done before, with the exception of Nasser and *Sawt al-Arab*.

Flourishing in the cracks

However, despite the potential (and real) power of transnational Arab broadcasting and despite the rapid growth and popularity of satellite TV in the Arab world, development has not emerged through any progressive pan-Arab policies.

The rise of transnational Arab satellite broadcasting has been the largest and most pervasive media challenge in contemporary history to state regime dominance. In many ways however, this challenge has largely been a product of indigenous mechanisms, which have allowed transnational TV to emerge and subsequent audience demand (and persistence) to access these channels, despite government attempts to prevent or thwart access.

State regimes initially made an important mistake regarding their initial media policies towards transnational satellite television: assuming that it was simply a more powerful form of domestic television. In other words, that it was a mass medium aiming to control the national population in the same way that domestic television was designed to do.

However, once it became clear that regular means of censorship could not work in a new technology ear, censorship battles have taken two different directions: increasingly through political and physical pressure.

The most successful censorship policy of most Arab states has been mass state control, whereby there is an understanding (whether legislated into policy or not) that states have the final say on broadcast content.

Indeed, it is apparent that Arab regimes intend on controlling the media, despite the difficulties this entails through new technology. While there appears to be a trend to simultaneously allowing more commercialization of stations (i.e., not in direct state hands), increasing pressure on channels to screen 'safe' material.

However, there is an apparent gap between the consistent attempts (in what ever form) of state regimes to control broadcasting and content actually aired. This gap appears to be a result of several important mechanisms or dynamics surrounding Arab media. There is a clear conflict between political interest and ratings and thus the stations with the freest hands, such as al-Jazeera, al-Arabiya, ANN and Abu Dhabi are the most popular.

More importantly, from the beginning of transnational Arab satellite TV, in particular stations such as al-Jazeera, an irreversible process of comparison and state delegitimization has occurred, whereby Arab viewers turn to non-state sources (al-Jazeera, ANN and others) for information, not state run programs. The process of delegitimization created a space for such channels that Arab leaders cannot easily remove without widespread opposition.

Indeed, a mixture of Arab domestic politics in individual states and technology has allowed the formation of satellite TV—indeed, *satellite television has grown through the cracks* represented by outdated censorship laws ad new technologies allowing international broadcasting, rather than any supportive structures in the Arab world.

In this regard, Lebanon, the U.A.E. and Qatar have provided the most important 'cracks'—the traditional role of small, often marginalized Arab states to acquire influence far beyond their population numbers or resources by exploiting the media for regional ends.

Lebanon's major crack has been both sensitivity regarding its legitimacy as a state, which has encouraged specifically 'Lebanese' cultural productions and its delicate sectarian balance, which has meant on a practical level, that each sectarian group runs its own television station with relatively little hindrance from the government (except where Syria is concerned). Nevertheless, these channels have developed according to their own dynamic to attract different audience groups possibly unrelated to their original viewership.

Qatar and the U.A.E., to a lesser degree have aimed to exert regional influence that only money can buy and that only the media can do. As I have noted earlier, broadcasting from tiny countries that do not have major influence in either intra-Gulf affairs or pan-Arab affairs allows critical news stations to overlook local/domestic news without losing much credibility on the pan-Arab screen.

Another important crack has been domestic strife, perhaps aligned to more influential Arab countries or financial revenue. This, with the right money and technology, has allowed the formation of Arab transnational broadcasting channels, which are tools of inter-Arab struggles for influence and power and simultaneously, a credible and critical news outlet.

Despite the return home of satellite TV stations as running costs become more significant, this does not appear to impact however on serious news outlets—which are principally a small few. These stations have flourished between the cracks I have mentioned, positioned into structures whereby their positions are safe: either in Qatar or the U.A.E., or broadcast from abroad (ANN), with no possibility of return to the Arab world.

However, flourishing between the cracks means that the novelty of serious news-based channels in the Arab world is still apparent. Conspiracy theories still abound about al-Jazeera, some of them taken quite seriously by al-Jazeera staff members and much of its highly educated public. However true or false these conspiracies may be, it certainly reflects a complexity, which is both new and healthy. For the first time, Arab media binaries are being broken.

Nevertheless, freedom of expression, not only transnational television technology as such, is crucial to media development. Satellite broadcasting provides a platform for greater freedom, but how the platform is used depends on laws, policies and habits. Satellite technology may have drawn attention to the dearth of uncensored media in the Arab world, but it has no intrinsic powers to change this situation (Sakr 2001) except for in several unique (and therefore inimitable) situations.

McArabism

Through this book, we variously noted that the implicatiosn of McArabism can be seen, although not yet qualitatively measured through the amount of people (increasingly so) participating in protests for Palestine through repeated assaults upon the West Bank and Gaza Strip; through the increasing legitimacy given to news broadcasts on transnational stations, chiefly al-Jazeera; through the increasing hostility (occasionally expressed through preventing transmission and removing press cards from journalists) via governments and their institutions towards transnational TV and finally, through the increasing desire for satellite dish ownership.

The pioneering steps of transnational Arab TV have impacted strongly on state regimes, eroding their sovereignty, forcing their positioning within a regional information market place, where most have floundered, despite cosmetic makeovers and entertainment program stacking.

Transnational TV and above all al-Jazeera, has impacted upon the Arab world, creating new visions of Islam, the Palestinian-Israeli conflict and Israel's positioning in the Arab world. It has created new dialogues about women in the Arab world; critiques on various levels of political relationships and on some level, foster civil society. Transnational TV, through its role as appealing to a mass market place, with competition firmly in place, is adopting the Turkish model of pushing social boundaries, broadcasting alternative realities of social relations, while also appealing to Muslims concerned with Islam through specific Islamic programs.

Interestingly, all satellite television stations have worked in varying degrees under the shadow of localization and globalisation. It has been those critical stations, or those most open socially, which have been closer to global, or regional models.

It is then no surprise that McArabism, as a creation of globalization or in this case, regionalization, is perhaps one of the most important by-products of satellite television and its respective technologies. The rise of regional information entities has reinvigorated a sense of common destiny among many in the Arab world. Put another way, it has fostered a *re*-imagination of Arab and Islamic communities, perhaps best symbolized by the shared concern satellite channels have fostered both about Palestine (Arab) and Afghanistan (Islam).

This common destiny is created on the regional pan-Arab scale that is common to all Arabs regardless of their location or place of residence. The key point of this process is accessibility to the regional or Arab transnational media. In addition, one impetus for McArabism is as interaction between Arabs and non-Arabs increases, so does the former group's awareness of its Arab identity in contrast to the latter group. Although none of this obviates their loyalties and identifications with their respective states, the increasing interaction Arabs have with non-Arab cultures and the manner in which they are treated by those cultures which see them as Arabs rather than as holders of specific nationalities, prompts Syrians, Moroccans, Iraqis, Saudis and other Arabs to embrace a heightened Arab identity *vis à vis* the outside world (Alterman 1998).

In this case, McArabism is a heightened identity constantly broadcasted through new technologies, seeking new audiences through media market competition, interpreted on local levels and as such, a dynamic, organic process, rather than a set of structures imposed from above (or on air), tending to loud or quiet deaths as they become slowly, more irrelevant.

Appendix 1
Nilesat TV Channels

SCR Name	IRD slot	TV Channel	Provider
EDUC-1	1	Primary Education	
EDUC-2	2	Preparatory Education	
EDUC-3	3	Secondary Education	
EDUC-4	4	Technical Education	
EDUC-5	5	Language Education	
EDUC-6	6	Al-Tanweer	
UNIV 1	7	University Education	
MNR	8	Manarah Science Channel	
Most-TV	9	Al Mustaqilah	
EDUC-7	10	Illiterate Education	
Hor-1	11	Hours Health information Channel	
Nef	12	Nefertiti information Channel	
HALL	13	Hallmark Channel	Showtime
Future	14	Future	Showtime
Zein	15	Zein	Showtime
ADSpace	16	Abu Dhabi Space	Showtime
Disney	17	Disney Channel	Showtime
SET	18	Sony Channel	Showtime
M TVI	19	MTV India	Showtime
TMC	20	The Movie Channel	Showtime
N/P	21	Nickelodeon Channel	Showtime
TVL	22	TV Land Channel	Showtime
MTV	23	Music TV	Showtime
Style	24	Style Channel	Showtime
BTV	25	Bloomberg TV	Showtime
DISC	26	Discovery Channel	Showtime

SCR Name	IRD slot	TV Channel	Provider
TMC-2	27	The Movie Channel-2	Showtime
T360	28	Reserved for future Use	Showtime
Zapper	29	Reserved for future Use	Showtime
Portal	30	Reserved for future Use	Showtime
VH-1	31	VH-1	Showtime
TCM	32	The Classical Movie Channel	Showtime
E!	33	Sony Entertainment TV	Showtime
TCN	34	The Carton Channel	Showtime
CNN	35	CNN	Showtime
PRM	36	Paramount Channel	Showtime
STsport	37	The Movie Channel-2	Showtime
Xsport	38	The Movie Channel-2	Showtime
ADSC	39	ADSC	Showtime
CNNfn	40	CNNfn	Showtime
Channel-1	41	ERTU National Channel-1	
Channel-2	42	ERTU National Channel-2	
ESC-2	43	Egyptian Space Channel-2	
CH1 SCR	44	Channel 1 SCR	
Nile TV	45	Nile TV	
ESC-1	46	Egyptian Space Channel-1	
Channel-3	47	CHANNEL-3	
Test	48	Reserved for future Use	
Test	49	Reserved for future Use	
Promo	50	Promo Channel	
BBCW	51	BBC World	
Channel-8	52	Channel-8	
Channel -5	53	Channel-5	
Nile News	54	Nile News Channel	
Nile Family	55	Nile Family Channel	
Nile variety	56	Nile Varieties Channel	
Nile Drama	57	Nile Drama Channel	
Nile Sport	58	Nile Sport Channel	
Sport+	59	Sport+	
Nile Culture	60	Nile Culture Channel	
MTC	61	Misr Tourist Channel	
Tanweer	62	Tanweer Channel	

SCR Name	IRD slot	TV Channel	Provider
ART-1	63	ART Varieties Channel	ART
AL Hekayat	64	Al Hekayat	ART
LBC\WOW	65	LBC \ WOW	ART
ART-3	66	ART-3	ART
ART-4	67	ART-4	ART
ART-5	68	ART-5	ART
Tarab	69	Tarab	ART
EDUC	70	Education	ART
Jordan	71	Jordan	ART
Iqra	72	Iqra	ART
BNTV	73	BNTV	ART
ART-1	74	ART-1	ART
ART-2	75	ART-2	ART
TFC	76	The Film Channel	ART
B4U	77	Indian Channel	ART
B4U-M	78	Indian Channel	ART
AP	79	Animal Planet	ART
RTV	80	Reality TV	ART
FSH	81	Fashion	ART
ESN	82	Fox Sport	ART
MUTV	83	MUTV	ART
MCM	84	Adventure	ART
ESP	85	Eurosport	ART
MBC	86	MBC Channel	ART
SSI	87	Supersport	ART
RM	88	Rail Madrid	ART
RTT	89	RTT	ART
SCI	90	SCI	ART
MCM	91	MCM	ART
ESN	92	Eurosport Newsdws	ART
ART	93	Test	ART
ART	94	Test	ART
ART	95	VIP Channels	ART
Iraq	96	Iraq Space Channel	
PSC	97	Palestine Space Channel	
ANN	98	Arab News Network	

SCR Name	IRD slot	TV Channel	Provider
MBC	99	Middle-East Broadcast Center	
Oman	100	Oman Space Channel	
Bahrain	101	Bahrain Space Channel	
Kuwait	102	Kuwait Space Channel	
Andalus	103	Andalus Space Channel	
Syria	104	Syria	
Mehwer	105	Mehwer TV	
Test	106	Test	
Kuwait Test	107	Kuwait Test	
TL	108	Tele. Liban	
NBN	109	NBN	
MTV Leba-non	110	MTV	
NTV	111 .	New TV	
Manar	112	Manar	
LBC	113	Lebanese Broadcasting Corporation	
Euronews	114	Euronews	
JSC	115	Al-Jazeera Space Channel	
EDTV Sport	116	Dubai Sport Channel	
EDTV Busi-ness	117	Dubai Business Channel	
EDTV Space	118	Dubai Space Channel	
EDTV Drama	119	Dubai Drama Channel	
Ajman	120	Ajman Space Channel	
Tamima	121	Tamima Shopping Channel	
STOON	122	Space Toon	
Majd	123	Al Majd Space Channel	
Test	124	Test	
Dream	125	Dream TV	
Dream2	126	Dream TV	
Test	127	Test	
TV5	128	French TV	
Test	129	Test	
Heya	130	Heya Channel	
DW-TV	131	DW	

SCR Name	IRD slot	TV Channel	Provider
JSC Feed	132	JSC Feed	
Feed1	133	Feed1	
Feed2	134	Feed2	
Video Cairo	135	Video Cairo	
Star World	136	Star World	ART
Vint	137	Channel V International	ART
NaGa	138	National Geographic	ART
Star Movies	139	Star Movies	ART
UKTV	140	UKTV	ART
CNBC	141	CNBC	ART
Sky N	142	Sky News	ART
HsFK	143	History / Fox	ART
FOX	144	FOX News	ART
STAR	145	Test	ART
STAR	146	Test	ART
STAR	147	Test	ART
HC-0	148	Home Cinema Preview	ShowTime
HC-1	149	Show Home Cinema1	ShowTime
HC-2	150	Show Home Cinema2	ShowTime
HC-3	151	Show Home Cinema3	ShowTime
HC-4	152	Show Home Cinema4	ShowTime
HC-5	153	Show Home Cinema5	ShowTime
HC-6	154	Show Home Cinema6	ShowTime
HC-7	155	Show Home Cinema7	ShowTime
HC-8	156	Show Home Cinema8	ShowTime
HC-9	157	Show Home Cinema9	ShowTime
HC-10	158	Show Home Cinema10	ShowTime
Line 1	159	Orbit Feed-1	Orbit
Line 2	160	Orbit Feed-2	Orbit
Test	161		Orbit

Appendix 2
Channels Available on Arabsat

ARABSAT 2-A at 26° East; Ku-Band

URL	TV Channels	Trans-Ponder	Freq. Mhz	Polarization
N/A	QATAR	1	12521	HORIZONTAL
moinfo.gov.kw	KUWAIT	2	12536	VERTICAL
art-tv.net	·ART	3	12562.77	HORIZONTAL
jrtv.com	JORDAN	4	12577.77	VERTICAL
art-tv.net	ART	5	12604.5	HORIZONTAL
ARABSAT.com	DIGITAL TV BOUQUET	6	12619.5	VERTICAL
art-tv.net	ART	7	12646.3	HORIZONTAL
ARABSAT.com	DIGITAL TV BOUQUET	8	12661.3	VERTICAL
almanar.com.lb	AL MANAR	9	12685.06	HORIZONTAL
ljbc.net	LYBIA	10	12700.06	VERTICAL
ARABSAT.com	INTERNET SERVICE	11	12720	HORIZONTAL
ARABSAT.com	DIGITAL TV BOUQUET	12	12735	VERTICAL

Medium C-Band

URL	TV Channels	Trans-Ponder	Freq. Mhz	Polarization
sharjahtv.net	SARJAH	1	3720.25	RHCP
lbcsat.com.lb	LBC	2	3740.75	LHCP
ertu.org/esc.htm	EGYPT	3	3761.25	RHCP
art-tv.net	ART	4	3781.75	LHCP
ertu.org/ Nile_Chan	NILE NEWS	5	3802.25	RHCP

URL	TV Channels	Trans-Ponder	Freq. Mhz	Polarization
/NL_news.html				
gna.gov.bh	BAHRAIN	6	3822.75	LHCP
cnn.com/CNNI	CNN	7	3843.25	RHCP
future.com.lb	FUTURE	8	3863.75	LHCP
orbit.net	ORBIT	9	3884.25	RHCP
sudantv .net	SUDAN	10	3904.75	LHCP
N/A	SAUDI 1	11	3925.25	RHCP
tv5.org	TV 5	12	3945.75	LHCP
N/A	SAUDI 2	13	3966.25	RHCP
emi. co.ae	EMIRATES MEDIA	14	3985.25	LHCP

High C-Band

URL	TV Channels	Trans-Ponder	Freq. Mhz	Polarization
emi.co.ae	ABU DHABI	15	4039.25	RHCP
edtv.com	DUBAI	16	4062.00	LHCP
moisyria.com	SYRIA	17	4080.25	RHCP
mbctvsat .com	MBC	18	4096.25	LHCP
aljazeera.net	ALJAZEERA	19	4122.75	RHCP
gna.gov.bh	OMAN	20	4139.50	LHCP
moinfo.gov.kw	KUWAIT	21	4166.75	RHCP
N/A	YEMEN	22	4180.50	LHCP

ARABSAT-2B at 26° East; Medium C-Band

URL	TV Channels	Trans-Ponder	Freq. Mhz	Polarization
N/A	MOROCCO TV	9	3876.75	RHCP
N/A	MAURITANIA TV	11	3917.50	RHCP

ARABSAT-2B at 26° East

High C-Band

URL	TV Channels	Trans-Ponder	Freq. Mhz	Polarization
ljbc.net	LIBYA	21	4166.75	RHCP

ARABSAT-3A at 26° East; Ku-Band

URL	TV Channels	Trans-Ponder	Freq. Mhz	Polarization
orbit.net	ORBIT	1	11727.48	HORIZONTAL
ARABSAT.com	ARABSAT BOUQUET	2	11746.66	VERTICAL
		3	11765.84	HORIZONTAL
ARABSAT.com	ARABSAT BOUQUET	4	11785.02	VERTICAL
orbit.net	ORBIT	5	11804.20	HORIZONTAL
		6	11823.38	VERTICAL
		7	11839.50	HORIZONTAL
emi.co.ae	ABU DHABI TV	8	11861.74	VERTICAL
		9	11880.92	HORIZONTAL
entv.dz	ALGERIA	10	11900.10	VERTICAL
orbit.net	.ORBIT	11	11919.28	HORIZONTAL
		12	11938.46	VERTICAL
orbit.net	ORBIT	13	11957.64	HORIZONTAL
		14	11976.82	VERTICAL
orbit.net	ORBIT	15	11996.00	HORIZONTAL
		16	12015.18	VERTICAL
		17	12034.36	HORIZONTAL
falconstream.com	FALCON STREAM	18	12053.54	VERTICAL
orbit.net	ORBIT	19	12072.72	HORIZONTAL
		20	12091.90	VERTICAL

List of TV Channels at 11746 MHz

URL TV	Channels
sharjahtv.net	SHARJAH
N/A	SAUDI 1
moinfo.gov.kw	KUWAIT
ljbc.net	LIBYA
sudan.tv.net	SUDAN
oman-tv.gov.om	OMAN
iraqtv.ws	IRAQ
almajdtv.com	Al-MAJD
emi.co.ae /television/adtv	ABU DHABI
N/A	SAUDI 2

List of TV Channels at 12661 MHz

URL TV	Channels
edtv.com	DUBAI
N/A	DUBAI SPORT
N/A	DUBAI BUSINESS
psctv.net	PALESTINE
aljazeera.net	ALJAZEERA
mbctvsat.com	MBC
ann-tv.com	ANN
N/A	AL MUSTAKILLAH
jrtv.com	JORDAN
moisyria.com	SYRIA

List of TV Channels at 11785 MHz

URL	TV Channels
almanar.com.lb	AL MANAR
future.com.lb	FUTURE
lbcsat.com.lb	LBCI
mtv.com.lb	MTV Lebanon
nbn.com.lb	NBN
N/A	New TV
teleliban.com.lb	TELE-LIBAN

Appendix 3
Channels Available on Nilesat Banquet

SCR Name	TV Channel
EDUC-1	Primary Education
EDUC-2	Preparatory Education
EDUC-3	Secondary Education
EDUC-4	Technical Education
EDUC-5	Language Education
EDUC-6	Al-Tanweer
UNIV 1	University Education
MNR	Manarah a science Channel
Most-TV	Al Mustaqilah
EDUC-7	Illiterate Education
Hor-1	Hours Health information Channel
Nef	Nefertiti information Channel
Ch-1	ERTU National Channel-1
Ch-2	ERTU National Channel-2
ESC-2	Egyptian Space Channel-2
CH1 SCR	Channel 1 SCR
Nile TV	Nile TV
ESC-1	Egyptian Space Channel-1
Ch-3	CHANNEL-3
Channel-8	Channel-8
Ch —5	Channel-5
Nile News	Nile News Channel
Nile Family	Nile Family Channel.
Nile variety	Nile Varieties Channel.
Nile Drama	Nile Drama Channel.
Nile Sport	Nile Sport Channel.

SCR Name	TV Channel
Nile Culture	Nile Culture Channel.
MTC	Misr Tourist Channel
Tanweer	Tanweer Channel.
Heya	Heya Channel
Dream	Dream TV
Dream2	Dream TV
Video Cairo	Video Cairo

Appendix 4
List of Governmental TV Stations

ABU DHABI
ALGERIA
BAHRAIN
DJIBOUTI
DUBAI
EGYPT 1 and 2.
IRAQ
JORDAN
KUWAIT
LEBANON
LIBYA
MASQAT
MAURITANIA
MOROCCO
OMAN
PALESTINE
QATAR
SAUDI 1 and 2
SHARJAH
SUDAN
SYRIA
TUNIS
YEMEN

Appendix 5
Channels Available on ART

ART-1	ART Varieties Channel
AL Hekayat	AL Hekayat
LBC\WOW	LBC \ WOW
ART-3	ART-3
ART-4	ART-4
ART-5	ART-5
Tarab	Tarab
EDUC	Education
Jordan	Jordan
Iqra	Iqra
BNTV	BNTV
ART-1	ART-1
ART-2	ART-2
TFC	The film Channel.
B4U	Indian Channel
B4U-M	Indian Channel
AP	Animal Planet
RTV	Reality TV
FSH	Fashion
ESN	Fox Sport
MUTV	MUTV
MCM	Adventure
ESP	Eurosport
MBC	MBC Channel.
SSI	Supersport
RM	Rail Madrid
RTT	RTT

ART-1	ART Varieties Channel
SCI	SCI
MCM	MCM
ESN	Eurosport Newsdws
ART	Test
ART	Test
ART	VIP Channels
Star W	Star World
Vint	Channel V International

NaGa	National Geographic
Star M	Star Movies
UKTV	UKTV
CNBC	CNBC
Sky N	Sky News
HsFK	History / Fox
FOX	FOX News
STAR	Test
STAR	Test
STAR	Test

Bibliography

Monographs

Alterman, J. B. 1998. *New media new politics? From satellite television to the internet in the Arab world.* The Washington Institute for Near East Policy, Washington: DC.

Anderson, B. 1993. *Imagined communities: Reflections on the Origin and Spread of Nationalism.* London, Verso.

Boulos, J.C. 1996. *La tele: quelle histoire!* Beirut, Fiches du Monde Arabe.

Boyd, D. 1993. *Broadcasting in the Arab world.* Philadelphia, Iowa State UP.

Boyd, D. 1982. *Broadcasting in the Arab world.* Philadelphia, Temple UP.

Chan, J. M. 1996. Television in greater China: structure, exports and market formation. in J. Sinclair, E. Jacka and S. Cunningham (eds.) *New patterns in global television: peripheral vision.* Oxford, Oxford UP.

Croteau, D. and Hoynes, W. 1997. *By invitation only: how the media limit political debate.* Maine: Common Courage Press.

Curran, J. & Park, M.J. 2000. (eds.), *De-westernizing media studies.* London and NY, Routledge.

Dahlgren, P. 2000. Media and power transitions in a small country: Sweden. in J. Curran and M.J. Park (eds.), *De-Westernizing Media Studies.* London and NY, Routledge, pp. 251-264.

El-'Aa'idi, A. 1999. *Arab media facing current challenges.* The Center for Strategic Studies in Abu Dhabi. Abu Dhabi.

Fahmy, A. 1997. Uses and gratifications of Egyptian women for satellite television. *The Egyptian Journal of Mass Communication Research,* volume 1, number 2.

Fiske, J. 1987. *Television culture.* London: Routledge.

Forrester, C. 1998. Digital television broadcasting: drivers for growth and pattern of uptake. Phillips Business Information.

Galtung, J. 1979. A structural theory of imperialism. in G. Modelski (ed.). *Transnational corporations and world order: readings in international political economy.* San Francisco, W.H. Freeman and Company, pp. 155-171.

Giddens, A. 1999. Runaway world: how globalization is reshaping our lives. London: Profile Books.

Habermas, J. 1991. *The structural transformation of the public sphere: an inquiry into a category of bourgeois society* (Studies in contemporary German social thought). Massachusetts: Massachusetts Institute of Technology (MIT) Press.

Hadid, D. 2000. Subaltern aspiration through popular political music in post-1990 Lebanon. Thesis.

Hallin, D. 2000. Media, political power, and democratization in Mexico. in J. Curran and M.J. Park (eds.), *De-Westernizing media studies*. London and NY, Routledge, pp. 97-100.

Hamelink, C.J. 1983. Cultural autonomy in global communications. NY, Longman.

Hourani, A. 1991. *A history of the Arab peoples*. Cambridge, Mass.: Harvard University Press.

Ismail, J. 2001. *Ben Laden, al-Jazeera and I*. Dar Al-Hurriah, Damascus.

Karam, G. 1999. *Arab media in the 21 Century*. Beirut, Lebanon.

Kazan, F.E. 1996. Mass media, modernity and development in Arab state of the Gulf. Westport, Coun: Praeger.

Kit-Wai Ma, E. 2000. Rethinking media studies: The case of China. in J. Curran and M.J. Park (ed.), *De-Westernizing media studies*. London and NY, Routledge.

Lee, C.C. 2000. State, capital, and media: The case of Taiwan. in J. Curran and M.J. Park (eds.), *De-Westernizing media studies*. London and NY, Routledge.

Link, J.H. 1984. Test of the cultural dependency hypothesis. in R. Stevenson and D. Shaw (eds.), *Foreign news and the new world information order*. Ames, Iowa State UP, pp.186-199.

Mackey, Sandra. 1989. *Lebanon: death of a nation*. New York: Anchor Doubleday.

Mattleart, A. 1994. *Mapping world communication*. Minneapolis, University of Minnesota Press.

McLuhan, M. 1964. Understanding media: the extensions of man. New York: McGraw-Hill.

McPhail, T.L. 1987. Electronic colonialism: The future of international broadcasting and communication. Newbury Park, CA, Sage.

Mellencamp, P. 1990. Indiscretions: avant-garde film, video, and feminism. Bloomington, Indiana UP.

Mohammadi, A. 1995. Cultural imperialism and cultural identity. in J. Downing, A. Mohammadi, and A. Sreberny-Mohammadi (eds.), 1995. *Questioning the media: a critical introduction*. London, Sage, pp. 362-378.

Mowlana, H. 1975. The multinational corporation and the diffusion of technology. in *The new sovereigns: multinational corporations as world powers*. (A. A. Said and L. R. Simmons, eds.), pp. 77-90. Prentice-Hall, Englewood Cliffs, New Jersey.

Park, M.J., Kim, C.N., and Sohn, B.W. 2000. Modernization, globalization, and the powerful state: The Korean media. in J. Curran and M.J. Park (eds.), *De-westernizing media studies*. London and NY, Routledge.

Raboy, M. 1997. *The world situation of public service broadcasting: overview and Analysis.* Dans public service broadcasting: cultural and educational dimensions. Paris: UNESCO.

Rogers, E. 1986. *Communication technology.* NY, The Free Press.

Rugh, W.A. 1979. The Arab press :news media and political process in the Arab world. Syracuse UP, NY.

Rugh, W. 2001. *President of the Amideast Foundation.* Personal interview, Cairo.

Rugh, W. 1987. The Arab press: News media and political process in the Arab world. Syracuse University Press, 1st edition.

Schramm, W. 1964. Mass Media and national development: The role of information in the developing countries. Stanford, California: Stanford University Press, and Paris: UNESCO.

Siebert, F. S., Peterson, and Schramm. 1963. *Four theories of the press.* Urbana: University of Illinois Press.

Schiller, H.I. 1976. *Communication and cultural domination.* NY, International Arts and Sciences Press.

Articles

Abu Laban, B. 1996."Factors in social control of the press in Lebanon. *Journalism Quarterly.* No. 43, pp. 510-518.

Al-Umran, H. 1996. 'MMDS- the cultural alternative to DTH', *Middle East broadcast and satellite,* September 19.

Ajami, F. 2001. What the Muslim world is watching. *New York Times.* NY, 18 November.

Al-Hitti, H. 2000. The international satellite broadcasting and its possible political effects in the Arab world. Al-*Mustaqbal Al-'Arabi.* No. 4. (Arabic)

Alterman, J. B. 1999. Transnational media and social change in the Arab world. in *Transnational Broadcasting Studies,* Spring, No. 2.

Amin, H. 2001. Arab women and satellite broadcasting. *Transnational Broadcasting Studies.* Spring, No.6.

Amin, H. 2000. The current situation of satellite broadcasting in the Middle East. *Transnational Broadcasting Studies,* Fall/Winter, No. 5.

Ayish, M. 2001. American-style journalism and Arab world television: an exploratory study of news selection at six Arab world satellite television channels. *Transnational Broadcasting Studies.* Spring, No.6.

Ayish, M. 1997. Arab television goes commercial: A case study of the Middle East broadcasting center. *Gazette: The International Journal of Mass Communication Studies,* Vol. 59, No. 6, pp. 473-494.

Ayish, M. 1995. Potential effects of direct satellite broadcasting on national television systems in the Arab region. *Journal of Humanities and Social Sciences,* Vol. 11, pp. 394-326 (Arabic).

Barber, B. 1982. Jihad Vs. McWorld. *The Atlantic Monthly.* Vol. 269, No. 3, March.

Barkey, M. 1996. Satellite TV: on the eve of revolution. *Arab Ad.* January, pp. 12-14.

Bulloch, C. 1995. Satellite TV in the Middle East. *Via Satellite.* March.

Chan, J.M. & Ma, E.K. 1996. Asian television: global trend and local processes. *Gazette: The International Journal of Mass Communication Studies*, Vol. 58 No. 5. pp. 45-60.

Dabbous, S. 1994. Egypt. in Kamalipour, Y. and H. Mowlana (eds.) *Mass media in the Middle East.* London, Greenwood Press.

Dajani, N. 1999. Satellite broadcasting in the Middle East and North Africa: regulations, access and impact. *Transnational Broadcasting Studies*, Spring, No. 2.

Fakhreddine, J. 2000. Pan-Arab satellite T\television: now the survival part. *Transnational Broadcasting Studies*, Fall, No. 5.

Fouda, Y. 2001. Al-Jazeera: here we stand; we can do no otherwise. *Transnational Broadcasting Studies*, No.6.

Ghareeb, E. & Mansour, K. 2000. Arab media in the 21 Century: between the hammer of the globalization and the anvil of the state. *Bahethat*, No. 6. (Arabic)

Harik, I. 1994. Pluralism in the Arab world. *Journal of Democracy*, No. 5, Vol. 3, pp. 43-56.

Hurrat, K & Leidig, L 1994. Iraq. in Kamalipour, Y. and H. Mowlana (eds.) *Mass media in the Middle East.* Greenwood Press, London.

Khairi, A. 2000. Echoes of Jerusalem fighting in Arab and world capitals. *Al-Hayat*, Oct. 15, p. 8. London.

Khoury, N. W. 1994. Arabsat: serving the Middle East. *Via Satellite*, February.

Kraidy, M. 1998. Broadcasting regulation and civil society in postwar Lebanon. *Journal of Broadcasting & Electronic Media*, Summer.

Kuttab, D. 1999. Satellite broadcasting in the Middle East and North Africa: regulations, access and impact. *Transnational Broadcasting Studies*, Spring, No. 2.

Lent, J. 1989. Mass communication in Asia and the Pacific. *Media Asia*, No. 16, Vol. 1, pp. 16-24.

Marghalani, Kh. and Boyd, D. 1998. The utilization of direct satellite broadcasting (DBS) in Saudi Arabia. *Journal of Broadcasting and Electronic Media*, volume 42, number 3.

Millichip, J. 1996. Sand castles: special satellite Middle East. *TV World*, April, pp. 45-50.

Nossek, H & Rinnawi, Kh. 2003. Censorship and freedom of the press under changing political regimes: Palestinian media from Israeli occupation to the Palestinian Authority. *Gazette*, Vol. 65(2): 181-200.

Owen, T. 1999. Regulating access to transnational satellite television shifting government policies in Northeast Asia. *Gazette: The International Journal of Mass Communication Studies*, Vol. 61 No. 3-4.

Rinnawi, Kh. 2003. Live Intifada: Arab satellite TV coverage of the Al-Aqsa Intifada. *Palestine-Israel Journal.* Vol. 10 No. 2.

Robins, K. Cornford. J. and Asu Aksoy. 1997. Overview: from cultural rights to cultural responsibilities. *Programming for people: from cultural rights to cultural responsibilities.* K. Robins, ed. Pp. 12-45. New York: United Nations World Television Forum.

Sakr, N. 2000. Optical illusions: television and censorship in the Arab world. *Transnational Broadcasting Studies.* Fall, No.5.

Schiller, H. 1991. Not yet the post-imperialist era. *Critical Studies in Mass Communication,* No. 8, pp. 13-28.

Schleifer, A. 1998. Media explosion in the Arab world: The Pan-Arab satellite broadcasters. *Transnational Broadcasting Studies,* Fall, No. 1.

Sreberny, A. 2001. Mediated culture in the Middle East: diffusion, democracy, difficulties. *Gazette: The International Journal of Mass Communication Studies,* Vol. 63, No. 2-3.

Sui-Nam Lee, P. 1988. Communication imperialism and dependency: A conceptual clarification. *Gazette: The International Journal of Mass Communication Studies,* No. 41, pp. 69-83.

Tagliabue, J. 1996. Tapping the power of satellite: three broadcasters aim for Arabic speakers around the world. *New York Times.* 15 April, pp. C1, C10.

Taylor, P. 2000. Introduction. European Journal of Communication (Special issue: The media and the Kosovo conflict), No. 15, Vol. 3, pp. 293-297.

Thomas, O. 1999. Regulating access to transnational satellite television: shifting government policies in Northeast Asia. *Gazette: The International Journal of Mass Communication Studies,* Vol. 63 No. 3-4.

Zednik, R. 2002. Inside Al-Jazeera. *Colombia Journalism Review.* May/June. [html].

Zureikat, D. 1999 Transnational broadcasting studies global conference coverage satellite broadcasting in the Middle East and North Africa: regulations, access and impact. *International seminar of Article 19, The International Center Against Censorship, Transnational Broadcasting Studies,* Spring, No. 2.

Reference Monographs

Ang, I. 1985. Watching "Dallas": soap opera and the melodramatic imagination. London, Methuen.

Baudrillard, J. 1995. *The Gulf war did not take place.* Bloomington, Indiana UP.

Boyd-Barrett, J.O. and Thussu, D.K. 1993. NWIO strategies and media imperialism: the case of regional news exchange. in K. Nordenstreng and H. Schiller (eds.), *Beyond national sovereignty: International communication in the 1990s.* Norwood, NJ, Ablex Publishing Corporation, pp. 177-192.

Boyd-Barrett, J.O. 1977. Media imperialism: towards an international framework for an analysis of media systems. in J. Curran, M. Gurevitch and J. Woollacott (eds.), *Mass Communication and Society.* London, Edward Arnold, pp. 116-135.

Capin J. 1980. *L'Elter Television* Ed. Grasset, Paris.

Caspi, D., & Limor, Y. 1999. *The in/outsiders: the media in Israel.* New Jersey, Hampton Press.

Cumings, B. 1993. *War and Television.* London, Verso.

Denton, Jr., R. E. 1993. Television as an instrument of war. in R. E. Denton, Jr. (ed.) *The Media and the Persian Gulf war.* London, Praeger, pp. 27-42.

Doane, M. A. 1990. Information, crisis, catastrophe. in P. Mellencamp (ed.) *Logics of Television.* Bloomington, Indiana UP, pp. 222-239.

Elasmar, M.G., and Hunter J. E. 1997. The impact of foreign TV on domestic audiences: A meta-analysis. in B.R. Burleson (ed.), *Communication Yearbook,* No. 20, pp. 47-69.

Flournoy, D. and Stewart, R. 1997. *CNN: making news in the lobal Market.* London, University of Luton Press.

Gerbner, G. 1992. Persian Gulf war, the movie. in H. Mowlana, G. Gerbner, and H. I. Schiller (eds.), *Triumph of the image: the media's war in the Persian Gulf: A global perspective.* Boulder, Westview Press, pp. 243-265.

Gillner, E. *Nations and Nationalism.* Newbury Park, CA, Sage, 1994.

Hachten, W. A. 1999. The world news prism: changing media of international communication. Ames, Iowa State UP.

Hallin, D. C. 1994. We keep America on top of the world. television journalism and the public sphere. NY, Routledge.

Hallin, D. C. and Gitlin, T. 1994. The Gulf war as popular culture and television drama. in W. L. Bennett and D. L. Paletz (eds.) *Taken by storm: the media, public opinion, and U.S. foreign policy in the Gulf war.* Chicago, University of Chicago Press, pp. 149-163.

Kitley, H. 1998. Television news rituals in new order Indonesia. M. Hitchcock & V. T. King, *Images of Malay and Indonesian identity.* Kuala Lumpur, Oxford UP.

Lerner, D. 2000. Toward a communication theory of modernization. in J. Curran and M.J. Park (eds.), *De-westernizing media studies.* London and NY, Routledge.

Livingston, S. 1998. Beyond the 'CNN Effect': The Media-Foreign Policy Dynamic. in P. Norris (ed.) *Politics and the Press: The News Media and Their Influence.* London, Lynne Rienner. pp. 291-318.

MacGregor, B. 1997. Live, direct, and biased? making television news in the satellite age. London, Arnold.

Manheim, J. B. 1994. Strategic public diplomacy: managing Kuwait's image during the Gulf war. in W. L. Bennett and D. L. Paletz (eds.) *Taken by storm: the media, public opinion, and U.S. foreign policy in the Gulf war.* Chicago, University of Chicago Press, pp. 131 - 148.

McAllister, M. 2000. From flick to flack: the increased emphasis on marketing by media entertainment corporations. in R. Anderson and L. A. Strate (eds.), *Critical Studies in Media Commercialism.* NY, Oxford UP, pp.101-122.

Mohammadi, A. 1997. *International communication and globalization.* London, Sage Publications.

Mowlana, H. 1992. Roots of war: the long road of intervention. in *triumph of the image: the media's war in the Persian Gulf: a global perspective.* Boulder, Westview Press, pp. 30-50.

Neuman, J. 1996. Lights, camera, and war: is media technology driving international politics? NY, St. Martin's Press.

Schiller, H.I. 1989. Culture, Inc.: The corporate takeover of public expression. NY, Oxford UP.

Seib, P. 1997. Headline diplomacy: how news coverage affects foreign policy. London, Praeger.

Shinar, D. 1996. Communicational technology and social changes. Tel Aviv, Open UP.

Tomlinson, J. 1991. *Cultural imperialism: a critical introduction.* Baltimore, Johns Hopkins UP.

Reference Articles

Al-Hail, A. 1989. The age of new media: the role of Al-Jazeera satellite TV in developing aspects of civil society in Qatar. *Transnational Broadcasting Studies*, Fall, No. 4 [html].

Ayish, M. 1989. News film in Jordan television's Arabic nightly newscasts. *Journal of Broadcasting and Electronic Media*, Vol. 33, No. 4, pp. 453-460.

Barnet, A. et al., 1999. .Globalization and international communication: an examination of monetary, telecommunications and trade networks. *Journal of International Communication*, No. 2, Vol. 6, December. Vol. 6.

Bennet, J. 1998. Bad vibes from the heartland launch fleet of finger-pointers. *New York Times.* 19 February.

Fejes Fejes, F. 1981. Media imperialism: an assessment. *Media, culture and society.* No. 3, pp. 281-289.

Hafez, K. 1999. Between globalism and beduism: mass media within social transition in the Arab world. *Proceedings of German-Arab media dialogue.* Rabat, June 8-9, pp. 70-77.

Jensen, E. 1999. CNN's home-front offensive. *Los Angeles Times.* 17 April, 1999 [Lexis-Nexis].

Kemoner, M. 2000. CNN continues personnel shake-up as replacement for US chief named. *The Atlanta Journal and Constitution.* 19 September [Lexis-Nexis].

Kwak, K. 1999. The context of the regulations of television broadcasting in East Asia. *Gazette: The International Journal of Mass Communication Studies*, Vol.61.

Livingston, S and Eachus, T. 1995. Humanitarian crises and U.S. foreign policy: Somalia and the CNN effects reconsidered. *Political Communication*, No. 12, pp. 413-429.

Mandaville, Peter. 2001. Reimagining Islam in Diaspora: The politics of mediated community. *Gazette: The International Journal of Mass Communication Studies*, Vol. 63

Robin, B. 1993. Asia survey: new technologies reach five barriers of media control. *Intermedia*, No. 21, Vol. 1, pp. 22-31.

Schleifer, A. 2001. Looks are deceiving: Arab talk shows and TV journalism. *Transnational Broadcasting Studies*, No. 6.

Schleifer, A. 2000. Egyptian media waxes and wanes in its attacks against Al-Jazeera. *Transnational Broadcasting Studies*, No. 2.

Semati, M. 2001. Reflections on the politics of the global 'rolling-news' television genre. *Transnational Broadcasting Studies*.

Sreberny-Mohammadi, A. 1992. The global and the local in international communications. in *The Media are American* Tunstall. NY.

Shoesmith, A. 1999. Transnational media in Asia. *Transnational Broadcasting Studies*. Spring, No. 2.

Sui-Nam Lee, P. 1995. A case against the thesis of communication imperialism: The audience's response to foreign TV in Hong Kong. *Australian Journal of Communication*, No. 22, pp. 63-81.

TBS. 1999. Transnational media and social change in the Arab world public opinion and Arab identity. *Transnational Broadcasting Studies*. Spring, No. 2.

Thussu, D. K. 2000. Legitimizing 'humanitarian intervention'? CNN, NATO, and the Kosovo crisis. *European Journal of Communication (Special Issue: The media and the Kosovo conflict)*, No. 15, Vol. 3, pp. 345-361.

Toensing, C. 2001. Bush administration's policies limit media coverage. *Merip*. 18 October.

Vincent, R. 2000. A narrative analysis of US press coverage of Slobodan Milosevic and the Serbs in Kosovo. *European Journal of Communication (Special Issue: The media and the Kosovo conflict)*, No. 15, Vol. 3, pp. 321-344.

Wheeler D. 2001. "The Internet and the public culture In Kuwait" *Gazette: The International Journal of Mass Communication Studies*, Vol. 63.

www.tbsjournal.org. [html]

www.al-mashriq.org [html] Al-Mashriq, 2002.

About the Author

Dr. Khalil Rinnawi is a lecturer in the School of Media and the Department of Behavioral Science in the College of Management in Tel Aviv. His research specialty is the Arab media and society and specifically transnational media in the Arab world. Dr. Rinnawi is the author of several articles on the Arab media. His recent publications include *The Social Agenda of the Palestinian Minority in Israel* and *Live Intifada: Arab Satellite TV Coverage of the Al-Aqsa Intifada*.
Email: krinnawi@hotmail.com

Index

Abu Dhabi, 75, 92, 96, 130, 172

Abu Dhabi TV, 16, 24, 25, 27, 57, 63, 64, 84, 91, 92, 123, 153, 163, 171, CNN format, 131, challenges al-Jazeera, 123, format similar to al-Jazeera, 92, internal changes, 63, pressure, 173

Adeeb, Emad, 67

access, 2, 14, 15, 18, 27, 28, 38, 40, 41, 42, 51, 53, 54, 55, 56, 57, 65, 67, 75, 83, 89, 90, 92, 93, 94, 95, 103, 108, 111, 143, 144, 151, 152, 155, 162, 163—164, 169, 170, 171, 179, 182

advertising—see revenue

Against The Current *(Didd al-Mawjah)*, 65

Akthar min Ra'iy—*see* More than One Opinion

'Ala Masu'liyati—see *My Responsibility*

Albaraka Group, 77, 98

Ala al-Hawa'—see *On Air*

Algeria, 11, 45, 51, 54, 62, 75, 84, 93, 94, 102, 107

Ali (-al), Jassem, 68

America, 132, 137, 138, 140, 141, 157, aid, 2, anti-, 87, 108, 148, army base, 117, attacks on Iraq, 119, brutality, 137, crusade—see crusade, American, embassy, 119, globalization, 69, influence, 87, interests, 24, 122, Marines, 143, media—see media, American, movies, 159, news, 39, 42, 143, 157, 174, officials, access to al-Jazeera, 108, officials, critical of al-Jazeera, 115, police series, 39, pressure, 172, programs, 70, 91, 110, 164, special forces, 120, strikes, 137, 146, Syrian understanding, 19, Taliban conflict, 146, values, 165

America, Voice of—see *Voice of America*

America Plus Channel, 67

Amman, 47, 51, 62, 98, 132,

Andalus (-al), 76

Andalusia, 10

Anglo-European binaries, 148, cultures, 70, 168, entertainment, 70, influence, 90, interests, 148, journalists, 145, media, 147, pressure, 90, products, 17, 91, radio stations, 34, states, 5, 9, 35, 44, 127, 147, television stations, 32, 35, 45, 146, 168

ANN (Arab News Network), 16, 25, 49, 57, 64, 72—73, 74, 79, 84, 87, 97, 112, 123, 158, 159, 161, 163, 176, 180, 181, breaks traditional mould, 161, challenges al-Jazeera, 73, 123, CNN format, 72, 157, finances, 72, 74, inter-Syrian struggle, 87, managed by Sawmar al-Assad, 72, ownership, 72, 79, , news, 72, *Thematic television stations*, 80, and Saudi Arabia, 73, and Syria, 73

Anti—see *She*

Arab Times, The, 117

Arab-Israeli conflict, 25, 62, 151, 156, 166—also see Palestinian conflict, conflict, impact on satellite television, 170 - 174, peace-talks, 61, war, 47

Arab Media Corporation, 78, 101

Arab nation-state—see nation-state

Arab Radio and Television (ART), 45, 51, 63, 64—67, 72, 80, 83, 84, 85, 87, 94, 97, 98, 100, 154, 159, 165, 166, headquarters, 67, 71, running costs, 65, news, 68, 112, ownership, 78, 101

ART Aflam—see *ART Movies*

ART Al-'Alamiyyah 1—see *ART Global Middle East*

ART Al-'Alamiyyah 2—see *ART Global America*

ART Australia, 65, 66

ART Curriculum (ART Manahij), 66, 66, 80

ART Drama (ART Hekayat), 65, 66, 67, 80

ART Global America (ART Al-'Alamiyyah 2), 65, 66, 67

ART Global Middle East (ART Al-'Alamiyyah 1), 65, 66, 67

ART Hekayat—see ART Drama

ART Latino, 65, 67

ART Manahij—see ART Curriculum

ART Movies (ART Aflam), 65, 66, 67, 80

ART Movies America, 65, 80

ART Music, 65, 66, 67, 80

ART Sport Land 1, 65, 80

ART Sport Land 2, 65, 80

ART Tarab, 65, 66, 80

ART Teenz, 65, 66, 67, 80

Arab Satellite Communications Organization (Arabsat), 44, 45, 46, 47, 48, 64, 72, 73, 76, 77, 83, 85, 86, 102

Arab world, 5, 16, 18, 20, 21, 22, 24, 25, 28, 35, 38, 39, 40, 41, 51, 56, 57, 58, 61, 62, 63, 65, 66, 67, 68, 69, 70, 72, 74, 86, 87, 91, 92, 95, 96, 97, 98, 99, 102, 104, 106, 107, 110, 111, 112, 115, 117, 121, 122, 123, 124, 125, 126, 127, 128, 130, 131, 132, 133, 147, 148, 151, 152, 153, 154, 155, 156, 158, 159, 161, 162, 163, 164, 168, 174, 175, 176, 179, 180, 181, 182, advertising, 18, censorship, 89 - 90, civil society, 169 - 170, classification of satellite television stations, 76 - 86, effect of transnational broadcasting, 55, emergence of satellite television, 41—49, media, 13, 36, 39, identical programming, 17, 18, Islamism, 19, 20, 164 - 167, imagined community, 9 - 12, language, 26, media technology, 31 - 35, and Palestine, 20, pan-Arabism, 19—28, penetration of satellite television, 51 - 55, transnational broadcasting, 15, 17, 31

Arabic Series Channel, The, 68

Arabiya (-al), 27, 63, 84, 91, 106, 124, 131, 158, 159, 161, 163, 171, 176, 180

Arafat, Yasser, 19, 72, 101, 106, 110, 133

Around the Issue (Madarat al-Ahdath), 66

Art Studio (Studio Funn), 70

Arwiqat al-Siyasah—see *Political Corridors*

Asia, 1, 15, 40, 49, 67, 77, 92, 96

Assad (-al), Hafiz, 22, 49, 72, 79, 175

Assad (-al), Bashar, 141

Assad (-al), Ra'fat, 49, 73, 79

Assad (-al), Sawmar, 72

assassination, 62, 138, 175

audience, 4, 12, 13, 14, 15, 17, 18, 21, 23, 24, 25, 26, 27, 35, 36, 39, 41, 43, 45, 46, 49, 51, 55, 56, 57, 58, 59, 61, 62, 63, 65, 66, 67, 68, 70, 71, 73, 75, 80, 83, 86, 89, 90, 92, 94, 103, 104, 108, 109, 111, 112, 115, 121, 122, 124, 125, 128, 130, 136, 142, 143, 144, 146, 151, 152, 153, 154, 155, 158, 159, 160, 164, 165, 166, 168, 169, 171, 172, 173, 174, 175, 176, 179, 181, 183, participation, 162—163

Audience Requests (Ma Yatlubuhu al-Mushahidun), 62

Avezzano, 45, 64, 71

Awa'el (-al), 85

Bahrain, 33, 34, 63, 75, 84, 165

ban, 61, 94, 95, 100, 109, 111, decoder, 94, al-Jazeera, 106, 109, LBC, 108, 109, satellite, 61, 65, 100, 111

Baramij Mutafareka—see *Program Variety*

Bass Kermalak—see *Only for You*

BBC, 31, 93, 100, 103, 116, 123, 133, 152, 157

BBC Arabic, 32, 68, 119, 157

Beirut, 22, 42, 51, 63, 68, 101, 108, *Beit al-'Anqabout*—see *Spider's Web, The*

Beiteddine, 66

Ben Laden, al-Jazeera and I, 118— also see Ismail, Jamal; 118

Ben Laden, Usama, 25, 118, 133

Berlin, 4

Bila Hudoud—see *Without Borders*

Bin Talal, al-Walid, 64, 66, 78, 101

binary, 87, 146, 148, 170, 181

Birri, Nabih, 76

Blair, Tony, 108

Book, The (Al-Kitab), 126

border, 11, 46, 87, 89, 90, 95, 143, 151, 153, 165, 173, 179, Arab state, 15, 16, 17, 27, 31, 34, 40, 111, 148, 159, closed, 36, geopolitical, 6, 56, 57, information, 23, 151, 152, 153, Israel, 145, Saudi Arabia, 100

bouquet, 45, 65, 84—85

Brazil, television programs, 3

Britain, 40, 63, 141—also see United Kingdom

British bombing, 109, comedies, 39, media, 91, news, 42, officials, 108, 115, presentation formats, 131

broadcasts, live, 124, 141, 154, television, 27, 33—35, 162, radio, 28, 31—33, 41, 55

broadcasters, 13, 18, Arab, 13, 156, government, 104, 153, Lebanese, 46, transnational, 14, 15

broadcasting agenda, 151, 154, analog, 85, Arab, 44, 70, 80, 86, 90, 102, 159, content, 35, 111, 162, 180, control, 36, digital, 85, diversity, 101, effects, 26, 12, 14, 152, 156, 167, tribal, 36— 41, 56—58, Palestinian, 101, patterns, 115, policies, 12, regulations, 80, 92—96, 96—97, 97—98, 98—99, 99—101, 101—105, , satellite, 13, 31, 43, 44, 45, 51, 54, 64, 67, 85, 90, 91, 92, 102, 105, 152, 160, 168, 169, 181, State, 55, 104, systems, 45, 64, technology, 112 , terrestrial, 71, 153, transnational, 5, 13, 14, 15, 17, 18, 24, 25, 26, 41, 89, 90, 105, 111, 170, 174, 179

Cairo, 32, 33, 41, 48, 51, 63, 65, 68, 77, 87, 99, 107, 109, 132

cable, 12, 53, 54, 73, 79, 84, 85, 86, 92, 93, 94, 95, 100

California, 3

capitalist, 3, 12, 17, 24

Cartage, 66

censor, 56, 67, 99

censorship, 13, 14, 16, 18, 36, 37,
     42, 46, 48, 55, 56, 57, 64, 87,
     89—90, 91, 98, 99, 101, 102,
     109, 112, 151, 159, 161, 164,
     171, 172, 179, 180, 181—also
     see interference , news, 79, 93,
     99, 105, 156, self, 96, 98, 101
children, 14, 21, 31, 48, 66, 70, 75,
     80, 117, 148, 167, 169
Christopher Ross, former U.S. am-
     bassador, 108
CIA, 69
cinema, 2, 47, 67
civil society, 2, 18, 23, 86, 145,
     151, 163, 167, 168, 169, 170,
     176, 182
citizen, 119, 121, 137, 152, 158,
     162, 163, 167, 169, Arab, 40, 55,
citizenship, 20
CNN, 31, 43, 44, 45, 70, 72, 93,
     109, 123, 153, 154, 155, 156,
     171, American network, 135,
     American perspective, 137, 142,
     and ANN, 157, comparison to
     al-Jazeera and Jordanian televi-
     sion, 115, 128, 129, 130, 131,
     132, 135, 136, 137—142, , and
     MBC, 62, 156, and al-Jazeera,
     69, 103, pro-American, 135, 137
colonial enterprises, 1, language,
     26, nations, 40, police, 148,
     powers, 32, 132, radio, 31
colonialism, 2, 18, 148
colonization, reverse, 3
commercialization, 13, 14, 58, 90,
     91, 105, 112, 159, 180
communication (also see *mass
     communication*), 3 , barriers, 56,
     era, 5, international, 5 , system,
     1, modern system, 1, networks,
     167, global, 3, technology, see
     technology,   communication,
     transnational, 4
Communication imperialism, 2

competition, 13, 14, 15, 32, 56, 58,
     63, 76, 92, 94, 99, 153, 161, 174,
     176, 182, 183
content, 13, 16, 17, 18, 24, 32, 34,
     35, 36, 37, 38, 44, 47, 48, 49, 55,
     56, 58, 61, 62, 67, 77, 78, 84, 90,
     92, 94, 98, 106, 111, 112, 132,
     148, 153, 154, 155, 157, 158,
     159, 160, 162, 164, 165, 168,
     169, 171, 180, American, 108,
     appropriate, 14, classification,
     80, identical, 27, media, 2, 3, 11,
     12, 14, 15, 27, 31, 37, 53, 58, 97,
     110, 152, 179, program, 15,
     Western genres, 15
correspondent, 61, 109, 116, 131,
     arrest, 106, al-Jazeera, 106, 118,
     199, 127, 132, 145, 157, MBC,
     207, program, 64, 127
*Creation and Invention (Ibtikarat
     wa Ikhtira'at),* 62
Critical theorists, 2
crusade, American, 136
cultural awareness, 57, community,
     4, 127, consumption, 24, con-
     text, 22, encounters, 3, events,
     64, 65, exchange, 4, groups, 20,
     hegemony, 10, imperialism, 1, 2,
     3, imperialism, American, 3,
     imperialism, and media—see
     Media and cultural imperialism,
     issues, 66, monopoly, 10, niches,
     4, phenomena, 24 , pluralism,
     revisionist, 1, products, 4, 14,
     19, 20, 22, 181, program, 64, 89,
     126, 128, 162, redlines, 14, 15,
     165, resistance, 3 , theories, 4,
     values—see values, cultural, 165
Cultural dependency and domina-
     tion, *2*
Cultural pluralism and globaliza-
     tion, *4*
Cultural synchronization, *2*
culture, Anglo-European, 70, 145,
     Arab-American,   17,   Arab-
     Islamic, 25, 91, 165, Eastern,

126, Egyptian, 47, indigenous, 6, local, 2, 3, mediated, 55, national, 4, non-Western, 3, North American, 145, pan-Arab, 169, 183, patriarchal, 55

Cyprus, 67, 84

Daher, Pierre, 69, 86, 108
Damascus, 93
decoder, 53, 83, 94, 100
dialogue, 126, 182, collective, 2, Islamic, 91, pan-Arab, 25, 43, with viewers, 75
diaspora, Arabs in, 9, 10, 31, 43, 46, 61, 162, 163
Didd al-Mawjah—see *Against The Current*
discourse, 171, 175, collective, 27, local, 6, political, 55, public, 39, 89
Disney Channel, 67
Debate of the Week (Hiwar al-Isbu'), 62
dependency, 2, 3
development, 1, 2, 3, 6, 9, 16, 25, 32, 40, Arab, 23, Arab media, 31, 41, 44, 47, 57, 84, 86, 87, 90, 91, 96, 99, 105, 111, 112, 157, 168, 169, 179, 181, civil society, 169, 170, Jordan, 158, Saudi Arabia, 77
Developmental media model, *158*
Din (-al) wal Hayat—see *Religion and Life*
Discussions on Sport (Hiwar Fi al-Riyada), 124
Djibouti, 75
Doha (-al), 27, 46, 68, 89, 102, 106
Dream TV, 99
Dubai, 27, 47, 75, 85, 104, 109, 156, media environment, 51, 53, 63, 68, 153, Media City, 63
Dubai Space, 84
Dubai Space Imaging, 85
Dubai Sport, 76
Durra (-al), Mohammed, 147

Economic Imperialism, 2
editor, 13, 39, 43, 108, 116, 119, 120, 147, 153
editorial, 21, 40, 42, 73, 135, dependence, 103, direction, MBC, 63, independence, 43, 104, 116, policy, 36, 102, 103, position, 102, 132, 136, staff, ART, 98, style, al-Jazeera, 109
editor-in-chief, 41, 108
Egypt, 11, 18, 19, 21, 22, 25, 26, 32, 33, 34, 35, 39, 41, 42, 44, 47, 48, 49, 51, 57, 65, 67, 69, 73, 75, 76, 77, 80, 83, 84, 87, 89, 91, 92, 93, 94, 97, 98, 99, 101, 103, 105, 109, 110, 111, 118, 119, 120, 122, 123, 125, 133, 136, 152, 153, 154, 155, 157, 166
Eighth Day, The (al-Youm al-Thamin), 70
Electronic Colonialism, 2
elite, Arab, 32, cultural, 6, 13, 15, intellectual, 169, political, 14, 37, 38, 155, 162, 170, religious, 12, 105, 165, 166, ruling, 39, 40, 58, 77, 97, 152, 158, secular, 165, 166, social, 13, 15, 105, 162, 170
Emirates-Dubai   Television (EDTV), 85
equipment, 34, 44, 53, 83, 93, 94
Esma'una—see *Listen to Us*
ESPN, 67
ethnic borders, 24, collective, 6, community, 11, diversity, 4, groups, 4, identity, 20, 25, language channels, 31, minority, 169, solidarity, 9
ethnocentrism, 2
Eutelsat Company, 53, 76, 77, 86, 95

Fahd, King of Saudi Arabia, 61, 63, 108
Fairouz, 22, 66

186 Index

Farah wa Marah—see *Fun and Games*
Faysal (-al), Toujan, 163
fax, 57, 66, 124, 145
FBI, 120
Fifty Years of the Arab-Israeli Conflict (Khamsuna 'Aman 'ala al-Sira' al-'Arabi al-Isra'ili), 62
Film Clip, 65
First, The (Al-Ula), 67
Firstnet, 85
For Women Only (Lil Nisaa'i Faqat), 125
free-to-air (FTA), 45, 64, 66, 67, 71, 74, 83, 84, 87, 104
freedom of expression, 1, 57, 68, 77, 98, 112, 181
Frankfurt, 4
From Washington (Min Washington), 125
Fucino, 64
Fun and Games (Farah wa Marah), 65
Future Television (al-Mustaqbal), 75, 79, 86

Game of Chance (Lu'bat Hazh), *68*
Globalization and localization bipolar model, *4, 5*
globalization, 1, 2, 3, 4, 5, 6, 9, 14, 174, American, 69, and McArabism, 9, 12, 15, 182
global homogenization, 2, market, 14, structures, 2, village, 4, 14
Good Morning Arabs! (Sabah al-Khayr ya 'Arab), 62s
Gulf War, The (Harb al-Khalij), 62

Hadith al-Sa'a—see *Latest Events*
Hadith al-Sa'ah—see *Talk of the Hour*
Hamad bin Jassem bin Jabr al-Thani, Sheikh, 117
Hamad bin Khalifa al-Thani, Sheikh, 115, 118

Hamad bin Thamir al-Thani, Sheikh, 116,
Hamas, 19, 20, 23, 62, 110, 138, 144, 167
Harb al-Khalij—see *Gulf War, The*
Harb (-al) al-Lubnaniyya—see *Lebanon War, The*
Hariri (-al), Rafiq, 76, 76, 79, 86, 102, 103, 108
Hayat (-al), 25, 42, 72, 91
Hiwar Fi al-Riyada—see *Discussions on Sport*
Hiwar al-Isbu'—see *Debate of the Week*
Hiwar Maftouh—see *Open Discussion*
Hiwar al-'Umur—see *Life Discussions*
Hizbollah, 19, 20, 49, 74, 75, 86, 133, 139, 166
hollywood, 79
How and Why (Kif w'Laysh), 70
Hot Bird, 73, 86, 73, 86
Hugo Interactive, 65
human rights, 18, 20, 121, 122, 167

Ibtikarat wa Ikhtira'at—see *Creation and Invention*
identity, 9, Arab, 16, 17, 19, 20, 22, 23, 148, 152, 159, 169, 170, 173, 176, 183, collective, 16, 40, 148, of diaspora communities, 4, Palestinian, 20, religious, 25, tribal, 6
Ideological Imperialism, 2
Ila Man Yahimmahu al-Amr—see *To Whom it May Concern*
imperial powers, 3, 20
imperialism, 2, 18, 20, 31, 147, 175
information, 2, 5, 13, 14, 16, 37, 39, 40, 51, 57, 58, 89, 90, 96, 146, 152, 153, 155, 167, 172, 172, 182, border, 23, 151, 152, 179, market, 176, 182, Ministry of, 32, 36, 78, 91, 95, 98, 99, 106, 107, 110, 115, 116, 120,

142, 143, 147, 152, 153, 154, 163, Minister, 56, 85, 108, policies, 102, political, 35, society, 168, source, 69, 93, 112, 120, 152, 175, 180

indigenous Arab minority, 9, 168, coverage, 171, culture, 6, mechanisms, 179, media, 175, nature, 20, 146, non-Western, 3, process, 91, 111, programs, 3, 15, structures, 143, 147

indoctrination, political, 1

independence, 20, 27, 32, 70, 110, editorial, 103, 104, 116, financial, 104, post, 2, Qatar, 115, 117, Arab, 9, 10, 18, 25, 56, 62, 72, 87, 121, 125, 148, 163, 169

interference, 57, 65, 160 —also see censorship

interview, 26, 62, 66, 67, 68, 69, 70, 76, 101, 102, 103, 108, 110, 117, 118, 119, 120, 121, 126, 127, 128, 131, 132, 134, 135, 136, 137, 142, 144, 156, 158, 166, 170, 174

Intifada, 21, 25, 72, 130, 166, 173, al-Aqsa, 21, 27, 72, 74, 107, 128, 130, 133, 135, 147, 162, 166, 167, 171, 172, 173, first, 19, 167, footage, 21, second— see Intifada, al-Aqsa, September 2000—see Intifada, al-Aqsa

investment, 40, 45, 78, 85, 97, 102, 105, 109, 111, 121

Iqra'—see Read

Iran, 33, 75, 84, 93

Iraq, 10, 19, 20, 21, 25, 27, 32, 33, 37, 51, 64, 73, 75, 106, 107, 109, 110, 119, 123, 132, 133, 137, 138, 140, 146, 148, 169, 172, 175, 183

Irhabiyoun—see *Terrorists*

'Ishir Ba'd 'Ishir, 68

Ishraqat—see *Shining/Eastern*

Islam, 10, 11, 15, 16, 18, 20, 23, 26, 49, 66, 74, 75, 93, 100, 107, 109, 118, 122, 125, 128, 132, 133, 135, 136, 137, 139, 140, 142, 151, 154, 164—167, 168, 173, 176, 176, 182, pan, 19, community, 11, movements, 20, 91, programs—see program, religious, values—see values, religious , world, 10, 25, 44, 160

Islamic Law and Life (al-Shari'a wal Hayat), 125

Israel, 10, 19, 21, 27, 42, 47, 49, 57, 62, 68, 69, 74, 75, 106, 107, 110, 130, 132, 133, 134, 135, 136, 137, 138, 139, 140, 143, 144, 145, 146, 147, 148, 151, also see Palestine, Arab-Israeli, boycott, 17, image in Arab world, 131, 156, 158, 170—174, 176, 182, normalization, 121, press, 42, Press Office, 143, and Qatar, 116, 117, 122

Issue of the Hour (Qadaya al-Sa'a), 125

Italy, 45, 64,

Ittijah (-al) al-Mu'akas—see Opposite Direction, The

Jar al-Qamar—see *Neighbor of the Moon*

Jarima (-al) al-Siyasiyya—see *Political Crime, The*

Jawa'iz 'al Hawa—see *Live Prizes*

Jazeera (-al), 16, 23, 24, 25, 45, 48, 57, 64, 67, 68, 70, 75, 79, 84, 89, 92, 102, 104, 106, 107, 108, 112, 115, 120, 123, 159, 160, advertising, 104, 105, 116, and Afghanistan, 108, 118, 120, 122, 137, 142, 143, 146, 147, 148, and Algeria, 107, anti-American, 135, 107, 108, 119, 133, 134, 135, 137—Also see al-Jazeera and United States, Arab audiences, 46, 69, 103, 108, 120, 123, 124, 142, 143, 163, 168, 182, and Arab identity, 23, 112,

123, 143, 176, anti-Israeli, 35, 133, 134, 135, 136, 172, and Arab-Israeli conflict, see al-Jazeera and Palestine, Arab rivalry, 112, 116, 118, 153, availability, 76, background, 115, bans, 106, and BBC, bias, 144 - 146, breaks traditional mould, 46, 161, boycott—see al-Jazeera, complaints , CNN format, 69, 131, comparison, 128 - 148, competition, 76, 122, 123, complaints, 17, 91, 102, 105, 106, 107, 108, 109, 110, 117, 120, 123, conspiracy theories, 115, 117, 118, 119, 120, 122, 181, delegitimization, 112, 115, 148, 163, 180, documentaries, 57, and Egypt, 107, 109, 118, 119, 122, 163, emergence, 63, even-handed, 76, global prominence, 69, hidden agenda, 69, 87, impact, 68, 108, 148, 152, 168, and Iraq, 106, 107, 109, and Israel 109, 116, 117, 120, 122, 133, 134, 143, 144, 145, 146, 148, 158, 170, 171—also see al-Jazeera and Palestine, and Jordan, 106, 107, 163, and Kuwait, 107, 109, 110, legitimacy—see al-Jazeera, popularity, and McArabism, 28, 115, 142, 146, 148, 176, 182, and Morocco, 110, motto, 68, news, 70, 103, 105, 106, 109, 123, 130, 131, 132, 133, 134, 135, 137, 142, 143, 144, 148, 151, 154, 157, news agenda, 103, and Pakistan, 120, 137, and Palestinian Authority, 106, 110, 144, and Palestine, 109, 116, 130, 133, 134, 135, 136, 137, 142, 143, 144, 146, 147, 148, 158, and pan-Arabism, 130 , pressure, 106, 107, 108, 109, 117, 122, 182, popularity, 66, 68, 69, 76, 112,

115, 123, 124, 142, 143, 146, 148, 180, 182, privately funded, 79, professionalism, 76, programs. Also see al-Jazeera, news; 69, 76, 124, 125, and Qatar, 112, 116, 117, 118, 119, Qatari news, 103, 116, 117, ratings, 76, and Saudi Arabia, 106, semi-private station, 78, 91, sensationalism, 147—148, spreads by word of mouth, 54, staff, 122, 123, 144, 146, staff trained in Anglo-European countries, 27, survey, 76, and Syria, 107, Taliban, 119, 120, thematic television station, 80, and Tunisia, 107, 132, and United States; 119, 120, 121, 122, 132, 134, 143, and Usama Ben Laden. Also see al-Jazeera and Taliban; 118, 119, 120, 132, Zionism, 120

Jerusalem, 22, 42, 62, 107, 132, 134, 144, 158, 167, 172, 173

jihad, 6, 9, 12, 15, 24, Islamic, 136, 144, 158

Jordan, 21, 40, 47, 54, 56, 75, 83, 84, 89, 90, 91, 92, 94, 97, 101, 109, 153, 154, 163, censorship, 105, 107, 120, Ministry of Information, 106, Press and Publications Law, 98, television ownership, 34, television, 115, 128, 130—142, 158, royal family, 57

Jordanization, 40

journalist, 13, 27, 37, 39, 96, 145, 146, 148, 152, 163, 168, 173, 182, Arab, 43, 69, 105, 111, 123, 132, 144, 147

journalism, 38, 116, 123, 143, 145, 148, 174, investigative, 22, 126, 142

Journey (Meshwar), 62

Kalam el-Nas—see *Talk of the People*

Kamel, Saleh, 64, 77, 98
Khalid bin 'Abdullah, Prince, 67, 72, 73
Khalid bin Sultan, Prince, 42, 67
Khalifa bin Hamad al-Thani, Sheikh, 118
*Khamsuna 'Aman 'ala al-Sira' al-'Arabi al-Isra'ili—*see *Fifty Years of the Arab-Israeli Conflict*
Kif w'Laysh—see *How and Why*
Kitab (-Al)—see *Book, The*
Koraa 2000, 65
Kuwait, 19, 40, 43, 45, 51, 68, 75, 84, 85, 89, 90, 93, 97, 102, 105, 106, 107, 109, 110, 120, 153, 169, 175

Late Hours, The (Sa'at Safaa), 65
Latest Events (Hadeeth al-Sa'a), 66
Latin America, 2, 35, 37
LBC, 24, 46, 67, 69—72, 81, 83, 86, 87, 92, 101, 102, 108, 112, 130, 131, 160, 161, 165, French-American, 70, popularity, 66, 67, 151, 159, 165, ratings, 58, 76, 104, 109
Lebanon, 21, 32, 35, 43, 46, 49, 51, 66, 67, 69, 71, 74, 75, 76, 79, 84, 101, 102, 103, 106, 133, 147, 153, 167, Audiovisual Media Law, 99, investment, 108, 109, Law 382/94, 100, media environment, 86, 89, 95, 97, 161, 164, 180, 181, Ministry of Information and Council of Ministers, 98, privately owned stations, 40, 47, 160, satellite access, 54, television ownership, 34, 152
Lebanon War, The (al-Harb al-Lubnaniyya), 57, 69
Lebanonization, 24, 40
Leil (-al) Leiltak—see *Night is Yours, The*

Leilkum Funn—see *Your Night is Art*
Libya, 34, 37, 75, 102, 106, 151
licence, 46, 73, 93, 95, 96, 97, 99, 100, 104
Life Discussions (Hiwar al-'Umur), 70
Lil Nisaa'i Faqat—see *For Women Only*
Listen to Us (Esma'una), 65
Live (Mubashir), 68
Live Prizes (Jawa'iz 'al Hawa), 62
Live Studio (Studio el Hawa), 65
localism, 6, 9, 12, 15, 158
London, 42, 43, 47, 49, 51, 61, 62, 68, 72, 79, 80, 107, 108
Lu'bat Hazh—see *Game of Chance*

Ma Yatlubuhu al-Mushahidun—see *Audience Requests*
Madarat al-Ahdath—see *Around the Issue*
Madrid, 19, 61
Majd (-al), 75
Malafat—see *Political Files*
Manbar al-Jazeera - see *Jazeera Pulpit*
Maronite, 69
Masqat, 75
Mawaqi' al-Hadath—see *Scene, The*
Maztha Ba'd?—see *What Next?*
management, 61, 99, ANN, 72, al-Jazeera, 103, MBC, 63, Orbit, 157, television, 58
Manar (-al), 20, 49, 74—75, 76, 79, 84, 86, 161, 166, 167, 171
Mas'ala ghayr Mahsuma—see *Undecided Case*
Mawarid Group, 67
Mauritania, 75, 123
Middle East Broadcasting Center (MBC), 24, 44, 45, 57, 61—64, 66, 67, 78, 80, 93, 95, 98, 106, 107, 110, 120, 123, 124, 130, 131, 159, 165, advertising, 83,

104, documentary, 62, Dubai Media City, 63, entertainment, 63, ownership, 64, 97, news, 62, 132, 142, 154, 156, 158, 161, programs, 62—63, 165, ratings, 51, 76, 83, 104, 108, 109, 151, Saudi following, 61, 109, subscriber fees, 83

McArabism, 5, 9, 11, 12, 16, 17, 18, 19, 23, 24, 25, 27, 28, 115, 166, 176, 182 - 3, and al-Jazeera, 142—8

Mecca, 33, 77, 123, 175

media access, 2, American, 91, alternative, 55, 97, 110, American content, 2, American media industry, 2, Arab, 16, 31, 36, 37, 41, 42, 43, 47, 51, 55, 56, 62, 96, 105, 106, 112, 122, 123, 151, 156, 163, 166, 170, 171, 180, Asia, 40, borders, 34, content, 11, 12, 14, 15, 24, 27, 36, 37, 53, 58, 80, 152, 164, 179, Corporations, 12, development, 1, 2, 6, 31, 112, 158, 181, effects, 5, Egypt, 47, 48, 99, 105, 107, 118, electronic, 13, environment, 3, 5, 33, 86, fourth estate, 86, free zone, 97, 98, globalization, 3, 14 , industry, 2, 17, 35, 90, 97, local, 3, 58, 96, 163—also see media, state, market, 17, 155, 183, mass, 2, 11, 12, 13, 31, 36, 37, 39, 58, 118, , ownership, 97, 159, policy, 32, 34, 37, 38, 46, 79, 89, 96, 99, 111, 112, 179, Production City, Egypt, 48, 99, professional, 13, 14, 18, 23, 38, 40, 47, 109, 125, 143, regulation—see media policy, state, 15, 16, 38, 78, 89, 97, 103, 105, 158, 159, 172, 174, 175—also see Arab media , technology, 5, 12, 13, 18, 31, 56, 153, 169 , transnational, 5, 6, 9, 10, 11, 12, 13, 14, 15, 16, 17, 22, 23, 24, 31, 34, 47, 48, 58, 75, 89, 90, 92, 94, 97, 105, 107, 152, 158, 163, 165, 169, 173, 175, 182, terrestrial, 14, 48, 169—also see local media, Arab media, state media, tribal—see tribal media, and women, 161

Media and cultural imperialism, 2, 4

Media globalization and localization in the Arab world , 5

Media imperialism, 3

Meshwar—see Journey

Mexicanization, 3

Mihwar (-al), 76

MMDS, 94, 111

Min Washington—see From Washington

Monajah—see Prayer

MTV Lebanon, 66, 67, 71, 76, 161

Mubashir—see Live

Mun Sayarbah al-Malyun?—see Who Wants to be a Millionaire?

Mordoch, Rupert, 67

More than One Opinion (Akthar min Ra'iy), 110, 115, 124

Morocco, 40, 84, 90, 95, 102, 105, 153, 155

Music Now, 68

Musicana, 63

Mustaqilah (-al), 75

Mustaqbal (-al)—see Future Television

My Responsibility ('Ala Masu'liyati), 62

Najem, Salah, 119

National development model, 1

nation, 9, building, 6, 32, 40, 158, 161, colonial, 40, European, 11, imagined community, 10, Islamic, 136, newly independent, 1, state, 4, 5, 11, 16, 24, 151, 158 (also see nation, state, state-regime, regime) , state, Arab, 6, 32, 33, 34, 37, 45, 159

national audience, 55, 111, borders, 27, 31, culture, 4, development, 40, frontiers, 4, identity, 16, 40, 159, markets, 31, policy, 5, public space, 58, 179, television, 15, 44, 45, 58, 152
nationhood, 20, 159
nationalism, 9, 10, Arab, 9
NBN, 76
New TV, 76
Nidaa' al-Salah—see Prayer Call
Night is Yours, The (al-Leil Leiltak), 70
Nile Television, 44, 48, 73—74, 76, 80, 103, 157
Nilesat, 45, 48, 49, 75, 76, 77, 80, 83, 84, 85, 86, 92, 94
Neighbour of the Moon (Jar al-Qamar), 68
Netanyahu, Benjamin, 68, 151
news—see program, news
nude, semi, 70, 161, 164, 165

Occupied Territories—see West Bank and Gaza Strip and Palestinian Territories
oil, 17, 43, 53, 102, 121, 122, 143
On Air (Ala al-Hawa'), 67 , 68
Only for You (Bass Kermalak), 66
Oman, 33, 51, 75, 84, 125
Omran, Hala, 63
Open Discussion (Hiwar Maftouh), 125
Open Soiree (Sahra Maftuha), 62
Opposite Direction, The (al-Ittijah al-Mu'akas), 69, 117, 123, 124, 151, 161
Orbit, 45, 63, 64, 65, 67—68, 78, 83, 84, 85, 87, 94, 97, 98, 100, 116, 151, 154, 157, 159, 165
Organization of Islamic Conferences, 11
Oscars, 66
Other Opinion, The (al-Ra'iy al-Akhar), 68, 69, 123,

ownership, 12, 27, 56, 61, 77, 80, 97, 159, ANN, 72, classification, 82, control, 96, 97, 98, government—see state ownership, al-Jazeera, 116 , private, 35, 41, satellite dish, 45, 53, 92, 93, 95, 111, 182, semi-private, 78, Showtime, 85, State, 13, 14, 37, 40, 41, 97, 111, television, 34, 56, 77, 104

Pakistan, 120, 127, 137, 140
Palestine, 20, 21, 75, 133, 135, 137, 138, 139, 140, 142, 145, 167, 173, 182, borders, 11, coverage, 130
Palestinian, 22, 51, 124, 130, 132, 133, 134, 135, 136, 137, 138, 139, 140, 144, 146, 147, 148, 158, 167, 170, 172, affairs, 62, 101, 142, Authority, 106, 110, 139, 144, 162, 167, broadcasting, 101, citizens of Israel, 121, conflict, 74, 109, 128, 133, 135, 137, 143, 145, 146, 166, 170, 171, 172, 174, 182—also see Arab-Israeli conflict, guerillas, 106, identity, 20, institutions, 145 , interests, 72, 133, Intifada—see Intifada, Islamist, 109, Islamic Resistance Movement—see Hamas, issue, 19, 23, 27, 137, 147, 167, 170, 172, officials, 145, police, 101, Preventative Security Forces, 106, refugee camp, 54, resistance, 130, 133, 170, sources, 144, spokespeople, 173, Territories, 124, 133, 136, 139, 140, 145, 147, 148, 173, uprising—see Intifada
pan-Arab, 5, 23, 24, 25, 27, 31, 44, 45, 47, 61, 70, 72, 74, 79, 86, 87, 90, 92, 102, 104, 123, 130, 132, 133, 135, 146, 154, 169, 171, 173, 179, 181, 182

pan-Arab audience, 24, 25, 43, 61, 154, 169, 172, identity, 17, 22, 170, coverage, 154, institution, 97, 106, and Islamic programs, 25, market, 17, media, 41, 42, 43, 55, 91, 151, 159, music, 25, radio, 42, Research Center, 109, 156, screen, 87, 181

pan-Arabism, 18, 19, 142, 159, 166, 175, and McArabism, 16, 18, Nasserite, 18, 19, 32, secular, 19

Pehla, 85

Political Corridors (Arwiqat al-Siyasah), 62

Political Crime, The *(al-Jarima al-Siyasiyya)*, 126

Political Files (Malafat), 75

political party, 14, 77, 79

politician, Arab, 15, 18, 62, 72, 103, Israeli, 58, 170, 171

Polisario, 110

Popular Front for the Liberation of Palestine (PLFP), 167

Portugal, 3

post-colonial, 16, 37

Powell, Colin, 108

Prayer (Monajah), 79, 166

Prayer Call (Nidaa' al-Salah), 75

presentation, 25 , attractive, 123, 142, format, American, 131, high quality, 84, news, 144

privatization, 13, 14, 35, 55, 58, 90, 91

program, 16, 21, 38, 39, 44, 49, 61, 63, 143, 154, 162, 163, 164, 169, adolescent, 65, 66, Anglo-European television, 35, analytical, 127, anti-Semitic, 110, Arab, 65, Arab-Islamic, 16, 25, authentic, 48, book, 126, business, 31, children, 31, 66, 70, 75, 80, content, 15, 58, controversial, 108, 161, correspondents, 127, culture, 64, 89, 126, 127, 128, 159, 161, current affairs, 39, 63, 64,

73, 80, 124, 125, 126, 127, 154, debate, 69, 123, 125, 127, 165, development, 158, dialogue, 75, 125, 162, 165, drama, 64, 65, 80, 156, documentary, 57, 62, 64, 69, 75, 102, 123, 126, 152, 158, 159, 169, educational, 31, 66, 73, 80, Egyptian, 47, entertainment, 25, 26, 27, 31, 33, 36, 44, 58, 63, 66, 67, 68, 70, 73, 75, 80, 91, 92, 151, 153, 154, 159, 165, 169, 170, 176, 182, erotic, 94, fashion, 156, film, 31, foreign, 74, 94, 159, game show, 68, 83, 165, health, 80, 156, historical, 126, 128, 166, immoral, 95, import, 35, 39, 164, indigenous, 3, interactive, 65, investigative, 64, 126, 132, journalism, 22, lifestyle, 156, live, 57, 64, 65, 124, 151, 159, 162, local, 35, 36, 64, 154, medical, 64, money, 156, music, 25, 66, 68, 70, 80, 154, 159, 161, 165, 170, news, 26, 31, 36, 38, 44, 68, 69, 70, 72, 73, 80, 89, 92, 98, 102, 132, 133, 152, 153, 154, 155, 156, 158, 169, 175, political, 23, 25, 35, 41, 66, 69, 72, 73, 89, 98, 102, 106, 108, 126, 127, 128, 154, 159, 161, 163, 175, press review, 64, 125, provocative, 69, 70, 123, 151, 161, radio, 35, religious, 33, 35, 44, 73, 74, 75, 80, 89, 107, 125, 128, 156, 158, 161, 166, 176, 182, scientific, 64, social, 35, 66, 154, 161, 163, sport, 62, 64, 66, 73, 80, 124, 125, 156, superficial, 105, talk show, 39, 57, 62, 64, 65, 66, 68, 72, 75, 124, 154, 159, 162, television, 3, tourism, 156, uninhibited, 72, Western-style, 47, women, 31, 125, 161

Program Variety (Baramij Mutafareka), 126

programmers, 18, 83, 153, Arab television, 35, 39

programming, 15, 17, 18, 36, 43, 44, 52, 55, 58, 64, 71, 79, 80, 90, 91, 93, 94, 100, 102, 110, 111, 153, 154, 155, 159, 160, 163, 164, 165, 166, agenda, 153, 154, American-style, 14, Arabic-language, 35, 46, 47, 54, 56, 65, 110, content, 37, English-language, 45, foreign, 56, inconsistent, 39, 160, international, 45, layout, 69, low-quality, 36, quality, 84, state-produced, 37, uncensored, 56

propaganda, 33, 35, 39, 74, 77, 110

Qadaya al-Sa'a—see *Issue of the Hour*

Qassem (-al), Faysal, 117, 124

Qatar, 27, 33, 45, 46, 68, 73, 75, 79, 81, 84, 87, 89, 91, 94, 97, 102, 103, 107, 108, 109, 110, 112, 115, 116—120, 121, 122, 152, 153, 157, 180, 181, and al-Jazeera—see Jazeera (-al), pro-American, 121, 122

Questions about Sport (Su'al Fi al-Riyada), 125

Ra'iy(-al) al-Akhar—see *Other Opinion, The*

radio, 2, 17, 21, 28, 31—33, 34, 35, 36, 37, 38, 39, 40, 41, 42, 44, 45, 46, 47, 55, 64, 77, 78, 80, 89, 94, 99, 108, 117, 122, 152, 155, 156, 159

Radio Corporation of America, 33

Read (Iqra'), 65, 66, 79, 80, 166

reception, 53, 92

redundancy, 160

regulation, 35, 37, 41, 58, 80, 89, 91—97, 98—99, 100, 112, 161, 162, 164

Religion and Life (al-Din wal Hayat), 75

report, 26, 68, 107, 118, 119, 121, 123, 125, 126, 129, 131, 132, 135, 146, 147, 148, 154, 155, 171, 176, news, 41, 62, 102, 127, 157, third-hand, 62

reporter, 26, 42, 116, 123, 126, 128, 132, 134, 135, 136, 137, 143, 144, 145, 146, 157, 172, format, 123, 131

reporting, 41, 96, 121, 133, 134, 142, 143, 147, 148, 158, 168, 172, 173, al-Jazeera, 106, 108, 109, 120, 144, critical, 101, 106, language, 25

Request and Choose (Utlub wa Ekhtar), 65

revenue, 87, 181, advertising, 68, 91, 104, 105, 121,159, subscriber fees, 83

Rice, Condoleeza, 108

Ritchie, Ian, 63

rivalry, 92, 111, 112, 116

Rome, 45, 64

Rotana, 66

Sa'at Safaa—see *Late Hours, The*

Sabah al-Khayr ya 'Arab—see *Good Morning Arabs!*

Sahra Maftuha—see *Open Soiree 'al-Sama'*, 68

Satellite Channels Coordinating Committee in the Arab States Broadcasting Union (ASBU), 106

satellite dish, 51, 53, 61, 94, access, 93, ban, 61, 93, 94, 95, 100, cost, 44, 53, ownership, 27, 45, 54, 92, 93, 95, 111, 182, private, 124, tax, 95

Saudi Arabia, 31, 33, 34, 35, 42, 43, 44, 45, 46, 47, 49, 51, 53, 61, 62, 64, 67, 68, 72, 73, 75, 76, 77, 78, 80, 84, 89, 92, 93, 94, 97, 98, 100, 101, 102, 104, 105, 106, 108, 109, 110, 111, 115, 120, 136, 151, 155, 157, 160, 161,

166, 169, 183, royal family, 44, 45, 61, 64, 78, 80, 97
Scene, The (Mawaqi' al-Hadath), 125
Second, The (al-Thaniyya), 67, 68
sectarian, 86, 98, 164, 181
Sehraya—see *Soiree*
shareholder, 78
Shari'a (-al) wal Hayat—see *Islamic Law and Life*
Sharjah, 73, 75
Sharq (-al), al-Awsat, 25, 42, 91
She (Anti), 62
Shiite, 20, 49, 74, 76, 86, 167
Shining/Eastern (Ishraqat), 126
Showtime, 45, 51, 79, 83, 84, 85
Sihtak Bi'l-Dunya—see *Your Health in this World*
Skermo, 65
Soiree (Sehraya), 65
soldier, 44 73, 134, 146, 147, 149, 158, 173
South America, 70
Spider's Web, The (Beit al-'Anqabout), 75
staff, media, 27, 43, 46, 62, 68, 72, 98, 102, 104, 107, 110, 116, 121, 157, 181
Star Select Company, 51, 67, 84—85
State (also see nation, nation state)
State, Arab-African, 162
State, Arab, 6, 13, 27, 31, 32, 33, 36, 37, 40, 41, 42, 46, 47, 48, 56, 57, 59, 69, 75, 77, 80, 85, 86, 90, 91, 93, 94, 96, 97, 106, 107, 109, 116, 118, 120, 121, 122, 128, 152, 153, 158, 162, 175, 176, 179, 182, Arab, satirized, 22, border, 15, 17, 23, 34, 40, 151, 159, 165, broadcasting authorities, 36, control over media, 35, of Emergency Law, 93, Gulf, 17, 18, 31, 45, 47, 62, 91, 104, 111, independent, 1, information apparatus, 36 , institutions, 36,

marginalized, 161, official, 53, 56, 99, Palestinian, 20, pressure, 96, 97, regime, 6, 10, 11, 19, 24, 36, 37, 38, 78, 89, 92, 94, 101, 112, 117, 148, 160, 163, 164, 168, 171, 172 (also see nation, nation state), Saudi, 100, sovereignty, 152
Structural imperialism, 2
Studio Audience (Studio Mushahadin), 66
Studio Funn—see *Art Studio*
Studio el Hawa—see *Live Studio*
Studio Mushahadin—see *Studio Audience*
Su'al Fi al-Riyada—see *Questions about Sport*
subsidy, 43, 78, 84, 87, 160
subscription, 45, 64, 67, 71, 84, 85, 87, 92, 94, 100
Sudan, 75, 93, 94, 163,
Sunni, 86
Super Movies, 67
Super Star, 70, 159
suppression, 92, 93, 94, 96
Syria, 11, 19, 22, 25, 34, 35, 37, 49, 51, 62, 72, 73, 75, 79, 84, 87, 89, 92, 93, 99, 101, 102, 106, 107, 108, 11, 130, 141, 147, 152, 153, 154, 155, 169, 172, 175, 181, 183

Taht al-Hisar—see *Under Siege*
Taht al-Majhar—see *Under the Microscope*
Talk of the Hour (Hadith al-Sa'ah), 75
Talk of the People (Kalam el-Nas), 70
tax, 47, 95
technology, communication, 4, 5, 59, 174
Tele-Lumiere, 79
telephone, 26, 57, 66, 107, 132
telenovela, 39, 70, 152,

television, 2, 3, 12, 13, 15, 17, 18, 21, 32, 34, 36, 38, 40, 41, 53, 55, 70, Algeria, 51, Arab channels, 19, Bahrain, 34   , broadcasting, 33—35, 41, 48, 90, 91, 96, 151, 162, 179, commercial, 31, 159, Egypt, 34, 47, 48, 49, 51, FTA, 83, 84, governmental—see terrestrial television , interactive, 162, Iraqi, 33, Jordan, 34, 115, 128, 129, 130, 131, 132, 133, 134, 135, 136, 137, 142, 143, 158, Kuwait, 51, Lebanon, 34, 46, 69, 76, license fees, 104 , management, 58, media institutions, 6, North Africa, 45, 49, Oman, 51, Palestine, 51, pay, 83, private, 76, 79, 84, 99, 101, production, 17 , programs, 35, 43, 44, 46, 53, 73, 91, religious, 79, satellite, 5, 15, 43, 44, 45, 46, 48, 49, 51, 54, 58, 61, 63, 64, 71, 74, 77, 79, 80, 84, 86, 87, 89, 90, 91, 92, 93, 95, 98, 101, 103, 105, 106, 107, 110, 151, 152, 153, 155, 161, 163, 167, 168, 169, 171, 174, 182, Saudi Arabia, 33, 34, 44, 49, 51, 78, screen, Arab, 25, semi-governmental, 31, station, 15, 20, 33, 40, station owners, 26, station, private ownership, 41, Syria, 51, 155

The Arab Times—see Arab Times, The, terrestrial, 31, 24, 25, 26, 32, 34, 35, 36, 37, 39, 40, 41, 44, 46, 47, 55, 56, 57, 58, 64, 76, 77, 80, 89, 98, 100, 121, 147, 148, 152, 154, 163, 168, 172, transnational, 23, 24, 25, 26, 27, 28, 31, 55, 56, 61, 70, 105, 106, 110, 111, 112, 152, 153, 160, 162, 165, 166, 168, 169, 170, 172, 179, 181—also see satellite television , U.A.E., 51

Terrorists (Irhabiyoun), 75

Thalitha (-al)—see Third, The
Thaniyya (-al)—see Second, The
Third, The (Thalitha (-al), 68
To Whom it May Concern (Ila Man Yahimmahu al-Amr), 66
Top 20, 66
tradition, 2, 161, Arab-Islamic, 15, local, 3
Transmission, 44, 63, 64, 71, 84, 90, 93, 94, 116, 165, of information, 16, 56 , prevention, 27, 111, 182, range, 45
tribal media, 6, 13, 15, 16, 36—41, 57, 59, 68, 128, 158, 159
Tunis, 45, 75, 84, 95, 102, 106, 107, 132, 163
Turkey, 4, 11, 136, 140
Turkish media model, 94, 176, 182
Turner, Ted, 56

Ula (-al) - see First, The
Umm Kalthoum, 41, 66
Undecided Case (Mas'ala ghayr Mahsuma), 65
Under the Microscope (Taht al-Majhar), 126
Under Siege (Taht al-Hisar), 124
UNESCO, 2
United Arab Emirates, 51, 53, 73, 81, 84, 85, 87, 91, 92, 95, 96, 97, 102, 153, 155, 180, 181
United Kingdom, 32, 73, 140, 141, 143, 148,
United States, 2, 25, 27, 42, 62, 69, 75, 87, 107, 110, 122, 135, 136, 138, 139, 140, 141, 142, 143, 144, 147, 156, 172, and Afghanistan, 118, 120, 132, 136, 137, 148, and Iraq, 43, 109, 133, and al-Jazeera, 108, 121, 125, 133
Utlub wa Ekhtar—see Request and Choose

values, Arab, 58, 110, 164, cultural, 38, 165, 39, 165, Islamic—see

religious values, journalistic, 163, local, 15, 35, political, 67, religious, 14, 15, 38, 39, 55, 67, 74, 110, 164, 165, social, 6, 14, 16, traditional, 15, 16, 58, 67, 99, 151
viewer, 15, 17, 18, 25, 26, 107, 143, 146, 158, 162, 163, 171— also see audience
Voice of America, 32

Wattan (-al), 109
Weekend, *66*
West, 3, 160
West Bank and Gaza Strip, 19, 27, 101, 123, 135, 136, 143, 158, 182
Western Asia, 77, content, 15, Europe, 83, 174, provocative-shock model, 70, style television, 47
What Next? (Maztha Ba'd?), 75
Who Wants to be a Millionaire? (Mun Sayarbah al-Malyun?), 63
Without Borders (Bila Hudoud), al-Jazeera program, 124
woman, 23, Western, 160
women, 14, 23, 26, 31, 58, 59, 62, 70, 125, 148, 151, 161, 162, 164, 165, 167, 168, 169, 176, 179, 182

Ya Leil Ya 'Ein, 58, 69, 70, 151, 165
Yemen, 37, 47, 75
Your Health in this World (Sihtak Bi'l-Dunya), 62
Your Night is Art (Leilkum Funn), 68
Youm (-al) al-Thamin—see *Eighth Day, The*

Zionist, 74, 110, 121
Zoubi (-al), Mahmoud, 93